Sleepaway

Sleepaway

Writings on Summer Camp

edited by
ERIC SIMONOFF

Riverhead Books
New York

THE BERKLEY PUBLISHING GROUP
Published by the Penguin Group
Penguin Group (USA) Inc.
375 Hudson Street, New York, New York 10014, USA
Penguin Group (Canada), 10 Alcorn Avenue, Toronto, Ontario M4V 3B2, Canada
(a division of Pearson Penguin Canada Inc.)
Penguin Books Ltd., 80 Strand, London WC2R 0RL, England
Penguin Group Ireland, 25 St. Stephen's Green, Dublin 2, Ireland
(a division of Penguin Books Ltd.)
Penguin Group (Australia), 250 Camberwell Road, Camberwell, Victoria 3124,
Australia (a division of Pearson Australia Group Pty. Ltd.)
Penguin Books India Pvt. Ltd., 11 Community Centre, Panchsheel Park,
New Delhi—110 017, India
Penguin Group (NZ), cnr Airborne and Rosedale Roads, Albany, Auckland 1310,
New Zealand (a division of Pearson New Zealand Ltd.)
Penguin Books (South Africa) (Pty.) Ltd., 24 Sturdee Avenue, Rosebank,
Johannesburg 2196, South Africa

Penguin Books Ltd., Registered Offices: 80 Strand, London WC2R 0RL, England

SLEEPAWAY

PRINTING HISTORY
First Riverhead trade paperback edition: June 2005
Riverhead trade paperback ISBN: 1-59448-088-5

This book has been catalogued with the Library of Congress.

PRINTED IN THE UNITED STATES OF AMERICA

10 9 8 7 6 5 4 3 2 1

*For David Samuel "Rosie" Rosenthal,
my best camp friend*

Acknowledgments

More so even than most books, an anthology is a group effort. I'd like to thank my friend and editor Cindy Spiegel, who turned a casual conversation into an actual book; my agent, Luke Janklow, the tall guy down the hall with whom I speak in code; my wife, Anne Sikora, who is smart in all the ways I am not; Deborah Treisman and Cressida Leyshon who introduced me to *New Yorker* archivist Jon Michaud, who generously gave of his time and resources; my assistant of fourteen years, Eadie Klemm, without whom the world would spin off its axis; Susan Ambler of Riverhead Books; my folks, Anne and Howard Simonoff, who did themselves and me a favor and sent me off to camp; the contributors to *Sleepaway*, of course, without whom there wouldn't be much of a book.

Special thanks to all my counselors at Camp Harlam.

Contents

Contents

Contents

Introduction

For ten consecutive summers, I attended the awkwardly named Joseph and Betty Harlam Camp in rural Kunkletown, Pennsylvania. I celebrated birthdays eight through eighteen there by eating a bland sheetcake that was wheeled to my bunk's table on a rickety steel serving cart while the ammonia-scented dining hall rang with the strains of "Happy Birthday." There was no place I would rather have been. Every year I bided my time during the intervening ten months, eagerly awaiting the day I could pack my ugly black cardboard trunk, stuff my sheets and scratchy army blankets into my duffel bag, load them into the family's Ford Country Squire station wagon, and head to the Poconos, where I knew I wouldn't be that weird, bookish kid who always had his hand up in class—where, instead, I would be the popular kid, the lifelong camper who knew all the counselors, all the camp songs, all the camp lore. I loved camp. Camp loved me. I was a diehard summer camper.

There are computer camps and drama camps, fat camps and cancer camps, music camps and soccer camps. Camp Harlam was a Jewish camp. My wife, who herself attended Camp Four-Winds-Westward-Ho in British Columbia (where all the girls were forced to wear midis and bloomers), has heard many many stories from my Camp Harlam days and now refers to it only as Jewish Sex Camp, as its all but stated purpose was to acclimate young Jews to the idea of marrying other Jews, by means of coed campouts, enforced Saturday socials, and a heavy emphasis on pairing off. In my case, they failed spectacularly: I married a half-Catholic/half-Protestant Scotch-German-Polish mix-breed from Canada. Then again, my wife fell for a Matt Dillon look-alike who worked with the kitchen staff at *her* camp—but that was a long time ago.

On the first day of my third summer at Camp Harlam I befriended a little curly-headed boy named David "Rosie" Rosenthal whom I saw standing all alone next to the equipment hut by the backstop of the boys' softball field, his shoulders shaking with his wracking sobs. At nine-going-on-ten, I was a grizzled veteran and felt it my duty to comfort the unfortunate greenhorn. We became inseparable friends over the course of eight summers. One literary wag of a counselor dubbed us Rosenkrantz and Guildenstern, which says more about the kinds of counselors Camp Harlam attracted than it does about our cravenness or tendency toward political assassination. It was at Camp Harlam that Rosie discovered that he could make people laugh. This would eventually lead him to become an extraordinarily successful writer and producer of sitcoms. Such is the power of summer camp. It wasn't until I attended his bar mitzvah that I discovered that no one in Rosie's hometown had any idea who Rosie was. From September to June he was David. He only became Rosie once safely en-sconced in Kunkletown.

As it was for so many of the authors whose work appears in this book, camp was for me a formative, or more accurately, a transfor-mative experience. Far away from home, removed from the con-straints of school, camp offers a rare opportunity for reinvention, a relatively safe atmosphere for the defiance of authority, and, what with the heat, the lake, the pool, the ceaseless chirping of bugs, and the sleeping arrangements, opportunities for exquisite sexual tension and exploration. There are certain constants that run through camp stories: bug juice and bug bites; the creaking of cot-springs and the chirping of crickets; homesickness and heartsick-ness; the lake and the canoes; the sing-alongs. I have endeavored to collect short stories and essays that encompass as many different aspects of summer camp as possible. For the reader who loved sum-mer camp, there are sweet evocations of summer idylls gone by. For the reader who hated summer camp, there are renderings of sadis-tic tentmates and unparalleled social competition. I hope there is something here for the eternal camper in each of us.

Eric Simonoff
Brooklyn, New York, 2004

Sleepaway

The Summer-Camp Bus Pulls Away from the Curb

Sharon Olds

Whatever he needs, he has or doesn't
have by now.
Whatever the world is going to do to him
it has started to do. With a pencil and two
Hardy Boys and a peanut butter sandwich and
grapes he is on his way, there is nothing
more we can do for him. Whatever is
stored in his heart, he can use, now.
Whatever he has laid up in his mind
he can call on. What he does not have
he can lack. The bus gets smaller and smaller, as one
folds a flag at the end of a ceremony,
onto itself, and onto itself, until

only a heavy wedge remains.
Whatever his exuberant soul
can do for him, it is doing right now.
Whatever his arrogance can do
it is doing to him. Everything
that's been done to him, he will now do.
Everything that's been placed in him
will come out, now, the contents of a trunk
unpacked and lined up on a bunk in the underpine light.

Death by Landscape

Margaret Atwood

Now that the boys are grown up and Rob is dead, Lois has moved to a condominium apartment in one of the newer waterfront developments. She is relieved not to have to worry about the lawn, or about the ivy pushing its muscular little suckers into the brickwork, or the squirrels gnawing their way into the attic and eating the insulation off the wiring, or about strange noises. This building has a security system, and the only plant life is in pots in the solarium.

Lois is glad she's been able to find an apartment big enough for her pictures. They were more crowded together than they were in the house, but this arrangement gives the walls a European look: blocks of pictures, above and beside one another, rather than one over the chesterfield, one over the fireplace, one in the front hall, in the old acceptable manner of sprinkling art around so it does not get too intrusive. This way has more of an impact. You know it's not supposed to be furniture.

None of the pictures is very large, which doesn't mean they aren't valuable. They are paintings, or sketches and drawings, by artists who were not nearly as well known when Lois began to buy them as they are now. Their work later turned up on stamps, or as silk-screen reproductions hung in the principals' offices of high schools, or as jigsaw puzzles, or on beautifully printed calendars sent out by corporations as Christmas gifts, to their less important clients. These artists painted mostly in the twenties and thirties and forties; they painted landscapes. Lois has two Tom Thomsons, three A. Y. Jacksons, a Lawren Harris. She has an Arthur Lismer, she has a J. E. H. MacDonald. She has a David Milne. They are pictures of convoluted tree trunks on an island of pink wave-smoothed stone, with more islands behind; of a lake with rough, bright, sparsely wooded cliffs; of a vivid river shore with a tangle of bush and two beached canoes, one red, one gray; of a yellow autumn woods with the ice-blue gleam of a pond half-seen through the interlaced branches.

It was Lois who'd chosen them. Rob had no interest in art, although he could see the necessity of having something on the walls. He left all the decorating decisions to her, while providing the money, of course. Because of this collection of hers, Lois's friends—especially the men—have given her the reputation of having a good nose for art investments.

But this is not why she bought the pictures, way back then. She bought them because she wanted them. She wanted something that was in them, although she could not have said at the time what it was. It was not peace: she does not find them peaceful in the least. Looking at them fills her with a wordless unease. Despite the fact that there are no people in them or even animals, it's as if there is something, or someone, looking back out.

When she was thirteen, Lois went on a canoe trip. She'd only been on overnights before. This was to be a long one, into the trackless wilderness, as Cappie put it. It was Lois's first canoe trip, and her last.

Cappie was the head of the summer camp to which Lois had been sent ever since she was nine. Camp Manitou, it was called; it was one of the better ones, for girls, though not the best. Girls of her age whose parents could afford it were routinely packed off to such camps, which bore a generic resemblance to one another. They favored Indian names and had hearty, energetic leaders, who were called Cappie or Skip, or Scottie. At these camps you learned to swim well and sail, and paddle a canoe, and perhaps ride a horse or play tennis. When you weren't doing these things you could do Arts and Crafts and turn out dingy, lumpish clay ashtrays for your mother—mothers smoked more, then—or bracelets made of colored braided string.

Cheerfulness was required at all times, even at breakfast. Loud shouting and the banging of spoons on the tables were allowed, and even encouraged, at ritual intervals. Chocolate bars were rationed, to control tooth decay and pimples. At night, after supper, in the dining hall or outside around a mosquito-infested campfire ring for special treats, there were singsongs. Lois can still remember all the words to "My Darling Clementine," and to "My Bonnie Lies over the Ocean," with acting-out gestures: a rippling of the hands for "the ocean," two hands together under the cheek for "lies." She will never be able to forget them, which is a sad thought.

Lois thinks she can recognize women who went to these camps, and were good at it. They have a hardness to their handshakes, even now; a way of standing, legs planted firmly and farther apart than usual; a way of sizing you up, to see if you'd be any good in a canoe—the front, not the back. They themselves would be in the back. They would call it the stern.

She knows that such camps still exist, although Camp Manitou does not. They are one of the few things that haven't changed much. They now offer copper enameling, and functionless pieces of stained glass baked in electric ovens, though judging from the productions of her friends' grandchildren the artistic standards have not improved.

To Lois, encountering it in the first year after the war, Camp Manitou seemed ancient. Its log-sided buildings with the white cement in between the half-logs, its flagpole ringed with whitewashed stones, its weathered gray dock jutting out into Lake Prospect, with its woven rope bumpers and its rusty rings for tying up, its prim round flowerbed of petunias near the office door, must surely have been there always. In truth it dated only from the first decade of the century; it had been founded by Cappie's parents, who'd thought of camping as bracing to the character, like cold showers, and had been passed along to her as an inheritance, and an obligation.

Lois realized, later, that it must have been a struggle for Cappie to keep Camp Manitou going, during the Depression and then the war, when money did not flow freely. If it had been a camp for the very rich, instead of the merely well off, there would have been fewer problems. But there must have been enough Old Girls, ones with daughters, to keep the thing in operation, though not entirely shipshape: furniture was battered, painted trim was peeling, roofs leaked. There were dim photographs of these Old Girls dotted around the dining hall, wearing ample woolen bathing suits and showing their fat, dimpled legs, or standing, arms twined, in odd tennis outfits with baggy skirts.

In the dining hall, over the stone fireplace that was never used, there was a huge molting stuffed moose head, which looked some-how carnivorous. It was a sort of mascot; its name was Monty Manitou. The older campers spread the story that it was haunted, and came to life in the dark, when the feeble and undependable lights had been turned off or, due to yet another generator failure, had gone out. Lois was afraid of it at first, but not after she got used to it.

Cappie was the same: you had to get used to her. Possibly she was forty, or thirty-five, or fifty. She had fawn-colored hair that looked as if it was cut with a bowl. Her head jutted forward, jig-gling like a chicken's as she strode around the camp, clutching notebooks and checking things off in them. She was like their minister in church: both of them smiled a lot and were anxious because they wanted things to go well; they both had the same overwashed skins and stringy necks. But all this disappeared when Cappie was leading a singsong, or otherwise leading. Then she was happy, sure of herself, her plain face almost luminous. She wanted to cause joy. At these times she was loved, at others merely trusted.

There were many things Lois didn't like about Camp Manitou, at first. She hated the noisy chaos and spoon-banging of the dining hall, the rowdy singsongs at which you were expected to yell in order to show that you were enjoying yourself. Hers was not a household that encouraged yelling. She hated the necessity of having to write dutiful letters to her parents claiming she was having fun. She could not complain, because camp cost so much money.

She didn't much like having to undress in a roomful of other girls, even in the dim light, although nobody paid any attention, or sleeping in a cabin with seven other girls, some of whom snored because they had adenoids or colds, some of whom had nightmares, or wet their beds and cried about it. Bottom bunks made her feel closed in, and she was afraid of falling out of top ones; she was afraid of heights. She got homesick, and suspected her parents of having a better time when she wasn't there than when she was, although her mother wrote her every week saying how much they missed her. All this was when she was nine. By the time she was thirteen she liked it. She was an old hand by then.

Lucy was her best friend at camp. Lois had other friends in winter, when there was school and itchy woolen clothing and darkness in the afternoons, but Lucy was her summer friend.

She turned up the second year, when Lois was ten, and a Bluejay. (Chickadees, Bluejays, Ravens, and Kingfishers—these were the names Camp Manitou assigned to the different age groups, a sort of totemic clan system. In those days, thinks Lois, it was birds for girls, animals for boys: wolves, and so forth. Though some animals and birds were suitable and some were not. Never vultures, for instance; never skunks, or rats.)

Lois helped Lucy to unpack her tin trunk and place the folded clothes on the wooden shelves, and to make up her bed. She put her in the top bunk right above her, where she could keep an eye on her. Already she knew that Lucy was an exception, to a good many rules; already she felt proprietorial.

Lucy was from the United States, where the comic books came from, and the movies. She wasn't from New York or Hollywood or Buffalo, the only American cities Lois knew the names of, but from Chicago. Her house was on the lakeshore and had gates to it, and grounds. They had a maid, all of the time. Lois's family only had a cleaning lady twice a week.

The only reason Lucy was being sent to *this* camp (she cast a look of minor scorn around the cabin, diminishing it and also offending Lois, while at the same time daunting her) was that her mother had been a camper here. Her mother had been a Canadian once, but had married her father, who had a patch over one eye, like a pirate. She showed Lois the picture of him in her wallet. He got the patch in the war. "Shrapnel," said Lucy. Lois, who was unsure about shrapnel, was so impressed she could only grunt. Her own two-eyed, unwounded father was tame by comparison.

"My father plays golf," she ventured at last.

"*Everyone* plays golf," said Lucy. "My *mother* plays golf."

Lois's mother did not. Lois took Lucy to see the outhouses and the swimming dock and the dining hall with Monty Manitou's baleful head, knowing in advance they would not measure up.

This was a bad beginning; but Lucy was good-natured, and accepted Camp Manitou with the same casual shrug with which she seemed to accept everything. She would make the best of it, without letting Lois forget that this was what she was doing.

However, there were things Lois knew that Lucy did not. Lucy scratched the tops off all her mosquito bites and had to be taken to the infirmary to be daubed with Ozonol. She took her T-shirt off while sailing, and although the counselor spotted her after a while and made her put it back on, she burnt spectacularly, bright red, with the X of her bathing-suit straps standing out in alarming white; she let Lois peel the sheets of whispery-thin burned skin off her shoulders. When they sang "Alouette" around the campfire, she did not know any of the French words. The difference was that Lucy did not care about the things she didn't know, whereas Lois did.

During the next winter, and subsequent winters, Lucy and Lois wrote to each other. They were both only children, at a time when this was thought to be a disadvantage, so in their letters they pretended to be sisters, or even twins. Lois had to strain a little over this, because Lucy was so blond, with translucent skin and large blue eyes like a doll's, and Lois was nothing out of the ordinary—just a tallish, thinnish, brownish person with freckles. They signed their letters LL, with the L's entwined together like the monograms on a towel. (Lois and Lucy, thinks Lois. How our names date us. Lois Lane, Superman's girlfriend, enterprising female reporter; *I Love Lucy*. Now we are obsolete, and it's little Jennifers, little Emilys, little Alexandras and Carolines and Tiffanys.)

They were more effusive in their letters than they ever were in person. They bordered their pages with X's and O's, but when they met again in the summers it was always a shock. They had changed so much, or Lucy had. It was like watching someone grow up in jolts. At first it would be hard to think up things to say.

But Lucy always had a surprise or two, something to show, some marvel to reveal. The first year she had a picture of herself in a tutu, her hair in a ballerina's knot on the top of her head; she pirouetted around the swimming dock, to show Lois how it was done, and almost fell off. The next year she had given that up and was taking horseback riding. (Camp Manitou did not have horses.) The next year her mother and father had been divorced, and she had a new stepfather, one with both eyes, and a new house, although the maid was the same. The next year, when they had graduated from Bluejays and entered Ravens, she got her period, right in the first week of camp. The two of then snitched some matches from their counselor, who smoked illegally, and made a small fire out behind the farthest outhouse, at dusk, using their flashlights. They could set all kinds of fires by now; they had learned how in Campcraft. On this fire they burned one of Lucy's used sanitary napkins. Lois is not sure why they did this, or whose idea it was. But she can remember the feeling of deep satisfaction it gave her as the white fluff singed and the blood sizzled, as if some wordless ritual had been fulfilled.

They did not get caught, but then they rarely got caught at any of their camp transgressions. Lucy had such large eyes, and was such an accomplished liar.

This year Lucy is different again; slower, more languorous. She is no longer interested in sneaking around after dark, purloining cigarettes from the counselor, dealing in black-market candy bars. She is pensive, and hard to wake in the mornings. She doesn't like her stepfather, but she doesn't want to live with her real father either, who has a new wife. She thinks her mother may be having a love affair with a doctor; she doesn't know for sure, but she's seen them smooching in his car, out on the driveway, when her stepfather wasn't there. It serves him right. She hates her private school. She has a boyfriend, who is sixteen and works as a gardener's assistant. This is how she met him: in the garden. She describes to Lois what it is like when he kisses her—rubbery at first, but then your knees go limp. She has been forbidden to see him, and threatened with boarding school. She wants to run away from home.

Lois has little to offer in return. Her own life is placid and satisfactory, but there is nothing much that can be said about happiness. "You're so lucky," Lucy tells her, a little smugly. She might as well say *boring* because this is how it makes Lois feel.

Lucy is apathetic about the canoe trip, so Lois has to disguise her own excitement. The evening before they are to leave, she slouches into the campfire ring as if coerced, and sits down with a sigh of endurance, just as Lucy does.

Every canoe trip that went out of the camp was given a special send-off by Cappie and the section leader and counselors, with the whole section in attendance. Cappie painted three streaks of red across each of her cheeks with a lipstick. They looked like three-fingered claw marks. She put a blue circle on her forehead with fountain-pen ink, and tied a twisted bandanna around her head and stuck a row of frazzle-ended feathers around it, and wrapped herself in a red-and-black Hudson's Bay blanket. The counselors, also in blankets but with only two streaks of red, beat on tom-toms made of round wooden cheese boxes with leather stretched over the top and nailed in place. Cappie was Chief Cappeosota. They all had to say "How!" when she walked into the circle and stood there with one hand raised.

Looking back on this, Lois finds it disquieting. She knows too much about Indians: this is why. She knows, for instance, that they should not even be called Indians, and that they have enough worries without other people taking their names and dressing up as them. It has all been a form of stealing.

But she remembers, too, that she was once ignorant of this. Once she loved the campfire, the flickering of light on the ring of faces, the sound of the fake tom-toms, heavy and fast like a sacred heartbeat; she loved Cappie in a red blanket and feathers, solemn, as a chief should be, raising her hand and saying, "Greetings, my Ravens." It was not funny, it was not making fun. She wanted to be an Indian. She wanted to be adventurous and pure, and aboriginal.

"You go on big water," says Cappie. This is her idea—all their ideas—of how Indians talk. "You go where no man has ever trod. You go many moons." This is not true. They are only going for a week, not many moons. The canoe route is clearly marked, they have gone over it on a map, and there are prepared campsites with names, which are used year after year. But when Cappie says this—and despite the way Lucy rolls up her eyes—Lois can feel the water stretching out, with the shores twisting away on either side, immense and a little frightening.

"You bring back much wampum," says Cappie. "Do good in war, my braves, and capture many scalps." This is another of her pretenses: that they are boys, and bloodthirsty. But such a game cannot be played by substituting the word *squaw*. It would not work at all.

Each of them has to stand up and step forward and have a red line drawn across her cheeks by Cappie. She tells them they must follow in the paths of their ancestors (who most certainly, thinks Lois, looking out the window of her apartment and remembering the family stash of daguerreotypes and sepia-colored portraits on her mother's dressing table, the stiff-shirted, black-coated, grim-faced men and the beflounced women with their severe hair and their corseted respectability, would never have considered heading off onto an open lake, in a canoe, just for fun).

At the end of the ceremony they all stood and held hands around the circle, and sang taps. This did not sound very Indian, thinks Lois. It sounded like a bugle call at a military post, in a movie. But Cappie was never one to be much concerned with consistency, or with archeology.

After breakfast the next morning they set out from the main dock, in four canoes, three in each. The lipstick stripes have not come off completely, and still show faintly pink, like healing burns. They wear their white denim sailing hats, because of the sun, and thin-striped T-shirts, and pale baggy shorts with the cuffs rolled up. The middle one kneels, propping her rear end against the rolled sleeping bags. The counselors going with them are Pat and Kip. Kip is no-nonsense; Pat is easier to wheedle, or fool.

There are white puffy clouds and a small breeze. Glints come from the little waves. Lois is in the bow of Kip's canoe. She still can't do a J-stroke very well, and she will have to be in the bow or the middle for the whole trip. Lucy is behind her; her own J-stroke is even worse. She splashes Lois with her paddle, quite a big splash.

"I'll get you back," says Lois.

"There was a stable fly on your shoulder," Lucy says.

Lois turns to look at her, to see if she's grinning. They're in the habit of splashing each other. Back there, the camp has vanished behind the first long point of rock and rough trees. Lois feels as if an invisible rope has broken. They're floating free, on their own, cut loose. Beneath the canoe the lake goes down, deeper and colder than it was a minute before.

"No horsing around in the canoe," says Kip. She's rolled her T-shirt sleeves up to the shoulder; her arms are brown and sinewy, her jaw determined, her stroke perfect. She looks as if she knows exactly what she is doing.

The four canoes keep close together. They sing, raucously and with defiance; they sing "The Quartermaster's Store," and "Clementine," and "Alouette." It is more like bellowing than singing.

After that the wind grows stronger, blowing slantwise against the bows, and they have to put all their energy into shoving themselves through the water.

Was there anything important, anything that would provide some sort of reason or clue to what happened next? Lois can remember everything, every detail; but it does her no good.

They stopped at noon for a swim and lunch, and went on in the afternoon. At last they reached Little Birch, which was the first campsite for overnight. Lois and Lucy made the fire, while the others pitched the heavy canvas tents. The fireplace was already there, flat stones piled into a U. A burned tin can and a beer bottle had been left in it. Their fire went out, and they had to restart it. "Hustle your bustle," said Kip. "We're starving."

The sun went down, and in the pink sunset light they brushed their teeth and spat the toothpaste froth into the lake. Kip and Pat put all the food that wasn't in cans into a packsack and slung it into a tree, in case of bears.

Lois and Lucy weren't sleeping in a tent. They'd begged to be allowed to sleep out; that way they could talk without the others hearing. If it rained, they told Kip, they promised not to crawl dripping into the tent over everyone's legs: they would get under the canoes. So they were out on the point.

Lois tried to get comfortable inside her sleeping bag, which smelled of musty storage and of earlier campers, a stale salty sweetness. She curled herself up, with her sweater rolled up under her head for a pillow and her flashlight inside her sleeping bag so it wouldn't roll away. The muscles of her sore arms were making small pings, like rubber bands breaking.

Beside her Lucy was rustling around. Lois could see the glimmering oval of her white face.

"I've got a rock poking into my back," said Lucy.

"So do I," said Lois. "You want to go into the tent?" She herself didn't but it was right to ask.

"No," said Lucy. She subsided into her sleeping bag. After a moment she said, "It would be nice not to go back."

"To camp?" said Lois.

"To Chicago," said Lucy. "I hate it there."

"What about your boyfriend?" said Lois. Lucy didn't answer. She was either asleep or pretending to be.

There was a moon, and a movement of the trees. In the sky there were stars, layers of stars that went down and down. Kip said that when the stars were bright like that instead of hazy it meant bad weather later on. Out on the lake there were two loons, calling to each other in their insane, mournful voices. At the time it did not sound like grief. It was just background.

The lake in the morning was flat calm. They skimmed along over the glassy surface, leaving V-shaped trails behind them; it felt like flying. As the sun rose higher it got hot, almost too hot. There were stable flies in the canoes, landing on a bare arm or leg for a quick sting. Lois hoped for wind.

They stopped for lunch at the next of the named campsites, Lookout Point. It was called this because, although the site itself was down near the water on a flat shelf of rock, there was a sheer cliff nearby and a trail that led up to the top. The top was the lookout, although what you were supposed to see from there was not clear. Kip said it was just a view.

Lois and Lucy decided to make the climb anyway. They didn't want to hang around waiting for lunch. It wasn't their turn to cook, though they hadn't avoided much by not doing it, because cooking lunch was no big deal, it was just unwrapping the cheese and getting out the bread and peanut butter, but Pat and Kip always had to do their woodsy act and boil up a billy tin for their own tea.

They told Kip where they were going. You had to tell Kip where you were going, even if it was only a little way into the woods to get dry twigs for kindling. You could never go anywhere without a buddy.

"Sure," said Kip, who was crouching over the fire, feeding driftwood into it. "Fifteen minutes to lunch."

"Where are they off to?" said Pat. She was bringing their billy tin of water from the lake.

"Lookout," said Kip.

"Be careful," said Pat. She said it as an afterthought, because it was what she always said.

"They're old hands," Kip said.

Lois looks at her watch: it's ten to twelve. She is the watchminder; Lucy is careless of time. They walk up the path, which is dry earth and rocks, big rounded pinky-gray boulders or split-open ones with jagged edges. Spindly balsam and spruce trees grow to either side, the lake is blue fragments to the left. The sun is right overhead; there are no shadows anywhere. The heat comes up at them as well as down. The forest is dry and crackly.

It isn't far, but it's a steep climb and they're sweating when they reach the top. They wipe their faces with their bare arms, sit gingerly down on a scorching-hot rock, five feet from the edge but too close for Lois. It's a lookout all right, a sheer drop to the lake and a long view over the water, back the way they've come. It's amazing to Lois that they've traveled so far, over all that water, with nothing to propel them but their own arms. It makes her feel strong. There are all kinds of things she is capable of doing.

"It would be quite a dive off here," says Lucy.

"You'd have to be nuts," says Lois.

"Why?" says Lucy. "It's really deep. It goes straight down." She stands up and takes a step nearer the edge. Lois gets a stab in her midriff, the kind she gets when a car goes too fast over a bump. "Don't," she says.

"Don't what?" says Lucy, glancing around at her mischievously. She knows how Lois feels about heights. But she turns back. "I really have to pee," she says.

"You have toilet paper?" says Lois, who is never without it. She digs in her shorts pocket.

"Thanks," says Lucy.

They are both adept at peeing in the woods: doing it fast so the mosquitoes don't get you, the underwear pulled up between the knees, the squat with the feet apart so you don't wet your legs, facing downhill. The exposed feeling of your bum, as if someone is looking at you from behind. The etiquette when you're with someone else is not to look. Lois stands up and starts to walk back down the path, to be out of sight.

"Wait for me?" says Lucy.

Lois climbed down, over and around the boulders, until she could not see Lucy; she waited. She could hear the voices of the others, talking and laughing, down near the shore. One voice was yelling, "Ants! Ants!" Someone must have sat on an ant hill. Off to the side, in the woods, a raven was croaking, a hoarse single note.

She looked at her watch: it was noon. This is when she heard the shout.

She has gone over and over it in her mind since, so many times that the first, real shout has been obliterated, like a footprint trampled by other footprints. But she is sure (she is almost positive, she is nearly certain) that it was not a shout of fear. Not a scream. More like a cry of surprise, cut off too soon. Short, like a dog's bark.

"Lucy?" Lois said. Then she called "Lucy!" By now she was clambering back up, over the stones of the path. Lucy was not up there. Or she was not in sight.

"Stop fooling around," Lois said. "It's lunchtime." But Lucy did not rise from behind a rock or step out, smiling, from behind a tree. The sunlight was all around; the rocks looked white. "This isn't funny!" Lois said, and it wasn't, panic was rising in her, the panic of a small child who does not know where the bigger ones are hidden. She could hear her own heart. She looked quickly around; she lay down on the ground and looked over the edge of the cliff. It made her feel cold. There was nothing.

She went back down the path, stumbling; she was breathing too quickly; she was too frightened to cry. She felt terrible—guilty and dismayed, as if she had done something very bad, by mistake. Something that could never be repaired. "Lucy's gone," she told Kip.

Kip looked up from her fire, annoyed. The water in the billy can was boiling. "What do you mean, gone?" she said. "Where did she go?"

"I don't know," said Lois. "She's just gone."

No one had heard the shout, but then no one had heard Lois calling, either. They had been talking among themselves, by the water.

Kip and Pat went up to the lookout and searched and called, and blew their whistles. Nothing answered.

Then they came back down, and Lois had to tell exactly what had happened. The other girls all sat in a circle and listened to her. Nobody said anything. They all looked frightened, especially Pat and Kip. They were the leaders. You did not just lose a camper like this, for no reason at all.

"Why did you leave her alone?" said Kip.

"I was just down the path," said Lois. "I told you. She had to go to the bathroom." She did not say *pee* in front of people older than herself.

Kip looked disgusted.

"Maybe she just walked off into the woods and got turned around," said one of the girls.

"Maybe she's doing it on purpose," said another.

Nobody believed either of these theories.

They took the canoes and searched around the base of the cliff, and peered down into the water. But there had been no sound of falling rock; there had been no splash. There was no clue, nothing at all. Lucy had simply vanished.

That was the end of the canoe trip. It took them the same two days to go back that it had taken coming in, even though they were short a paddler. They did not sing.

After that, the police went in a motorboat, with dogs; they were the Mounties and the dogs were German shepherds, trained to follow trails in the woods. But it had rained since, and they could find nothing.

Lois is sitting in Cappie's office. Her face is bloated with crying, she's seen that in the mirror. By now she feels numbed; she feels as if she has drowned. She can't stay here. It has been too much of a shock. Tomorrow her parents are coming to take her away. Several of the other girls who were on the canoe trip are also being collected. The others will have to stay, because their parents are in Europe, or cannot be reached.

Cappie is grim. They've tried to hush it up, but of course everyone in camp knows. Soon the papers will know too. You can't keep it quiet, but what can be said? What can be said that makes any sense? "Girl vanished in broad daylight, without a trace." It can't be believed. Other things, worse things, will be suspected. Negligence, at the very least. But they have always taken such care. Bad luck will gather around Camp Manitou like a fog; parents will avoid it, in favor of other, luckier places. Lois can see Cappie thinking all this, even through her numbness. It's what anyone would think.

Lois sits on the hard wooden chair in Cappie's office, beside the old wooden desk, over which hangs the thumbtacked bulletin board of normal camp routine, and gazes at Cappie, through her puffy eyelids. Cappie is now smiling what is supposed to be a reassuring smile. Her manner is too casual: she's after something. Lois has seen this look on Cappie's face when she's been sniffing out contraband chocolate bars, hunting down those rumored to have snuck out of their cabins at night.

"Tell me again," says Cappie, "from the beginning."

Lois has told her story so many times by now, to Pat and Kip, to Cappie, to the police, that she knows it word for word. She knows it, but she no longer believes it. It has become a story. "I told you," she said. "She wanted to go to the bathroom. I gave her my toilet paper. I went down the path, I waited for her. I heard this kind of shout . . ."

"Yes," says Cappie, smiling confidingly, "but before that. What did you say to one another?"

Lois thinks. Nobody has asked her this before. "She said you could dive off there. She said it went straight down."

"And what did you say?"

"I said you'd have to be nuts."

"Were you mad at Lucy?" says Cappie, in an encouraging voice.

"No," says Lois. "Why would I be mad at Lucy? I wasn't ever mad at Lucy." She feels like crying again. The times when she has in fact been mad at Lucy have been erased already. Lucy was always perfect.

"Sometimes we're angry when we don't know we're angry," says Cappie, as if to herself. "Sometimes we get really mad and we don't even know it. Sometimes we might do a thing without meaning to, or without knowing what will happen. We lose our tempers."

Lois is only thirteen, but it doesn't take her long to figure out that Cappie is not including herself in any of this. By *we* she means Lois. She is accusing Lois of pushing Lucy off the cliff. The unfairness of this hits her like a slap. "I didn't!" she says.

"Didn't what?" says Cappie softly. "Didn't what, Lois?"

Lois does the worst thing, she begins to cry. Cappie gives her a look like a pounce. She's got what she wanted.

Later when she was grown up, Lois was able to understand what this interview had been about. She could see Cappie's desperation, her need for a story, a real story with a reason in it; anything but the senseless vacancy Lucy had left for her to deal with. Cappie wanted Lois to supply the reason, to be the reason. It wasn't even for the newspapers or the parents, because she could never make such an accusation without proof. It was for herself: something to explain the loss of Camp Manitou and of all she had worked for, the years of entertaining spoiled children and buttering up parents and making a fool of herself with feathers stuck in her hair. Camp Manitou was in fact lost. It did not survive.

Lois worked all this out, twenty years later. But it was far too late. It was too late even ten minutes afterwards, when she'd left Cappie's office and was walking slowly back to her cabin to pack. Lucy's clothes were still there, folded on the shelves, as if waiting. She felt the other girls in the cabin watching her with speculation in their eyes. *Could she have done it? She must have done it.* For the rest of her life, she has caught people watching her in this way.

Maybe they weren't thinking this. Maybe they were merely sorry for her. But she felt she had been tried and sentenced, and this is what has stayed with her: the knowledge that she had been singled out, condemned for something that was not her fault.

Lois sits in the living room of her apartment, drinking a cup of tea. Through the knee-to-ceiling window she has a wide view of Lake Ontario, with its skin of wrinkled blue-gray light, and the willows of Centre Island shaken by the wind, which is silent at this distance, and on this side of the glass. When there isn't too much pollution she can see the far shore, the foreign shore; though today it is obscured.

Possibly she could go out, go downstairs, do some shopping; there isn't much in the refrigerator. The boys say she doesn't get out enough. But she isn't hungry, and moving, stirring from this space, is increasingly an effort.

She can hardly remember, now, having her two boys in the hospital, nursing them as babies; she can hardly remember getting married, or what Rob looked like. Even at the time she never felt she was paying full attention. She was tired a lot, as if she was living not one life but two: her own, and another, shadowy life that hovered around her and would not let itself be realized—the life of what would have happened if Lucy had not stepped sideways, and disappeared from time.

She would never go up north, to Rob's family cottage or to any place with wild lakes and wild trees and the calls of loons. She would never go anywhere near. Still, it was as if she was always listening for another voice, the voice of a person who should have been there but was not. An echo.

While Rob was alive, while the boys were growing up, she could pretend she didn't hear it, this empty space in sound. But now there is nothing much left to distract her.

She turns away from the window and looks at her pictures. There is the pinkish island, in the lake, with the intertwisted trees. It's the same landscape they paddled through, that distant summer. She's seen travelogues of this country, aerial photographs; it looks different from above, bigger, more hopeless; lake after lake, random blue puddles in dark green bush, the trees like bristles.

How could you ever find anything there, once it was lost? Maybe if they cut it all down, drained it all away, they might find Lucy's bones, some time, wherever they are hidden. A few bones, some buttons, the buckle from her shorts.

But a dead person is a body; a body occupies space, it exists somewhere. You can see it; you put it in a box and bury it in the ground, and then it's in a box in the ground. But Lucy is not in a box, or in the ground. Because she is nowhere definite, she could be anywhere.

And these paintings are not landscape paintings. Because there aren't any landscapes up there, not in the old, tidy European sense, with a gentle hill, a curving river, a cottage, a mountain in the background, a golden evening sky. Instead there's a tangle, a receding maze, in which you can become lost almost as soon as you step off the path. There are no backgrounds in any of these paintings, no vistas; only a great deal of foreground that goes back and back, endlessly, involving you in its twists and turns of tree and branch and rock. No matter how far back in you go, there will be more. And the trees themselves are hardly trees; they are currents of energy, charged with violent color.

Who knows how many trees there were on the cliff just before Lucy disappeared? Who counted? Maybe there was one more, afterwards.

Lois sits in her chair and does not move. Her hand with the cup is raised halfway to her mouth. She hears something, almost hears it: a shout of recognition, or of joy.

She looks at the paintings, she looks into them. Every one of them is a picture of Lucy. You can't see her exactly, but she's there, in behind the pink stone island or the one behind that. In the picture of the cliff she is hidden by the clutch of fallen rocks toward the bottom, in the one of the river shore she is crouching beneath the overturned canoe. In the yellow autumn woods she's behind the tree that cannot be seen because of the other trees, over beside the blue sliver of pond; but if you walked into the picture and found the tree, it would be the wrong one, because the right one would be further on.

Everyone has to be somewhere, and this is where Lucy is. She is in Lois's apartment, in the holes that open inwards on the wall, not like windows but like doors. She is here. She is entirely alive.

At August's End:
Serving Time in Leftist
Summer Camps

Mark Oppenheimer

When I was eight years old, my father sent me to a nudist camp.

Not a nudist colony—mine was a nudist camp, a summer camp where people sometimes went without clothes. We wore clothes to the dining hall to eat, and we wore them again to play rough sports and hike in the steep and tangled woods. We wore clothes in the rain and in the cold of night. In truth, we were clothed more often than not. Swimming was the time for nakedness. But so, too, was walking from the lake back to the cabin or from the cabin to the outdoor showers. The camp brochure put it something like this, with an odd patriotism: "We at Farm and Wilderness believe in peace and respect for the environment. We believe too, remembering President Roosevelt's Four Freedoms, in a 'fifth freedom': the freedom from clothes." Nudity was not required, clothes were not required. A boy could follow his heart.

Farm and Wilderness is a Quaker camp in Plymouth, Vermont, a wooded steeple-church town near the New Hampshire line. It actually is a complex of five small and distinct camps: Saltash Mountain, Tamarack Farm, Indian Brook, Flying Cloud, and Timberlake. Each has a theme: Flying Cloud, for example, attempts to re-create traditional Native American life. The campers and counselors live in tepees, learn indigenous crafts, and assume "Indian names." An alumni note in the quarterly newsletter might read as follows: "Haskell Childs (Plays in the Water '87) recently found himself at a hockey game in Boston seated next to his old tepee-mate, Jim Gold (Watches the Moon '87). Turns out they're both working for Jobs with Justice—Haskell in Lowell, Jim in the Boston office." Indian Brook, which does not have an Indian theme, is the girls' camp, and Timberlake, my camp that summer, is for boys.

I turned eight in the summer of 1982, so when I say that there was nothing erotic about the communal nudity, the skinny-dipping boys and their freely tanning lifeguards on the shores of the lake, it may be my youth talking. I never returned for another summer, so if the adolescent campers escaped to the other side of the lake for moonlit trysts with Indian Brook's naked girls, I never knew. They probably did. I imagine that the gay boys found each other, too. I do know this: One night, toward the end of my four-week stay, some cabin-mates and I escaped after bedtime to spy on our counselors. We knew that there was an all-staff square dance that evening, with counselors from the five camps converging on the grassy clearing in the middle of Timberlake. Leftists play instruments, and a bluegrass band had formed for the night's music. Four of us, I think, waited until the rest of our cabin was soundly asleep, and then stole away, following the sound of the twang and laughter floating in from the distance. It was a warm night, warm in that northern New England way that has a lining of cold, which catches you in the back of the throat when you breathe deeply. As we approached the clearing, we took care to crouch low and hug the treeline of the woods, playing the cloak-and-dagger aspect of our mission to the hilt.

The first things I saw, I remember, were the halter tops, cut-off denim shorts, clogs and keychains littering the ground at the edge of the field. Like a camera, I panned upward and outward, slowly taking in the unshod feet, then the calves, thighs, and hips, then the hanging men and bushy women. Here the pan accelerated, shot straight past their chests to the faces of the men and women: our counselors, activity directors, chefs and lifeguards and nurses, all naked and twirling to the sounds of the guitars and banjo and fiddle. There was a caller yelling, "Do-si-do!" and "Bow da yer pardner!" They were square dancing in their birthday suits. The four of us, all about eight years old, looked at each other and giggled loudly, unafraid that we would be noticed. We looked back at the spectacle, and stared for minutes. As young as we were, we knew somehow that this was a momentous moment, to be savored. We knew that eight more years of life, and then sixteen and twenty-four would all pass without our ever again seeing something quite so awesome as a hundred nude, square-dancing Quakers.

. . .

My father had always felt ambivalent about the monied skin of his German-Jewish background. Like an ill-fitting coat, it kept him warm and protected him from the elements but caused discomfort. When he wed my mother, the daughter of leftist school teachers and union activists, it was he who was marrying up. My parents married in San Antonio, where the army reserves had taken him. After a stint in New York City for my father's law school, they moved to New England so that he could begin a teaching career and they could raise a family.

After New York, the narrow world of Springfield, Massachusetts, imposed on my parents a claustrophobia that they still have not escaped. But they did manage to find like minds. In Springfield, the tiny leftist community—those most likely to ignore the impending Bicentennial—came together around Mudpie, a "daycare cooperative" housed, without intentional irony, in the Tudor auditorium of a local Episcopalian church. Besides one full-time teacher, the only staff was the parents: every couple had to take several shifts a week sitting the children. Fathers as well as mothers worked there, and they took care to use "nonsexist, nonracist language." In 1978, before such linguistic matters had felt the hot light of close scrutiny, I was chastened by one mother for showing off my watercolor of a "mailman." Reeducation came swiftly at Mudpie: "The proper term is 'letter carrier,'" I was told.

To separate oneself from the bourgeoisie, it is enough to be among either the elite or the lumpen, the shoeshined or the shoeless. The socialist parents of my daycare cooperative were cut from the former, more expensive of those cloths. The ink on my father's Columbia Law diploma was barely dry. Another father was a Unitarian minister (who also, it happens, had a law degree from Columbia). There was the father about to enter law school and a mother who went several years thereafter. I do remember a mailman—letter carrier—among the parents, but he had found that career only after his Amherst graduation. The sole interracial couple of the bunch sported two doctorates between them. There was a chemistry professor and there were several law professors. Remember, too, that the money never traveled far from the education: this family had old Protestant money anchored in the leafy hills above Detroit, that family, old Jewish money skulking in the New York suburbs.

So they could afford summer camps. When I was in second grade, old enough for sleepaway camp, my parents turned to old Mudpie friends for advice. One couple suggested a Quaker camp in the mountains of Vermont. If any word has more luster for a leftist than "Quaker," it is surely "Vermont," and my fate was probably sealed right there. Still, we attended a perfunctory information session hosted by a family nearby. There we saw slides of naked boys and girls lounging on sun-drenched lakesides, emerging from tepees, playing frisbee. I was a modest child but brazen enough to ask, in the darkened room filled with prospective campers and their agreeable parents, if I would be allowed to wear clothes. Our host chuckled, and assured me that we could and often would wear clothes. "It all depends on how you feel. Whatever makes you comfortable. Like dinner, for example: usually we dress for dinner, but you don't have to."

That did not make me comfortable. I was a normal kind of boy.

I traded baseball cards with my best friends and was excited to sign up for Little League. My eccentric streak extended to local chess tournaments and a love of books, two facts of my life best hidden from the kids on the block. Swimming naked around other boys—while all well and good in the nineteenth century, in the waterhole of a Laura Ingalls Wilder plot—did not fit neatly into my summer plans.

When my friend Adam, whose parents had told mine about the camp, decided to go, I reconsidered. Adam was big and tough and had been my best friend since our Mudpie days. He lived in the house behind mine, and a gap in the ivied fence allowed us to visit without walking around the block. We traded baseball cards, listened to Hall and Oates, and both hoped to own Camaros someday. If he was going, maybe I could. When my father heard that I would think about it, he smiled and said, "That's all we ask."

Nothing beat the square-dancing vision. If every day had given me a sight so bizarre, I would have returned for more summers. Five or six years later, nearing high school and desperately wanting a girlfriend, it occurred to me that the Farm and Wilderness camps were probably just the place to go—Tamarack Farm, one of the five, was nudist and *coed*. I stayed away, though, and have never gone back. Like Telemachus at sea, I have reason to fear what would await me.

The camp's proprietor was an old woman named Susan Webb. She was rumored to have a husband, a sick one; nobody ever saw him. They were Quakers, or at least their ancestors were, probably the original seventeenth-century kind who had been the first

Friends to channel their antinomianism into nudity. When I got to college and began to study religion, I learned that the Friends were passionately Christian people who, when filled with the Inner Light, developed strange antinomian tendencies, which some of them took as license to do anything they pleased. George Fox was condemned as a heretic to the Anglican church for his teachings. The camp run by the Webbs had kept the antinomianism but, so far as I could see, had ditched the Christianity. Like the Unitarians, who initially had shocked traditional Congregationalists by denying the Trinity, or the Universalists, who had had the temerity to preach universal salvation, the Quakers were born of Christian descent but have become in this day mostly a sect of leftists drawn to certain libertine aspects of their tradition. At Timberlake, I heard nothing about pacifism, but there was a lot of talk about the Five Freedoms. At the Webbs' camp, the real Quaker heritage was not so much elided as ignored.

I do remember endless Meetings. Every morning, after breakfast, we gathered at a circle of benches planted amid tall evergreens. There we sat, for a long time. (I can truthfully say that I do not know how long Meeting lasted. It may have been as little as fifteen minutes, but it felt like an hour or more. I just don't know.) Nobody ever told me that Meeting was part of the Quaker tradition; I knew only that it was my least favorite part of the camp's tradition. Most mornings, nobody spoke. We sat there, for minute after minute of silence. I assumed that we had to bow our heads. One morning, however, I dared to look up, and saw others looking up. Some mornings, I fell asleep.

On a good day, somebody would do something. I remember

one truly slow morning, when I had to pee and wanted to go back to sleep. It was a feeling I would meet again years later, in college classes that lasted for two hours. As I began softly to curse my parents, I heard a bench creaking ninety degrees of the circle to my left. I looked over and saw an old bearded man rising unsteadily to his feet. He looked around at the camp family, the campers and staff and our assortment of bearded men who served no purpose, just arrived every morning and lent authenticity to the proceedings, like extras on a movie set. The old man started to speak, but the New England morning cold gripped his throat, and he paused. The trees shivered from the breeze, and dew rained down, waking me a little. I stared intently at this man, so thankful that he was about to do something to attenuate my boredom. He continued to cast his eyes around the circle, and the eyes widened as they scanned. Looking back, I think that maybe he was genuinely overcome by the Inner Light. His mouth turned up at the corners, and he broke into a wildly cackling laugh, one that scared me. I was afraid that he had gone mad, and I looked over at the row of counselors sitting on the bench to my right. They were nodding their approval, unfazed, and one or two were stroking their chins in silent meditation. The man kept cackling, louder now, and I grew frightened, very frightened. Just as I was about to ask someone—I don't know whom—if the old man was okay, he stopped. Now people were nodding and smiling, and I began to panic because I didn't understand. I, who was the brightest boy in every class, who had been taught adult things, like why Ronald Reagan was bad and what a picket line was for, simply could not make sense of the nods and smiles and the old man's cackle. I felt a lump in my throat and decided that I would get up and leave the circle. As the courage to move tried to spread its way down to my feet, it was distracted, again now by the old man. He had begun to sing. In a creaky, tired bass, he sang a line that I had never heard: "Kumbaya, my Lord, Kumbaya."

"Beginning in the early 1920s," historian Paul Mishler writes, "Communist-organized children's activities were designed to transmit the values and ideology of the movement to, what they hoped, would be the next generation of radicals. These activities ranged from children's organizations, such as the young pioneers of America, to a variety of after-school programs, cultural groups, and summer camps." In 1956, the State of New York, unable to shake its McCarthyite grippe, launched an investigation of communist camps within its borders. It found twenty-seven, some privately run, some owned by organizations like the Fur and Leather Workers Union. One of the private camps was Camp Kinderland, then thirty years old. Founded originally by members of the Workmen's Circle of New York City, it had for its first decade tried to effect a mix of radical politics and secular *Yiddishkeit;* Yiddish classes had through the 1930s been mandatory. In 1937, Sholom Aleichem's widow had visited the camp; Soviet Yiddish writer Itzak Feffer had managed a visit before being executed, by Stalin, in 1940; Paul Robeson visited the campers.

We don't know what Robeson said to the young Communists, but he probably sang. Folksongs are the leitmotiv of leftist camps. I learned as much when, three years after my ill-starred summer at Timberlake, my parents suggested another camp, recommended by different friends, and it was Camp Kinderland. Closer to home (it is now in Tolland, Massachusetts), this was, they promised, a more buttoned-down affair. No nudity, no Quaker Meetings. I was reluctant but ever-trusting, and they sold me on the idea— packed me up and shipped me out, once more unto the breach. My first week had not yet elapsed when we were gathered by the Paul Robeson Playhouse for some old-time religion. We sang "Kumbaya," "If I Had a Hammer," "Blowin' in the Wind," "We Shall Overcome," and "We Shall Not Be Moved"—a compilation of folk's greatest hits, Leadbelly to Guthrie to Dylan. I had forgotten the words learned at Timberlake, but the tunes were the same. As in Wagner's *Ring*, so in leftist camps: the same melodies kept cropping up, ever pregnant with meaning and ideology and, after a while, predictable.

For the comrades of Camp Kinderland, Woody Guthrie was not only a songwriter, sage, and minor prophet. He was a cabin. A ramshackle, weather-beaten cabin, but one fit for shelter nonetheless. I did not live in Woody Guthrie. I lived for four weeks in Eugene V. Debs, which sat ten yards from the other eleven-year-old boys' bunk, Joe Hill. I always wanted to spy on the girls in Pablo Neruda. But I would have been caught by the girls across the way in Roberto Clemente. That might have forced me to hide in Anne Frank or plot an uprising in Bar Kochba.

But even after they had told us that Roberto Clemente had died en route to aid the victims of an earthquake in Nicaragua, I still thought of my father's beloved Pirates every time I passed by the building. Even after living near Anne Frank, the cabin, she remained for me an author and Holocaust victim. Or sometimes metaphors work too well, lose their power to represent and instead just become: because I first heard of Pablo Neruda as a building, I cannot really think of him as a poet. At Camp Kinderland, nobody ever read us a poem by Neruda. It was sufficient that he had his building.

I think historians are born and not made, and I would have been interested in the history of the camp. Nobody told me about the history. I didn't know that in the early years, campers had saluted a red flag after breakfast and bunk cleanup. Nor that Camp Kinderland had been the object, in its first year, of a tug of war between leftists and rightists—probably Communists and Socialists—in the Workmen's Circle. I absorbed instead other memes of cultural trivia: why it was a progressive stand to live in Park Slope or not to buy from Nestlé. My peers repeated what their parents told them, not Old Left propaganda but smug facsimiles, ink smudged in the process until unrecognizable as politics at all.

We played sports at Camp Kinderland, with a twist. Nobody ever won or lost—everything ended in a "Kinderland Tie." The Kinderland Tie was achieved by not matching teams as evenly as possible or by neglecting to keep score. One time, we began a volleyball match, diligently keeping track of the points. Within fifteen minutes, our server was calling "thirteen serving two," and serving an ace, bringing us to match point. He then simply served again, without calling out the score. I knew our team was on the verge of winning; indeed, everyone must have known, because after we won the ultimate point, we all stopped playing, recognizing that a game had just ended. Nobody, however, congratulated the winning team or consoled the losers. Everybody screamed, "Kinderland Tie!" and hugged each other.

Although the deception was badly surreal for me at the time, the practice gains a certain burnish through the prism of memory. How nice, I see now, that we could play for the pure joy of athleticism. A man I recently met learned that I had gone to Camp Kinderland. "Oh, a great place," he told me. "My oldest boy is legally blind, and I sent him there. It was the only camp where he ever felt comfortable playing sports."

Still, I didn't understand: why then keep score at all? Perhaps they—I, we, all of us—were competitive. Volleyball and softball and Ping-Pong are more fun with scoring. My fellow Kinderlanders knew this but would never admit it. Their sporting lives, too, were governed by congenital utopian fantasies about human nature, fantasies that they refused to relinquish even after being mugged by reality. An hour and a half of full-court hoops under the August sun? Sure, it might be fun to keep score for a while, but really, do we need a winner?

I did. I didn't need to win, but I insisted that somebody did. When after match point everybody threw their hands in the air, proclaimed a "Kinderland Tie!" and rushed under the volleyball net to hug their dead-matched competitors, I slunk away from the party. More than once I found myself standing at the edge of the volleyball court or basketball court or softball field, smiling gamely but annoyed to the core. As the revelers dispersed and headed to the showers, someone would always tousle my long bowl-cut hair and tell me to "get with the spirit."

For I was not unpopular. They treated me with all the affection and warmth granted a retarded boy, which in a sense I was. My consciousness was yet unraised, but that could hardly be my fault, and I had come to the right place. My leftist sympathies simply had yet to bloom, stunted in their growth by some unknown allergen in the air of Springfield. A vast number of the campers and counselors lived on the Upper West Side or in the right parts of Brooklyn, where the soil nourished well the proper tendencies. Western Massachusetts was a fine retreat for summer play but hardly fit for year-round living; and people seemed surprised when I told them where I lived when August ended.

There was an exception to this law of return, and it afforded me a minor celebrity. Michael and Robert Meeropol, the sons of Julius and Ethel Rosenberg, also lived with their families in western Massachusetts where they were close friends of my parents. The Meeropols sent their children to Kinderland (and probably were the ones who told my parents about the place). One of Michael's sons was counselor to a group of boys my age, though he was not my counselor. He was exceptional not just for his lineage but for his kindness. His cousin was also a camper at Kinderland that summer, likeable and, as I remember, unconcerned with the shibboleths of authenticity that seemed to consume the masses. I was wise enough even then to divine the root of their comfort: they had nothing to prove. Like the counselor who knew Pete Seeger or the elderly hanger-on who had known a victim of the Triangle Shirtwaist fire, their loyalty was beyond question. In later years, I have often wondered that what saved me from outright hostility was my fellow-traveler status. I was a friend of the Meeropols, and so the party line may have slackened in deference.

. . .

Obviously, I did not have the faith. The camp could read my stubbornness in the turn of my head, the raised eyebrows, and the doubting mien. One rainy day, the boys of Eugene V. Debs were crowded into a shed and handed writing paper and pens. The counselor told us that we would be writing letters to congressmen, advocating a position of our choice. A camper could, if he so chose, demand an end to aid to the Contras. He could, if he so chose, demand an end to the Cuban embargo. He, if he chose, could demand an end to our involvement in El Salvador. Now get to it, boys, we only have an hour until lunch. I muttered that this was a stupid idea. I wanted to play in the rain. The counselor heard me. A week later, on a luminous, breeze-bathed August noontime, the boys of Eugene V. Debs were herded into that same shed and introduced to Chaika. Chaika looked healthy for a ninety-year-old, though I was later told that she was seventy. For an hour we ten boys listened to her Methuselan face lecture us about the joys of Yiddish. None of us knew any Yiddish beyond the Yiddish that all Americans know, and the camp, now past the 1930s, ventured no pretense of teaching us. Her talk—that one hour carved from a long month—was the requisite homage to Kinderland's legacy of "secular Judaism." Wasn't it a wonderful lecture? my counselor asked me later. Not really, I said. He frowned. Yet people indulged me, decided that my resistance to their dogma was a function of youth or hometown.

The summer might in fact have been no worse than a pleasant, quirky romp but for three incidents that my memory keeps in relief, perpetually caught in my mind's eye, fixed:

It is a cool mountain evening, the temperature diving toward night. I rummage through my trunk to find armor against the cold. I pull out a deep crimson velour sweatshirt. My mother just bought it for me because I wanted a sweater like the one my dad wears to rake the leaves. I pull it over my head, bend down and tie my shoelaces, and walk over to the all-camp meeting that daily precedes dinner. As I near the crowd, Alice, the camp director, approaches me with a smile. She looks me up and down, and laughs. "Jesus Christ, Mark," she says. "You look just like a golfer."

Today they load us into camp vans and drive us thirty miles to the nearest cineplex—an unexpected treat. We all watch *Back to the Future*, with Michael J. Fox, one of the biggest TV stars. I love the movie, and that's really cool because I think that now I have something in common with my bunkmates, something we can talk and laugh about. As we pile back into the vans for the trip home, I am lucky enough to get shotgun, so I sit next to Jon, one of our counselors. "Wasn't that movie cool, Jon?" I say. "No, I thought it was really awful," he says. "So racist. The character sweeping the floor in the diner, he's *black*, of course. And the terrorists are Libyan, of course." I keep my eyes on the road. I try to think of something to say back, but can only think to reply, "I thought it was okay."

There is that boy named Hunde—I think he is named after some foreign word. He and I haven't been getting along, and yesterday he hit me. When I told Jon about it, he said he would speak to Alice, who is in charge. But I guess they didn't say anything to Hunde, because today I say something mean to him and he attacks me, throws me to the floor of the cabin, and starts punching me. They finally pull him off me, and I am screaming and crying, which makes me ashamed in front of the other boys. I ask Jon if anything will happen to Hunde, if he'll be kicked out or at least punished so he won't hit me again. Jon says that Hunde is troubled, and his home life is not so good, and in the future I'll just have to be more careful. I manage to laugh bitterly through my tears, and I wonder if Hunde's punching me while I try to shield my face will be regarded as a Kinderland Tie.

John Irving has written that "one can always imagine a better detail than the one we can remember." Joseph Mitchell aimed "not to be factual but to be truthful." Adam Larrabee, who sat across the table in Mrs. Archibald's senior English class at Loomis, promised me once, as I agonized over an autobiographical paper, "You have to lie to tell the truth." The best I can say about Timberlake and Kinderland is that they proved all these maxims wholly false. No fiction writer, no matter how cosmic and Merlinesque his or her powers, could conjure details and color better than what I actually experienced at the lefty camps. I've never lacked a crazy story of my childhood or one that makes my past seem more exotic than it was. My truth is stranger than almost any fiction.

What my truth, the two summers I was caught in propaganda's gunsight, could not do was make me a leftist. The songs, the unclothed anomie, the cabins, and the eponymous martyrs—I remember none of them so well as the self-righteousness of the people sleeping next to me on those summer nights in the mountains. It seemed odd that Debs had suffered imprisonment—spoken out against the Great War and been jailed for his speech—so that I might be mocked for wearing velour. Or that Woody Guthrie, were he alive, would chide me for enjoying a good movie just as I enjoyed his songs. The leftists I met that summer were so keen to preach the good news of tolerance. They just couldn't brook someone's doubting their gospel.

In those days, I had a naive belief, because the leftists I knew were my decent and nurturing relatives, that people who talked about tolerance and freedom did first by example. That had been my experience. So Camp Kinderland—where sports contests had no winners, brutal beatings no consequences—seemed even at the time more absurd than cruel. I distanced myself, stood outside their glass bowl, watching as the fish inside played with water. It was, in a sense, an education. Few of us have the opportunity to live for long in a world whose working assumptions differ so wildly from our own: the kind of world where a young boy with no racist, sexist, or even capitalist impulses arouses suspicion because he enjoys a movie or wears the wrong kind of shirt.

My memory has completed the work of transforming those people from strange and unknowable ideologues into sad sacks. They are the true believers whose gods have failed, and in their summers—still, for the camp thrives today—they work to stem the tide of apostates. The great danger is not the right but the seductive allure of apolitical respectability; it is not the Christian Coalition that siphons off members, it is the Democrats. They see the turncoats, like David Horowitz shouting into his own wind, and the thousands more who simply choose to be respectable. My desire just to have a fun summer, to swim and play and laugh, was thus the most subversive of statements, for it denied the ubiquity of politics. Not *our* children, Camp Kinderland says. And so everything is political, even for the very young, even the buildings where they sleep.

I might have manufactured more understanding, more critical perspective, at the time had someone during that month of Camp Kinderland sat us down and told us the history of the camp, about the red-flag salutes and Widow Aleichem's visit. The problem is that utopians begin anew—they level history and live without it. To talk about the visits in days past, from Aleichem to Robeson to Seeger, would have been seductive and gorgeous, and would have made me feel that I stood on hallowed ground. Which would have defeated the purpose. Until the revolution has come, the point is to let no ground be sacred but to turn it and till it until it births something new. So they never looked back and never shared the history, just kept singing the songs.

What shone through all the clouds of ideology was my parents' simple belief that children are an end, not a means. My parents did not have children to add more footsoldiers to the cause. My father had genuinely wanted me to have summer experiences richer than those in his past, and he hurt for me when he read my unhappy letters home. At the end of August, he came to fetch me from Camp Kinderland, and I, shy about disappointing him, said that I would not return for another summer; he agreed. He was, I think, just a little glad to realize that his son wasn't about to get his political views from camp counselors and peer pressure. Camp

Kinderland, and Timberlake far off in the distant past, were two experiences among an infinite number, and they would have their say in who I became. My liberalism would come to be a different creature, one admixed with the history that I now study, spiced with the knowledge that the world is a fallen place, not suitable for utopian schemes. That's an easy thing to see when you've met some utopians.

The Days of the Thunderbirds

Andrea Lee

When the Thunderbirds arrived at Camp Grayfeather, Ellen, Chen-cheu, and I were waiting for them, lounging on the splintery steps of the recreation hall. Behind us, a big fly with a weary August note to its buzz banged against the screen door. In front of us, under a level evening sun, the straw-colored Delaware countryside—pointedly referred to as "Wyeth Territory" in the camp catalogue—rolled off from our own wooded hillside toward the bluish haze that was Maryland. It was a Tuesday and just after dinner, the tranquil period in a camp day, when the woods are filled with the soft clanging of bells announcing evening activities and the air still holds a whiff of tuna casserole. After dinner was supposed to be journal-writing time for the three dozen or so fourteen-year-olds who made up the rank and file at Grayfeather, but Chen-cheu, Ellen, and I had slipped out of our tent in order to witness the coming of the Thunderbirds. It was an event we were awaiting with the same kind of horrified delight as that with which Biblical adolescents, as deep in glandular boredom as we ourselves were, must have greeted a plague of locusts. The Thunderbirds were a black teenage gang, one of many that battled in the close brick streets of Wilmington, and, through some obscure adult arrangement, they were coming to spend a week with us at camp.

"Do you think they'll have knives, Sarah?" Chen-cheu asked me, rubbing an array of chigger bites on her ankle.

Chen-cheu was the camp beauty, a Chinese-American girl from Oberlin, Ohio, whose solid-cheeked, suntanned face had an almost frightening exotic loveliness above her muscular swimmer's shoulders. She had, however, a calm, practical personality that belied her thrilling looks, and she talked with a flat Midwestern accent, as if she'd been brought up in a soddy.

"Nah," I said. "Gangs use guns these days."

In fact, my only knowledge of the habits of gangs came from seeing the movie *West Side Story*, but, like the other black kids at Grayfeather, most of us the overprotected or dreadfully spoiled products of comfortable suburban childhoods, I had been affecting an intimate knowledge of street life ever since I'd heard about the Thunderbirds.

"Maybe we'll end up massacred," said Ellen, in a hopeful voice, unwrapping a stick of gum.

Ellen was always chewing gum, though it was against camp rules; she had come to Grayfeather with about a thousand packages of Wrigley's hidden in her trunk, and even, to the derision of her bunkmates, made little chains of the wrappers. She chewed so much that her father, a Reform rabbi in Baltimore, once made her walk around a shopping mall with a wad of gum stuck to her forehead. She and Chen-cheu and I had been close friends all summer—a brisk female triumvirate who liked to think of ourselves as Maid Marians, both lawless and seductive. (In reality, it was only Chen-cheu who provided the physical charms, since Ellen and I were peaky, bookworm types.) The three of us made a point of being on the spot whenever anything interesting or scandalous happened at the camp, and the arrival of the Thunderbirds was certainly the most riveting event of the summer.

They were not the first visitors we'd had at Grayfeather: already we'd played host to a morose quartet of Peruvian flute players and a troop of impossibly pink-cheeked Icelandic scouts. The Thunderbirds represented, however, the most ambitious attempt to incarnate the camp motto, which was "Adventures in Understanding." As Ellen once remarked, instead of being a tennis camp or a weight-loss camp, Grayfeather was an integration camp. The campers—most of whose fathers were professors, like Chen-cheu's, or clergymen, like mine—had been carefully selected to form a motley collection of colors and religions, so that our massed assemblies at meals, chapel, and campfires looked like illustrations for UNICEF posters.

It was at chapel the previous Sunday that Ned Woolworth, the camp director, had announced the coming of the Thunderbirds. "During the next week, you'll be more than just kids relating to kids," he said, strolling up and down between the rows of split-log benches, scanning our dubious fourteen-year-old faces with his benign, abstracted gaze, his big, gnarled knees (his nickname was Monster Legs) working below his khaki shorts. Woolworth was tall and looked like Teddy Roosevelt, and had an astonishing talent for not knowing things. He ignored the generally unenthusiastic silence, as his campers coldly pondered the ramifications of doubling up in tents with their comrades-to-be, and passed over the muttered lamentations of the camp misfit, a Nigerian diplomat's son named Femi. He read us a few lines from "The Prophet," and then told us we would be like ambassadors, bridging a gap that society had created. It appeared that the staff had already written and gotten permission from all of our parents.

The arrival of the Thunderbirds at Grayfeather was signalled by a grinding of gears and a confused yelling from far down the dirt road that led through six miles of woods to the camp. As Ellen, Chen-cheu, and I poked each other in excitement, a battered yellow school bus, covered with a tangle of long-stemmed graffiti, rattled into the clearing and swerved into the dusty parking lot beside the rec hall. The bus ground its gears once more, shuddered, and seemed to expire. The doors flew open and the Thunderbirds poured down the steps into the evening sunlight.

"They're so *small!*" Ellen whispered to me.

There were ten boys and seven girls (the girls forming, as we later found out, a sort of women's auxiliary of the Thunderbirds)—brown-skinned teenagers with mature faces and bodies and stunted, childish legs that gave the boys, with their well-developed shoulders and short thighs, the look of bantam cocks.

One of the boys came up to Chen-cheu, Ellen, and me and

stood rocking on his heels. "Hello, ladies," he said. "My name is Marvin Jones."

He wore tight black pants and a green T-shirt that was printed with the words "KING FUNK," and he had an astonishing Afro pompadour that bobbed like a cresting wave over his mobile, trickster's face. Above his left eye, he had dyed a platinum streak in his hair, and down one brown cheek ran a deep scar. Looking at him, I had the feeling that something unbelievable was happening in front of me.

"Hello," said Chen-cheu, Ellen, and I in a faint chorus.

In a minute, Ned Woolworth and the rest of the staff were there organizing things. The sleepy little camp clearing, with its square of sunbleached turf and its cluster of low, green-painted buildings, seemed suddenly frantic and overcrowded. Radios weren't allowed at Grayfeather, but one of the Thunderbirds had brought a big portable receiver that filled the air with a Motown beat. Martha and the Vandellas were singing, their shrill, sweet voices crackling with static, and the Thunderbirds were bouncing to the beat while they eyed the camp, shoved each other, picked up their abbreviated luggage, and shouted back and forth. Meanwhile, the rest of the Grayfeather campers had slipped unobtrusively, even furtively, out of the woods, like an indigenous tribe showing itself to explorers; they settled on the steps and porches of the rec hall, to swing their feet and observe. Little Nick Silver, a math whiz from Toughkenamon, Pennsylvania, who at a precocious twelve years old was the youngest kid at camp, sat down next to me. "You have *got* to be joking," he whispered. "They'll eat us for breakfast!"

With the Thunderbirds had come a counsellor from the social

agency that had sponsored their visit: a tall, sallow white man with thinning curly hair and a weary, skeptical way of regarding the woods, the camp buildings, the evening sky, and his charges. He talked with Ned Woolworth for a few minutes and then climbed back inside the battered school bus, turning around only once to smile sardonically at the Thunderbirds. "See you later, guys," he called out. "Behave yourselves." The Thunderbirds responded with a kind of roar, and then the school bus started up with another wrench of gears and rattled off through the trees.

Once the newcomers had filed down the path into the woods, to put their bags away in the tents, one of the counsellors rang the evening-activities bell. "We'll have introductions at campfire," she announced. "Be friendly!"

We campers simply looked at one another. With the Thunderbirds gone from the clearing, a powerful current of noise and energy had suddenly been shut off. Bats flitted across the darkening sky, and a breeze from the lake carried the smell of damp leaf mold. While the others were lining up, I went over to inspect a far corner of the dining hall, where I'd seen a group of the Thunderbirds clustering. There, scratched deeply into the green paint, was a miniature version of the same long-stemmed, weirdly elegant graffiti that had covered the school bus, and that I had seen spray-painted on decrepit buildings on trips to the city. It read: "T BIRDZ RULE."

Marvin Jones was the leader of the Thunderbirds. At the get-acquainted campfire, it was his command that galvanized his troops into standing up and stepping forward, one by one, to give their names. (L. T. LaWanda. Doze. Brother Willy.) He himself stood by in the firelight with a crazy tremor running through his body, wearing a rubber-lipped showman's smirk, like a black Mick Jagger. (Stretch. Dewey. Belinda. Guy.) In the bright circle of hot moving light that baked our faces and knees and left our backs chilled with the damp breath of the big pine grove behind us, we campers studied the Thunderbirds and they studied us. Both groups had the same peculiar expression: not hostility but a wary reservation of judgment. As bits of ash danced like a swarm of glowing insects in the draft of the fire—a big log-cabin fire, built especially for the occasion by the woodcrafts class—Ned Woolworth, his cheerful, freckled wife, Hannah, and the rest of the staff guided us all through a number of cheers and folk songs.

Most of the counsellors looked eager and uneasy. The near-instantaneous grapevine among the campers had already reported that the Thunderbirds had gotten into trouble immediately after their arrival, as they walked down the path to the boys' tents. Marvin Jones and two others had shinnied up a tall, skinny tree—one of the birches, unusual in that area, and beloved by the nature counsellors—swinging on it and pulling it down with their combined weight until it seemed likely to break. When one of the counsellors asked them to stop, Marvin Jones, laughing crazily and hanging on to the birch, responded, "This is the *woods*, man! Ain't *no* law against climbing no tree in the woods!"

That night, the Thunderbird girls who had been assigned to share our tent refused to undress until the light was turned out. There were three of them: a pair of tiny, frail-boned twins named Cookie and June, who had large almond-shaped eyes, hair done identically in an intricately braided puff over each ear, and small breasts in sharp, pointed brassieres that stuck out like Dixie Cups through the clinging nylon of their blouses, and Belinda, a stocky girl who looked twenty years old and had a slight squint, straightened hair bleached a bright orange-red in the front, and a loud, unbridled tongue (I had heard Belinda laughing and cursing above the others when they got off the bus). She was subdued now, as were Cookie and June, the three of them sitting bolt upright on the tightly stretched army blankets of the cots that had been set up for them, muttering replies to the kindly chitchat of our counsellor, Molly. Molly was from Jamaica—a student with an anxious, plump face and a delightful habit of shaking her head at her campers and exclaiming, "Girls, you are becoming hardened in your ways!"

The three Thunderbird girls responded to Molly with a sudden opacity of gaze, glances among themselves, and abrupt fits of shy giggling. We campers were stricken with shyness ourselves: there was none of our usual roughhousing, or bedtime ballets in our underwear. Instead, we undressed quickly in our bunks, turning away from each other, painfully conscious of the contrast between the lavishly equipped trunks from which we drew our pajamas and the small vinyl bags that our guests had brought. Once Molly had turned off the single yellow bulb that illuminated the tent and had strolled off up the path to a staff meeting at the rec hall, the tent was unnaturally silent.

I arranged myself on my lumpy top bunk as I always did—with the sheet over my head to keep off mosquitoes—and breathed in the scent of slightly mildewed canvas from the rolled sides of the tent. From the bunk beneath me, Chen-cheu, an instant and sound sleeper, gave an adenoidal snore, and I could hear little clicks and rustlings that meant the Thunderbird girls were undressing. There was a cool breeze blowing with a steady rushing sound in the trees, and I wondered what the girls from the city were thinking as they listened, perhaps for the first time in their lives, to the noises of the wild night. Never had I been so aware of the woods as a living place around me. Over the stubborn saw of the crickets, I heard two hoots from a white-faced owl that lived in a tree near our tent, and a gradually intensifying gray light in the direction of the lake meant the moon was rising. In my mind, the moon mingled with the yellow school bus that had brought the Thunderbirds, and then suddenly I found myself sliding quickly out of the vision, knowing that I'd been asleep.

What had awakened me was a soft voice. It was the new girl June, calling out to her sister in a whisper. "Cookie—Cookie—are you up? I hear a noise."

There was a creak as Cookie got up and crept over to her sister's cot. I leaned my head out slightly from my bunk, and in the dim moonlight caught a glimpse of the tiny girl, her hair greased and braided for the night, dressed in her underwear. It hadn't occurred to me until then that perhaps the Thunderbird girls didn't have pajamas. "Hush, girl," whispered Cookie to her sister, sitting lightly down on the cot. "Hush up! You want these bitches to hear you?"

"But there's a noise," whimpered June.

"Hush up, girl. It's just trees, that's all. Just trees."

There was silence, and when after a few minutes I edged my head out of the bunk to have another look I saw that Cookie had lain down on her sister's cot, and that the two girls were sleeping with their heads close together on the pillow.

At breakfast, Ned Woolworth announced to a chorus of groans from the campers that instead of swimming or canoeing or tennis we would divide up into small groups for what he called rap sessions. My group included Ellen; Jackie Murdock, a camper notorious throughout Grayfeather for his prolonged belches at mealtimes; a round-faced Thunderbird named Ricky; and a skinnier Thunderbird named Les, who wore a peculiar rust-colored bowler hat. There was also Marvin Jones, the Thunderbird leader, who wore an Army fatigue jacket, open to show his gleaming bronze chest, and sat slumped, wiggling his feet, an expression of exaggerated forbearance on his face. The six of us met with a counsellor in a grove of pin oaks near the chapel. It was one of those clear, dry, autumnal days that occasionally leap ahead of their time into the middle of August. The sky was a sharp blue, crisp moving shadows checkered the ground, and in the eyes of all of the kids sitting there was a skittish, inattentive look, as if they might dash off suddenly into the breezy woods.

A green acorn plopped down near Ricky, the Thunderbird sitting beside Ellen. "Wha's that?" he asked her, pointing.

"That's an acorn," said Ellen scornfully, tossing back her red hair. "Didn't you ever see an acorn before?"

"No, Sweet Thighs," said Ricky, giving her a lascivious, cherubic smile that showed a broken front tooth. He picked up the acorn and put it carefully in his pocket.

The counsellor clapped her hands. She was a diving coach, with a pugnacious sunburned face and a blunt, bossy way of talking. "This morning, we're going to discuss friendship," she said. "We all have friends, so let's talk about them—who they are, and what they mean to us—"

"I don't have friends," interrupted Marvin Jones.

"What?" said the counsellor.

"I said I don't have friends," said Marvin Jones, looking at her seriously, the platinum streak in his hair glittering in the sunlight through the treetops. "Yeah, that's right, Miss. I mean, shit— scuse me, Miss—I got my *men*. Spike is my *man*. Ricky is my *man*. And L.T., that dude with the sunglasses and the FREE AFRICA T-shirt, he's my *main* man. I mean, them dudes will cut for me. But they don't be no *friends*. And then we got the Thunderbird Queens—I mean our ladies."

"*They're* not your friends, of course," said the counsellor acidly.

"No. Like I said, we don't have no friends. We got enemies, though—the Twelfth and Diamond Street gang. You ever hear of them?"

"No."

"Well, that's good, 'cause the T-birds are on top. Wait a minute—I'll show you something."

He gave a curt, imperious nod to Ricky and the other Thunderbird beside him, and an odd tension seemed to seize all three of them. The woods seemed very quiet for a minute, and all at once, synchronized, they stood up, snapping their fingers. In high, plaintive voices, they broke into words and rhythms that were not quite a song, not quite a chant: "What the word/Thunderbird . . ."

It was a strange mixture: a little bit of Motown, a bit of the interlocking verses all kids use to choose sides for games, a bit of the bouncy silliness of football and basketball cheers, all bound together quite naturally with swearwords—words that we Grayfeather campers all knew and used enthusiastically among ourselves, in spite of what parents and teachers and counsellors had to say. The Thunderbird song could have been ridiculous, but instead it was thrilling, carrying with it, to those of us who sat listening, all the resonance of a dangerous young life in the city. It was clear that the song was not intended as an entertainment for us but was presented as a kind of credential, like the letters scratched into the paint of the rec hall. Ellen and I punched each other excitedly in the ribs, and tried to remember every word. When the song was finished, Marvin Jones and the two other Thunderbirds flopped down abruptly at the base of a tree, their faces full of restrained pride.

"That was great, fellows," said the counsellor. She was trying to seem cordial, but it was clear that she was uncomfortable, almost angry, about what had just happened. "Let's see if you can do a little more talking now, so that we can get to know you."

Marvin Jones picked up a twig from the ground and tapped the toes of his sneakers with it—one, two, three. "Lady, you just got to know us," he said.

. . .

Down at the lake that afternoon, Jimmy Terkel, the boating counsellor, gave a briefing on canoeing to an assembled group of campers and Thunderbirds. Jimmy Terkel was a dark, soft-spoken young man who loved the little irregular lake, with its cedar water and clustering lilies; all summer he had made canoeing into an austere rite, embarking on solitary voyages at dawn or sunset, an angular silhouette at the far corner of the water. The afternoon had grown overcast, and as Jimmy Terkel talked about water safety and demonstrated the proper way to dip and feather a paddle—the lecture was chiefly for the newcomers, since the campers had been handling canoes all summer—swarms of audacious gnats made forays at our eyes and ears.

Suddenly, in the middle of the talk, Marvin Jones strode over to one of the aluminum canoes on the shore and began to push it toward the water. "I want to go for a ride, Mister," he said politely to Jimmy Terkel. "I know how to do this. I see it all the time on TV."

Three other Thunderbirds grabbed paddles and rushed over to the canoe, pushing it through the shallows to deeper water, and tilting it dangerously when they all climbed in, about fifteen yards from shore.

"That's too many in a boat, fellows!" called Jimmy Terkel, coming forward.

The gunwales of the overloaded canoe were riding about six inches above the surface of the lake, and the boat shipped water as the passengers thrashed about trying to position themselves; miraculously, the canoe did not capsize. There was an argument between two of the Thunderbirds ("You on my *arm*, man!"), and then the canoe took off with an irregular splayed motion, as Marvin Jones and a second Thunderbird paddled with great splashing thrusts.

"Oh, *no!*" Jimmy Terkel muttered, glancing automatically at the heap of orange life preservers on the shore. But no disaster occurred. The canoe made its awkward, lunging way into the cluster of lily pads, and we heard the delighted yells of the novice canoeists as they yanked up the tough-stemmed blossoms—an act that the camp staff, ardent conservationists all, had raised in our minds to the level of a felony. Then the boys in the boat all took off their shirts, and Marvin Jones stood precariously upright to paddle like a gondolier, a big lily coiled dripping around his neck. There was something barbaric and absurd about the sight of him paddling that overloaded canoe, which, as it wobbled heavily over the dark water, seemed a parody of a boat, something out of a nursery rhyme. As I watched, there came to me out of nowhere a surge of pure happiness. The other campers seemed to feel it as well; the faces of the kids around me were contorted with crazy laughter, and some of them were jumping up and down. Out of the corner of my eye, I saw one of the campers, from pure joie de vivre as it were, pick up a handful of sand and rub it into the hair of his bunkmate. Just for a minute, it seemed that the camp was a place where any mad thing could happen. While Jimmy Terkel stood on the shore with an angry smile on his face, campers and Thunderbirds alike were almost dying with glee.

That was the last, really the only, good time we had with the Thunderbirds. Later that afternoon, a scuffle broke out near the camp infirmary between two of the gang members and a stable-boy. A burly counsellor from Honolulu broke up the fight, which was just a matter of shoving and name-calling. The participants were made to stand face to face and explain themselves, and in the process they quite spontaneously shook hands and apologized. In ten minutes, the grapevine had telegraphed news of the scuffle to all parts of Grayfeather. It seemed that everyone involved in the fight had laughed it off except for Ned Woolworth, who had rushed to the scene and glared at the three boys as if he wanted to knock them all down.

The staff had scheduled a hayride for that night. Normally, the campers looked forward to hayrides: the dusky country roads, shrill with insects; the creaky wagon and plodding, pungent horses; the deep, scratchy hay that offered the opportunity for a little romantic improvisation (though Grayfeather, a camp of overeducated fourteen-year-olds, was notoriously backward in that department). Early in the evening, a subtle intelligence flashed through the ranks of the campers, a kind of mass intuition that suggested that things would be much better if we let the Thunderbirds go hayriding on their own. To the bewilderment of our counsellors, who had no way of forcing us to accept a treat, all of the campers, gently but immovably, refused to go.

After dinner, Ellen, Chen-cheu, and I and the other girls from our tent took part in a desultory sunset game of Capture the Flag, as the Thunderbirds and their girls, escorted by Grayfeather staff members, boarded the wagon. An hour and a half later, the returning wagon creaked slowly up to the recreation hall. Norah Pfleisch, an excitable junior counsellor, rushed inside and burst into tears on the shoulder of Ned Woolworth's wife, Hannah, who was directing a spur-of-the-moment Ping-Pong tournament.

"I've never, *never* had anything like this happen," sobbed Norah, resisting Hannah's efforts to lead her out of the rec hall and away from the fascinated gaze of forty campers. "They—fornicated! They lay in the hay like animals and just . . . did it! It started when we went under the old covered bridge. It was such a beautiful night. Usually we *sing* on hayrides, but this time I didn't know *where* to look, or *what* to listen to!"

We all rushed to the door of the rec hall. Outside, under a clear night sky streaked with meteor showers, the Thunderbirds and their girls, chattering loudly and innocently, were climbing out of the wagon, pulling hay out of each other's clothes.

Things fell apart completely the next day. That morning at swimming class, another fight broke out—this one between Femi, the camper from Nigeria, and an agile, pale-skinned, sullen-faced Thunderbird. On the shore in front of the swimming area of the lake, as the white rope and bright floats of the lane dividers bobbed gaily in the morning sun, two counsellors held back the two struggling boys in bathing suits, Femi with a swollen nostril leaking blood. "I'll kill that filthy little nigger bastard," panted Femi in his Mayfair accent, wiping his nose with his coal-black arm. "I'll smear his dirty little arse all over the beach. He called me a monkey!"

"He spit on me," the Thunderbird was muttering, scuffling his feet in the sand.

Marvin Jones, his platinum streak glowing brilliantly in the blinding sunlight, was called over to make peace. "This ain't no way to act," he began, but his tone was insincere, the tone of a showman bent on pleasing everyone. He sent a quick, shifty grin over to the Thunderbirds standing near him, and one of them suddenly shoved a camper, who went sprawling into the lake. In the boys' swim group, a general melee broke out between campers and Thunderbirds, the tanned bodies of the campers mingling wildly with the small, dark, muscular Thunderbirds. The two counsellors were themselves dragged in. Pairs of boys bolted, yelling threats, and ran off into the woods.

The girls at the lake, both Thunderbirds and campers, were quickly marched away to our tents, where we were told to sit quietly. Looking into her trunk, Chen-cheu found that someone had taken three of her prettiest T-shirts and a new bathing suit. When she complained loudly about it, she found herself surrounded by the three Thunderbird girls who shared the tent with us. They began to jostle Chen-cheu, and to pluck at her long, black hair. Chen-cheu promptly socked Belinda in the stomach. Our counsellor, Molly, came running down the path from the rec hall at precisely the moment when Chen-cheu, propelled by a nasty push, came flying out of the tent and sprawled in the dust, shrieking out a string of curses that even Ellen and I had never before heard her use. Her beautiful face was contorted and almost purple with rage, but she wasn't crying. None of us were. After that, we were separated from the Thunderbird girls.

Meanwhile, the boys were being rounded up. I heard later that a number of them were found grappling in twos and threes in the woods; there were surprisingly few injuries beyond a few black eyes and bloody noses. "We had a plan," one of the boy campers said afterward. "We were going to barricade ourselves in the infirmary and fight 'em off from there. Firebomb 'em."

The Thunderbird boys, escorted by several strapping counsellors called in from a tennis camp across the lake, were confined to the rec hall. By eleven o'clock on a fine, sharp, hot August morning, Camp Grayfeather had settled into a stillness in which the only sounds were those of a sublimely untroubled nature: birdsong, the harsh whirring of cicadas, the light slapping of waves on the lake shore.

None of us were surprised to discover that the Thunderbirds were to be sent home. I sat with nine other girls on the sagging bunks of our tent as Hannah Woolworth, her kindly face pale and drawn with strain beneath its sunburn and freckles, talked to us. "We all feel that it would be better and safer for everyone," she said. "We don't want any of you kids getting hurt."

When she said "you kids," it was clear that she did not mean the Thunderbirds.

I looked at Ellen and Chen-cheu, and they looked back at me. Events were passing, as usual, into the unreachable sphere of adult justice, and though there was a certain relief in that, it also seemed sad. For a day and a half, the Thunderbirds, like a small natural disaster, had given an edge of crazy danger to life at Grayfeather; now the same powers that had brought them to us were taking them away.

"We didn't even get a chance to learn all their names," said Ellen slowly, after Hannah Woolworth had left.

A flicker of resentment ran though the group of girls crowded together in the tent, and Ellen and I began, with an obscure feeling of defiance, to teach the others the song that the Thunderbirds had sung for us under the oak trees the day before.

In about two hours, after we'd eaten a large pile of bologna sandwiches on horrid white bread, sandwiches that the camp cook had provided as a sort of emergency takeout lunch, we heard through the woods the unmistakable sound of a bus. "We've *got* to see this," I said.

Five of us—Ellen, Chen-cheu, and I, and two other girls—jumped up and, against the strict instructions left us by our absent counsellor, took off toward the rec hall. We didn't take the path, but ran, dodging like Indian scouts, through the underbrush, stifling occasional nervous giggles and trying to avoid the poison ivy. When we got to the edge of the clearing, we stood discreetly back in the bushes and observed the scene. The midday sun gave the clearing a close, sleepy feeling. The Thunderbirds, their spirits apparently undaunted, stood in a rambunctious platoon behind a grim-faced Ned Woolworth, and the familiar graffiti-covered school bus was just coming to a halt in the parking lot.

We could see that the same tall, curly-haired man who had delivered the Thunderbirds was coming to pick them up; this time, he was wearing a green eyeshade, as if he'd been interrupted during a stretch of desk work. He came quickly down the bus steps and strode over to stand in front of the assembled Thunderbirds. "Well," he said, clapping his hands together. "What the hell have you guys been doing *now?*"

The Thunderbirds, all of them, broke into loud laughter, as if he had just told them the best joke in the world.

"We ain't been doing *nothing*, man," answered Marvin Jones, rocking on his heels. "Just being ourselves!"

The curly-haired man pulled off his visor and sighed so that even we could hear him, fixing his weary, skeptical gaze for a second on Marvin Jones' scarred face, and then on the golden hills and fields of the Delaware countryside rolling into the distance. He talked to Ned Woolworth in a low voice for a few minutes, and then turned back to his charges and sighed again. "Come on, get on the bus," he said. "We're going back to the city."

When we five girls heard the bus start up, we did something we hadn't planned to do. Without anyone suggesting it, we all took to our heels again and ran through the woods to a dusty crossroads far from the clearing, a spot where we knew the bus had to pass. Through some extraordinary, even magical, coincidence, the same plan had occurred to each one of us. When the bus came rattling up to the crossroads a few seconds after we got there, the five of us, like guerrilla fighters, dashed out of the bushes onto the road. "Stop the bus! Stop for a minute!" we shouted.

The bus slowed and halted, with a squeal of brakes, and the Thunderbirds stuck their heads out of the windows. We could see Marvin Jones' platinum streak shining beside Belinda's patch of dyed red hair.

"We wanted to sing your song," said Ellen, and without further ado we all began clapping our hands and chanting the profane verses that belonged to the Thunderbirds. "What the word/ Thunderbird . . ."

We probably looked ridiculous—five girls in cutoffs, football T-shirts, and moccasins, clapping and trying to perform like a group of tough guys on a city street corner—but we felt natural, synchronized, as if we were doing a good job.

When we had finished, the Thunderbirds—still hanging out of the windows of the bus—gave us a burst of grave, polite applause. Marvin Jones leaned farther forward out of the window. "That sounded good," he said. "And we're sorry to leave."

The two groups looked at each other, and it seemed for a minute that some obscure misunderstanding was about to be cleared up, and then the bus started up and moved slowly away through the trees.

The Devoted at Lake Delavan

Wendy McClure

In the chapel at Lake Delavan Christian Youth Camp there was an enormous fireplace, the kind you'd expect to see in a ski lodge: rough quarry rock and a deep, charred hearth. On the long, slab-like mantel rested a crown of thorns. The crown of thorns was not made of actual thorns but was carved out of wood—two or three pieces crafted to form spiky branches that interlocked like a grim craft puzzle.

It was difficult to tell whether the crown could fit an ordinary human head. As far as I knew no one ever tried it on during the three years I attended summer camp at Lake Delavan—either because it was in unspeakably poor taste to do so or else because the thorns were so long they could take out an eye.

The thorns were easily longer than my fingers. The wood was pale and unfinished and sanded smooth; the thorns looked bleached and dry, and it was hard to imagine what kind of thorny plant they simulated. More than anything, the thorns resembled antlers, and on the big rustic mantel they were not out of place.

Colette Molloy was the primary reason why I joined Pioneer Girls in the first place—Colette, and to a very slight extent, the word *pioneer*, which brought to my third grade mind notions of Laura Ingalls Wilder and a certain simplicity that I'd come to crave. I'd read almost all the *Little House* books over the past two years and had become so smitten with its single-room schoolhouses, ironed pinafores, and floorboards swept clean that, whenever I looked up from the pages, my own world seemed irremediably cluttered and shoddy and garish. Why did groceries have so many brand names and cartoon mascots; why did T-shirts *say* things; why did school have "pod" classrooms with desks arranged in awkward cluster formations; why did we use *tape*?

I couldn't quite imagine the kind of existence I wanted instead; just that I would know it when I saw it, and my first summer at Lake Delavan, Wisconsin, I felt a twinge of recognition as soon as I found my cabin. My frontier heart sang: a *cabin!* I was destined to love the rafters, the paneling, the row of five sturdy bunk beds made from thick wooden beams and planks.

At camp, you brought one suitcase and one sleeping bag; you had the *one* pillow. Everything had a purpose and a place. You had the single sentimental item that you'd display propped up on your pillow or against your bunk post, and it would be just as if you'd had only that one stuffed animal your whole life, the way Laura Ingalls Wilder had only a doll made from a corncob.

For a while I loved this dismantled life. The heaviest things I had were my gym shoes, a flashlight, and a Bible.

We went to Chapel twice a day. Attending Chapel wasn't quite like going to church—more like a big, Jesus-themed assembly. Morning Chapel consisted mostly of singing and announcements. Evening Chapel had verse recitations, testimonials from the staff and the older campers, and an inspirational talk. These were given by visiting youth ministers who had entertaining gimmicks such as juggling or banjo playing, though one summer there was a man who gave a weeklong slide presentation about the life of John Bunyan and *Pilgrim's Progress* and it was sort of over our heads. The week after that they were sure to bring back the camp favorite, Reverend Dale, who always brought an easel and drew on it with big, squeaky markers to illustrate the parables he told.

There were Devotions every afternoon at 3:16, when we had to report back to our cabins and stay inside with our Bibles for forty-five minutes. Every summer we were assigned Psalms to memorize and we'd lounge on our sleeping bags and mumble them to ourselves. Most days, Devotions followed our afternoon swims; in our bunks we'd still feel the motion of the water as if we carried the spirit of the lake in our limbs.

Colette Molloy had been my best friend since the beginning of third grade. She had bushy auburn hair and when you looked closely at her eyes you could see how the pupils flickered back and forth. ("It's called *nystagmus*," she'd say, wearily, whenever anyone asked her.) We'd had two sleepovers and an excursion to see *The Muppet Movie* together, and now she had invited me to Pioneer Girls. I didn't know what it was, just that it met after school someplace where Colette's mom would drive us.

"You're Christian, right?" she asked. "Because it's sort of religious."

"We're not Catholic," I told her. "Or Jewish." I knew that much. Our church was called First United Congregational Something-or-Other of Oak Park. It sounded sort of like a bank. "I think it's okay," I said.

I would go the next Tuesday with Colette and her mom to Riverside Bible Chapel in Maywood, a small '60s-era church building that looked like an especially pointy ranch house; it had a spire like a wedge driven through the roof. Pioneer Girls met in the basement.

There were about twenty girls altogether. They came from different schools in the area; some came with their mothers, who, like Mrs. Molloy, helped set up folding chairs and serve snacks. We had a Bible lesson, sang song lyrics printed neatly in marker on posterboard, and then we sat at the long brown folding tables and made decorative bookmarks with rubber stamp letters. Afterward, while the adults were cleaning up, Colette and I went into the ladies' room and put a dime in the Modess machine and when the tampon came out we unwrapped it and took it apart.

The Tuesday after that I went back again.

"They do Bible stories," I'd told my mom. Our family hadn't attended church in a year, other than Christmas and Easter. My mom was in graduate school and sometimes she sat at the desk in the spare bedroom and typed and cried at the same time.

"You mean you're *interested* in that?" she said. "Last time you swore you wanted to go back to Sunday School and then two weeks later you couldn't care less."

"This is on *Tuesdays*," I told my mom. "And you wouldn't have to take me."

"And what religion are they again?" she asked.

"They're the same as us," I told her. I knew they weren't but I couldn't explain the difference.

Once I started going to Pioneer Girls, being around Colette was sort of like doing the Hidden Pictures page in *Highlights* magazine, where you'd look at a drawing of an ordinary scene and try to find the objects camouflaged in the pen-and-ink lines: the comb in the grass, the spoon in the wood grain. When it came to Colette, all the hidden things were Christian things. She carried a canvas tote bag with a fish drawing on it that she said stood for Jesus; the lion on one of her favorite sweatshirts stood for Jesus, too, and even *I* knew that the ceramic lamb figurine on her dresser meant Jesus.

The Molloy's living room didn't look much different from ours, with earth tones and macramé plant hangers. Her parents had a wooden crate filled with records; in between Beatles and John Denver records were albums with titles like "The Word" and "Galilee." Scripture quotes were everywhere—printed on notepads, on refrigerator magnets; as graceful italic captions to the nature scenes on a wall calendar. They got their pictures developed at Calvary Camera and picked up their dry-cleaning across town at The King's Cleaners. From the Molloys I learned that nearly every kind of diversion—movies, music, magazines—was available in a Jesus flavor.

One day at school Colette took out a new notebook; the cover had a picture of a horse with flowers in its mane. I asked her what it was.

"What is *what?*" Colette said.

"That," I said, pointing to the animal. Because there was a chance it was Jesus' donkey.

"It's a horse," said Colette.

"So what does it mean?"

"That I *like horses*," she said, giving me a pained look.

The way I figured, it didn't hurt to guess about these things. Especially not after the birthday slumber party I'd held that spring, when I'd invited four girls, including Colette, and somehow our game of indoor tag had taken an unexpected and ultimately controversial turn inspired by the Swedish modern lamp on the bookshelf on our stairway landing.

"That lamp is freaky," my friend Dawn had said. We'd both been tagged and we had to sit on the landing and count to a hundred before we could join the game again. "Really. It looks like it has special powers."

It was simply a frosted glass globe perched on an orange cube. It had a cold, space-age look to it. I nodded and kept counting, but Dawn darted back down the stairs and by the time I was done counting the rules had changed. Now, instead of counting, we had to face the lamp and say "I believe" a hundred times.

"Only then will the space light let you go," Dawn explained.

The game got even better when, instead of just tagging me, Karen Bradford said, "Now you must be *taken* to Space Light," and yanked me brutishly toward the stairs.

"*Never!*" I heard myself say, as if on cue.

"Take her!" ordered Dawn.

We sensed not only the theatrical possibilities of the situation but the genre as well, and soon our game of tag became high drama with just a touch of Spanish Inquisition thrown in for kink. Those of us who weren't tagged were the unconverted; those who were tagged again had displeased Space Light and needed to answer to It.

We dragged each other up and down the carpeted stairs to the lair of the lamp; we made each other bow down before it. We developed our own personal subplots, too: Colette's encounters with Space Lamp left her with tragic amnesia while Karen had impressive seizures. Emily leached power from the lamp with her fingertips, and Dawn kept walking trancelike into my older brother's room. I opted for hypnosis and gazed at the globe until my sight was gilded with bright spots. We persisted for maybe two hours until we realized the TV required considerably less from us, and so we forsook the lamp.

"It was really bad what we did," Colette told me a few days later at school. Her voice was grave. Her parents didn't want her sleeping over at my house anymore, she said. "We were worshipping something and it wasn't God."

"But we were pretending," I protested. We weren't *making* another god; we were just girls.

"I know," she said. "But still."

The last Pioneer Girls meeting before school ended consisted of pizza, singing, and a simple ceremony where we were called up one by one and given hugs and small presents. Colette got a book of devotional stories with a laminated bookmark; Nancy Yarborough, who sometimes carpooled with us, got a ceramic plaque that read *God Answers Prayer*.

My gift was a Bible; a New International Version. It was as thick as a block of Velveeta. The hardbound cover was creamy white mock leather with gold stamping; it was very much like the lid of my ballerina jewelry box. The front illustration showed Jesus holding a lamb while three exuberant children reached out to pet the lamb or maybe even Jesus himself, since his long hair flowed as appealingly as a pony's mane.

There was an envelope stuck inside. I opened it and pulled out a brochure and some kind of certificate that had been filled out by hand. My name was written on one line, "$30 off" on another. I didn't know what it meant, so I showed it to Mrs. Molloy.

"Give it to your mom and dad," she said. "It's for summer camp. Would you like to go?" Colette and Nancy were going, she said. They hoped I could come, too.

The first summer I was in a bunk under Colette. On Initiation Day we had to wear our clothes backward and seasoned campers could smack us on the butt if they wanted. I passed the intermediate swimming test and memorized the Twenty-third Psalm. My favorite craft project was a plaster wall ornament that I'd painted for my mom: a smiling apple, for the kitchen. I knew that people were "saved" but I wasn't sure how they got that way, much less whether I had to be saved anytime soon.

The second summer our cabin placed third in the camp Olympics. Colette and I got in trouble for running across the two-lane highway between the camp and the lake instead of waiting for the rest of the group. I bunked next to a girl who sprayed her feet every night with Dr. Scholl's and it made me cough. I learned that being saved meant that you asked Jesus to come into your heart, which seemed so simple that I *thought* I was saved and I said so whenever anyone asked.

The place in my mind where I prayed became clearer to me. It was like an auditorium, empty and spacious, and I would be there all by myself. In the acoustic darkness of my head I would speak from my heart, bravely, but with pauses for uncertainty, like I'd seen in plays or on the TV show *Fame* whenever a character was facing a tough audition. I'd speak and then someone would over-hear me, someone else I hadn't known was there.

"Your brother said you asked him the other day if he was saved," my mom said one afternoon. This was after the second summer and before the third.

"I was just curious," I said. It was true: how did other kids get saved when they didn't go to Bible camp, anyway?

"Well, that's *his* business," my mom said.

She was training to be a therapist and was very concerned with things like *boundaries* and *bad strokes*. I knew that when she talked like this I wasn't exactly in trouble but that I shouldn't do whatever I did in the first place to cause the concern.

"Are *you*, you know, saved?" she asked me.

"I don't think so," I said. I didn't want to lie. Secretly I was glad the truth wasn't *yes*.

In the church basement where Pioneer Girls was held hung a framed print of Jesus knocking on a door, at the threshold of what appeared to be a cozy little cottage. Since it was a picture about Jesus that actually *showed* Jesus I hadn't asked anyone what it meant. To me it depicted a sort of everyday Jesus in a quiet interval between miraculous deeds. I liked it until at camp I saw *another* painting of another Jesus, at another door, and then I knew something was up.

That third summer Colette and Nancy were in my cabin again, along with two other girls from Pioneer Girls, Laurie and Jessica, and also Jessica's friend Merritt. There were two sisters, Cindy and Diane Pardo, and Marie Elena Herrera, who was shy enough to perpetuate the general impression that she didn't speak much English.

There was Robin, who had a stuffed toy chimpanzee named Doris. Doris had a distressingly realistic molded plastic ape face and Robin dressed her daily in baby clothes she'd brought in a doll suitcase. Robin couldn't sleep without Doris, a fact she spoke of as if it were a medical condition like asthma.

"One time I left Doris at my grandma's house and my dad had to get her at three in the morning," she said somberly, fidgeting with the ruffles on Doris's gingham dress. "He drove twenty miles."

"Aww, just for your *monkey baby*," said Cindy Pardo, just sweetly enough.

Cindy was a year older than her sister Diane; they were both tiny, like gymnasts, and there was something vaguely feral about them, though they were never violent with anyone except each other. Laurie had shared a room with the Pardo sisters at the Winter Weekend Retreat, and said the two had fought so viciously they'd attacked each other with ice skates, swung by the laces like nunchuks.

Our counselor was Miss Alice, who was in her sixties. She had pasty arms and was unfortunately too dull to have much grandmotherly appeal. Her voice was mournful and tremulous but in the mornings she tried singing "Jesus Loves Me" in order to wake us up; at lights-out she attempted to read aloud passages from the book *Joni*, the true story of a Christian teenager who had been paralyzed in a diving accident. Miss Alice stumbled over the sentences and plowed tonelessly through the dialogue. *"What's your name the nurse asked. Joni. Joanie. No, Joni, I said. Joni can you move your legs. No."*

We were palpably envious of the girls on the other side of our duplex cabin because they had Miss Debbie, who was in college and had feathered hair and who had Done Drugs before she'd been saved, according to the testimony she'd given the first night in Evening Chapel. Miss Alice never gave a testimony; as far as we could tell she'd just *always* loved Jesus. When she talked about her own girlhood the details were unconvincing, as if they'd been cribbed from *Anne of Green Gables*. "Oh, I loved skirts with pleats," she told us. "Do you know what *pleats* are?"

She seemed bewildered by us, by the shrieks we made when we laughed, by our terrycloth halter tops, and by the way we staged reenactments of Joni's fateful dive using Doris the Monkey Baby and one of the upper bunks.

Joni was abandoned after four nights and two chapters and we were left to ourselves. The night dimensions of the cabin were familiar by now: the bedposts, the bathroom light. We told stories: rounds of anecdotes whispered in turn about teachers, or dogs, or disasters. Stories about tornado drills at school or other people's neighbors' house fires were popular lights-out entertainment.

Tonight in my bottom bunk I felt like I was sinking gently. Someone—Laurie—was talking, and in between the sounds of her voice my thoughts made little chimes of their own. I was both listening and not listening. Whatever story she was telling me struck me as sad, though I couldn't say why. My mind was taking the words and playing them to a soft dirge.

Someone was whispering. Someone was whispering back.

And then Cindy called out, "Do you hear that?" Loudly, as if there was someone else besides us to interrupt.

"Hear what?"

"Music?" Laurie said.

"*Shhh!*" Cindy said. "Yes."

Merrit heard it and so did Jessica.

Nancy said, "Wait!" and then she said she heard it.

Of course I heard it. I'd been hearing it all along.

We held our breaths. It was hard to tell what kind of music it was, just that it came from very far away. There were bass mumblings and thin treble notes that could almost have been wind.

"Who else hears it?" Nancy asked.

For a moment I was convinced the dark of the cabin was the same as inside my head. I was sure that some terrible reversal had occurred; that the world was flooded with my thoughts, that my head was submerged like a broken boat. I thought, briefly, that I was responsible.

"Wendy," said Colette. I could barely make out her face in the bunk across from mine. "You hear it, too?"

"Yes," I whispered.

"It sounds like sad music," said Diane.

"Like an organ," said Cindy.

It wasn't coming from the chapel. It was coming from the opposite direction—from somewhere around the fields, the woods, the trail to the lake. But it sounded like an organ when Cindy said it did, and when Robin said she thought it was a piano, somehow it sounded like that, too.

"You guys?" Cindy said. "We can't go outside. *Don't* go outside."

"I just want to know what it *is*," said Nancy.

"I sort of like it," said Robin, her voice tiny.

Who was scared? Nancy wasn't; Laurie was; Merrit was *sort of*.

Below Merritt, Marie Elena Herrera was either asleep or pretending to be asleep.

"Cindy?" Jessica asked.

"We have to stay inside," said Cindy. "It might be a trap."

None of us had any idea what she was talking about, though in the corner Diane suddenly turned over and faced the wall.

Cindy claimed she had seen it on the news: A woman had been lured outside and murdered in cold blood. The killer had *played a radio*.

"Stop it," Diane cried from her bunk. Her voice was a muffled bleat.

"This was in a movie?" Merrit said.

"No this was *real*," Cindy replied. "I heard the story and so did Diane. Right?"

"Are you okay?" Laurie asked Diane, who was in the bunk next to her.

Cindy went on. "It was the middle of the night so he played the radio really soft so her neighbors wouldn't hear. She went outside. And then he attacked her."

"Stop-it-shut-up!" Diane said.

"He *stabbed* her."

"God, Cindy," hissed Jessica. "Shut up."

"She had the knife in her throat. She actually choked to death."

"*Gross*," said Nancy.

The noises Diane was making into her pillow sounded almost like barking. The sounds grew longer into screeches and finally broke into crying. In a moment her sobs were joined by Laurie's.

"Oh, God," someone said. We were turning on our flashlights and pointing them over to Diane's bunk.

"You guys?" said Robin in a loud whisper. "Marie Elena's crying, too." Our flashlight beams found her as she lay flat on her back, shuddering, her face crumpled.

It didn't seem to matter that the music we heard was so tinny and low it could be drowned out by Diane's and Laurie's soft crying. We had all heard it; it had to mean something—*whatever* it meant we wanted to be part of it; to conduct it and carry it in ourselves. If some of us had become hysterical we knew that by the same turn some of us would be brave.

"You guys?" said Nancy. "The Lord is my shepherd."

Nobody said anything.

"Psalm twenty-three. *You guys*. Maybe we should say it," said Nancy.

Colette started: *"The Lord is my shepherd I shall not want—"*

Nancy joined in: *"—he maketh me lie down in green pastures.* Guys?"

Nancy and Colette and Robin and I tried our best to recite in unison, though it was hard to keep up with Nancy's rapidly spiraling cadence, and Colette began to stress the *eth* verb endings, as if this were a situation where only the King James Version would do. The cabin had fallen quiet. But by the time we plodded through the third verse someone wept even more audibly than before, and let forth a keening, prolonged cry. It was Cindy.

"You guys?" she said. She was shaking. "I am really fucking scared now."

· · ·

Someone had started to howl *Miss Alice!* She and Miss Debbie shared the small adjacent room between our cabin and Cabin 4.

"I don't think she can hear us," said Merrit, and, in fact, Miss Alice's age and singing voice had given us reason to believe she was sort of deaf. Someone would have to go to her door.

"Someone, please?" Cindy begged.

It was going to have to be someone from the bottom bunks.

"Wendy is the tallest," said Robin.

"Wendy, *please?*" bawled Cindy.

I had to extract my legs from my sleeping bag and put my feet on the concrete floor. "Colette?" I whispered. I couldn't see her.

"*Go-oh!*" someone howled, and I padded across the room to Miss Alice's door.

Miss Alice was already sitting up in bed. She wore a crumpled bonnet that looked like a shower cap and she looked cartoonish as she blinked at my flashlight. When she heard the crying she said, "Oh my dear."

"There's music outside," I told her. She only nodded and kept blinking.

"You have to get up," I said, and suddenly I felt like I would start crying, too. It felt like my soul was in my throat as I ran back to my bunk.

Miss Alice was there for us in her quilted robe; we'd hoped Miss Debbie might come in, too, but Miss Alice had sent her to fetch an acquaintance of hers instead, a counselor from Cabin 6 who was, of course, as old as Miss Alice. Neither one of them seemed to understand how we'd become so upset. The two of them wandered up and down the bunk aisles holding open Bibles and flashlights.

Miss Alice thought we'd been telling ghost stories, and her cohort began searching for Bible passages to explain that the only life after death was Heaven, and that therefore there couldn't be ghosts.

"Jesus was not in the tomb! He was *alive!*" the old woman said, almost breathlessly, as she hovered over Marie Elena's bunk.

Diane spoke up from her corner. "We didn't think there was a *ghost*," she said, sounding remarkably sober after her histronics. "We thought there was a killer outside."

"Playing music," added Laurie.

"Music?" The women held still for a moment. We all listened, but there was no sound now, and we hadn't known quite when it had stopped.

Miss Alice turned to the other counselor. "Who's over in the east field tonight?" she asked. They went over by the windows.

"We didn't hear *people*," said Cindy, to no one in particular.

Miss Alice had retrieved her clipboard and she and the other counselor were reading it with their flashlights. "The junior high girls," said Miss Alice. "They're with Denise."

Miss Denise was the music counselor, who conducted campfire sing-alongs with her guitar, and sometimes, an autoharp.

"That must be it," said the old woman counselor. She raised her voice to address us all. "That's what you heard, right? The junior high girls?"

"No," Cindy muttered.

Robin spoke up. "It wasn't singing we heard. We swear."

The two women looked at each other. "Are you sure?" Miss Alice asked.

Yes, we replied from the bunks.

"It wasn't singing," Miss Alice repeated, incredulous.

Colette spoke up for the first time. "And it wasn't *happy*," she said.

Jesus would come and knock on the door to your heart, so to speak. By my last summer at Lake Delavan I understood what those paintings meant—the dozens of them, all showing the same scene. You could paint it yourself if you wanted; you could pick out the plaster plaque in the craft room and fill in the colors, and put your name on the back. I liked to believe Jesus visited all those doors, as if all of humanity was simply a neighborhood that He had to canvass. Though I knew He transcended time and place, I wondered if being saved came from knowing the precise moment He'd knock, or if He was there all the time and you simply opened the door when you were ready.

I asked Miss Alice about it at the end of the summer. "He's there all the time," she said, gently. "But He would *like* for you to be ready."

They brought us outside; just a few feet out into the small clearing that the ring of cabins enclosed. The security lamp next to Cabin 8 buzzed faintly. I was barefoot and I stretched my legs in big strides from the concrete stoop to the closest patch of grass I could find. The other cabin windows were dark, though there were a few faces peering out at us from Cabin 4 next door.

"Listen," said Miss Alice, though we didn't think it would start again.

But the old woman counselor whispered, "There!" and Miss Alice lightly tapped my shoulder and then Colette's, though by then we could hear it, too. The insistent *strum-strum-strum* and then the opening strains of "Happiness Is the Lord," sung by a very earthly choir.

"Now isn't this what you heard?" Miss Alice asked us. While the song went on nobody answered.

"That's singing," she said. "Now who could think it was anything else? Those are *girls*."

We knew who was singing in the distance. They were all twelve and thirteen, and their legs were long, and their shirts had bra lines. Their bodies were clearly more intricate than ours, as if they were of a higher order. They were mostly kind.

Miss Alice spoke up. "Who heard them singing before?" she asked. "Please raise your hands."

For a moment we didn't move. The girls' singing sounded nothing like the sad music we'd heard in the cabin, though it was possible that those things we'd stumbled across in terror had simply changed form, that they called to us now in voices like our own.

"Girls?" Miss Alice asked us again. "We don't have all night."

And we raised our hands to save ourselves.

I didn't go back to camp the next year; after the night of the music I understood that I would never be *ready*, and for years I imagined the world was waiting for me to explain why. But my mother never asked, and Colette went on to Pioneer Girls without me.

The Order of the Arrow

Steven Rinehart

Heitman, the homosexual, the insane, is my tentmate. Again.

Porter, the fat kid who cries a lot, cried again this morning, saying he didn't want to tent with Heitman ever again. Last night Heitman put ticks on Porter's eyelashes while he slept. This morning our scoutmaster, Casper, had to pluck them off with tweezers, since the hot-match trick was too dangerous that close to his eyeball. The ticks came away with tiny chunks of Porter's eyelid clasped in their jaws, like grains of sand. Casper said this was good; if the head stayed in, Porter could lose the eye. He told Heitman one more time and he was out. As soon as he left the tent, Heitman dropped his pants and pretended to masturbate violently in Casper's direction.

Two nights ago Heitman leapt off his cot in the middle of the night and onto my back, bucking frantically. "Bergie," he cried, "Oh, Bergie, Bergie, Bergie, you hunk of a man." I tried to curl up and beat him off with my fists, but he knew where to put his knees.

"You bastard," I cried, "get off me," but Heitman was laughing and slapping the back of my head.

"We're buddies, aren't we?" Heitman said. "Say we're hunch buddies, Bergman. Hunch buddies forever." He stopped suddenly, before I could say anything, and got off me. I turned over and saw that the moon was out and shining through the fabric of the roof. Heitman was half dressed. He stood bent over, peering out the front flap of the tent. His shoelaces were untied and his shirt was off. He had his Scout neckerchief tucked in the back pocket of his jeans. He turned around, his black hair in his eyes, and said, loud over the crickets, "Let's go out, Bergman. Let's go explore."

"Heitman," I tell him, "you can't catch fish with your hands. It's impossible." He ignores me and wades out farther into the stream in his underwear, the moonlight reflecting around where his knees disappear into the current. He rises up and sinks down, stepping on hidden shelves and rock formations, not seeming to worry about his balance. He stops on a high spot and squats down, his hands in front of him.

"They're sleeping," he says. "You sneak up on them while they're sleeping." I can see his rounded back and the row of tiny knobs that runs up to his neck. The rippling water of the stream makes his back look strange. It looks striped like a trout, or maybe like he's been whipped.

I settle back and look up at the sky, listening to the screaming of the frogs and crickets. My eyes are just starting to close when something cold and spiny hits me on the throat, falls to the ground, and lies there flipping in the dirt. Heitman sloshes back to the bank and climbs out. He squats next to the fish. It has stopped moving, its upturned eye brilliantly white against the dark ground. It arches its tail and lets it fall. Its gills open and close and its mouth flexes, the moon reflecting off the edges of its scales. Heitman picks it up and walks over to the water.

"Don't hold it tight," I tell him. "Just let it go easy. If you hold it tight then its scales will rot away." It's something my grandfather told me. He never touched the fish he threw back; he cut his best hooks apart with wire trimmers rather than tear up their mouths. He tried to save the small ones but still when he let them go some just arced over slow and slid away.

Heitman turns and bends sideways at the waist and launches the fish straight up into the sky. It disappears and for a second there is no sound, just the crickets and the rustling water, then the fish hits the ground next to me like a dropped stone. Its body doesn't move but its mouth opens and closes, slower than before. Its eye is now dark and may be gone, I can't tell. I pick it up and walk over to the edge of the stream. The fish is bone-rigid in my hand, frozen in an arc. I bend down and wash the dirt off. But the eye is still black, and I throw it up gently over the water. Seconds later it hits with a small splash, shattering the reflection of the moon, and disappears.

Heitman is furious. "That's fine," he says, shaking water from his arms. "That's just great. Now what do I have to show?" He grabs his pants and starts up the path. He doesn't say a word to me all the way back to camp.

The next day around the steam tables everyone talks about Friday night, the Order of the Arrow ceremony, and if they'll be Tapped Out. The generator is on and Old Willy is watching television under the bus tarp. Old Willy is Casper's father, and he invented the steam tables and the water heater and fixed up the old school bus that takes us around. We know that no other scout troop has an electrical generator, no other troop gets to wear jeans and not wear shirts and smoke cigarettes just about whenever they please. We are lucky. Casper has always preferred a more natural, Indian-style philosophy. According to Casper the old army scouts were just half-ass Indians at best, and he considers most of the standard Boy Scout stuff silly. Summer camp is the only organized camp he lets his troop attend, because of the Order of the Arrow ceremony, where each troop selects a few of its boys to be transformed into men, the way the Indians used to.

"Merit badges are for pussies," Casper says. "Uniforms are for mailmen. I should make you all get tattoos instead." Casper has tattoos, up and down both arms. He wears boots with metal toes. He is a Korean veteran, the seniors say. He has a medal for valor against the enemy, and a scar on his shoulder from a Chinese bayonet. He's tough, but fair, he likes to say. Every kid gets a fair shake.

Casper's right-hand men are the senior troop leaders. They're in high school and they don't eat with the rest of us, the small ones. The only one of us they can tolerate is Heitman, who they get a charge out of. They've learned that Heitman will do almost anything anyone dares him to do; he eats small animals raw, sets his hair on fire, that kind of thing. He eats at their fire but they won't let him sleep with them in their canopy tent. Heitman has been known to howl at night; an unearthly cry, like rutting hyenas at a fire drill, Casper says. The only time Heitman can be sure not to howl is in my tent, so he mostly sleeps with me. He tells everyone I'm his official hunch buddy, and whatever they think, everybody pretty much leaves me alone. When I walk by they whisper to each other. I know what I am called. I am Heitman's girlfriend.

The seniors spend most of their time sitting around their own fire, smoking cigarettes and telling stories about women they've molested. Chadwell is the biggest. He has removable front teeth and long black hair parted in the middle. In camp he wears feathers in it, two of them that dangle just next to his ear. Sometimes he soots the area under his eyes. Garcia is only slightly smaller, but with bigger shoulders. He sits next to Chadwell and breaks the wood that goes into the fire with his bare hands, sometimes using the arch of his shoulders for leverage. He once hit me in the back of the head for leaving grease in one of the big pots I was cleaning. The next day he came up to me and told me a sex joke that I didn't really get, and I've been friends with him ever since. I give him the cigarettes I steal from my mother but don't smoke.

Heitman has gotten ahold of some Mace from somewhere. His father is a mailman, he says, but I know he's lying. Heitman lives on the street behind mine and everybody on the block knows that his father stays home all day, looking after his chinchillas. Mr. Heitman has a patent on a chinchilla-killing machine that hooks up to a car battery. He calls it the Chilla-Killa. You clamp one end on the chinchilla's nose and stick the other in its anus, then throw the switch. They stiffen right up, Mr. Heitman told me once when I'd come around, right up like a big furry dick. It's not the volts, he said, it's the amps. He shook a dead chinchilla in my face and laughed when I screamed.

We sit on a stone wall by the front gate to the camp, and Heitman hides the Mace behind the wall from a line of scouts who are marching in to use the lake. They're from the rich kids' troop. We're out of uniform so their scoutmaster doesn't even acknowledge us. He knows what troop we're from, and he hates Casper. Earlier in the week he tried to get us kicked out of the camp, on account of our conduct at Taps, but nobody did anything. They were too afraid of us. Every night the other troop stands at attention while the flag is lowered, while we put our hands in our pockets and whistle over the pathetic hooting of their fat-faced bugler. Their scoutmaster closes his eyes in fury, and when the sound dies he marches his kids quickly down the hill to his own camp.

The troop passes the stone wall and Heitman maces the last kid in line as he marches by, eyes forward. It's quick and the kid doesn't seem to know what it is, he just wipes his neck and marches on. They tromp out of sight around the corner of the pool, the kid shaking his head, and Heitman stashes the Mace under a loose stone that has fallen from the wall. "Crap doesn't work," he says. "Wouldn't you know?" We walk the long way back to camp and Heitman traps a black rat snake next to the path. Back in the tent we put it in a box and collect tree toads. The snake swallows four toads before Heitman throws it into the hot-water tank. It boils and turns gray and hard as a spring, its eyes completely white.

The seniors are grimly practicing being Indians for the ceremony when the scoutmaster from the other troop marches in, red-faced. He walks up to Casper, his forefinger shaking, and wants to see all of the troop. One of his boys got sent to the hospital after being shot in the face with something. It might have been acid, he says. He'll know the boys who did it when he sees them. He knows they're here.

I come out of the tent in full uniform, more or less, trying to disguise myself. Heitman is nowhere to be found. Casper lines us up and the scoutmaster starts at one end, looking each of us up and down for a long time, then moving on to the next. His face is still red, and his mouth set, but after a few kids it's clear he's not cut out for this sort of thing. He's starting to lose his nerve; he's too soft. Even fat Porter senses it and seems to sneer at him. Casper follows next to him and tries to keep him moving along the line. He's on our side.

There is a noise behind me and Heitman moves in next to me, naked except for his gray underpants. He stands rigid, almost not breathing, perfectly at attention. His bony chest is thrust out and the hollows above his collarbone are so deep they're shadowed. The scoutmaster gets even with me, takes one look, and taps Casper on the shoulder. "That's one of them," he says, pointing at me. I look at Casper and his face is stone.

"Which was he," he says, "the one with the can or the other one?"

"The other one," says the scoutmaster, already moving on. He stops and squints at Heitman. He looks at Heitman's face but not at the rest of him. Heitman's face is cold, reptilian. His eyes don't blink and don't focus. The scoutmaster draws away for a second, then leans forward, close to Heitman's face. "Have you got a problem, young man, standing here in your underpants?" Heitman smiles softly, then looks the scoutmaster in the eye. Up close, the scoutmaster's face is soft and freckled, and his eyelashes are just wisps of white above his eyes. He has a sparse moustache that sticks out slightly, trying to hide a harelip. The moustache quivers, like a rabbit, and it is a second before I realize that it is something the scoutmaster can't control. He stands there, staring at Heitman, and everyone knows after a couple of seconds he doesn't have the courage to call him out.

Sure enough, he moves on and finishes the line. Under the bus tarp the seniors have quit being Indians and sit around a table, playing cards loud and smoking cigarettes. When they notice the scoutmaster looking at them, they lower their cards and stare at him. The scoutmaster looks for a moment as if he might go over, but thinks the better of it and turns around. He sees Casper walk up to me and slap me hard across the face.

"Who was it?" Casper says. "Talk to me and I won't kick the living shit out of you."

"Hey," says the scoutmaster, "there's no need for that." I hold my face and start to cry. The scoutmaster shoves in front of Casper and bends down at the waist, his hand on my shoulder. "No one's going to hurt you," he says. He's breathing hard and his hand shakes on my shoulder. "I have a boy in the hospital," he says. "You understand?" I shake my head and my throat snags when I breathe in.

The scoutmaster turns to Casper. "I mean, he's going to be all right and everything. It's just the idea." Casper looks at him without saying anything. The scoutmaster shakes his head; his face is terrible to look at. "I mean," he says, "I mean the boy is *hurt*." He looks at all of us but nobody says a word, and after a moment he just walks off the way he came. Casper watches him go and when the scoutmaster is out of sight he sighs. He puts a hand on my shoulder but I can tell he doesn't like touching me.

"Show me the can, you stupid shit," he says, his voice almost gentle. I look up at him with gratitude, but he's not looking at me. He stands with his hand on my neck but looks at Heitman, who is still at attention, his underwear sagging in front.

"Heitman," he says, "one more time and that's it."

Casper walks me back along the path to the stone wall, and I point out the can, under its rock. He picks it up, hefts it, and puts it in his pocket. After a moment he sits down on the wall and I sit next to him. He picks up his legs and crosses them under him, his elbows on his thighs, his metal-toed boot tips tucked behind his knees.

"Heitman's crazy, you know," he says. He stares down the road where the other troop came from. "I used to never think kids could be crazy, but that kid's crazy."

He looks at me like I should explain and I know I have to say something. I think of Heitman at the river in the moonlight and say the first thing I think of.

"He's got scars," I whisper.

Casper is quiet for a second. "Where?"

I tell him and he sighs softly. His shoulders sag and he closes his eyes, just for a moment.

"You know," he says, "I was thinking of tapping him out tomorrow night. I thought it might be just the thing for him."

"Maybe," I say.

His voice drops low and his face gets dreamy. "The Indians used to make their boys go out into the wilderness for months, just living off the land. When they came back they were men. That's what the Order of the Arrow ceremony is based on."

"Alone?" I say.

He looks at me sharply. "They look for their spirit guide," he says. "An animal, like an eagle or a mountain lion, to lead them. Then they become one."

I want to correct him. He doesn't know Heitman the way I do. I know what Heitman would do to any animal that tried to lead him anywhere, or become one with him. Instead I say nothing, and Casper shakes his head and looks away from me. A second later he gets up and walks back up the path to camp. I follow him, not too far behind.

When we get back to the camp Heitman is sitting with the seniors, smoking, looking pleased with himself. Casper walks up and takes his cigarette away and throws it into the cooking fire. He walks behind him and looks at his back. I know what he's looking for, and I can't remember for the life of me why I told him that. Casper shoots me a dark look and goes inside his tent and pulls the flaps shut. Chadwell hands Heitman another cigarette and Heitman lights it directly from the fire, his face nearly in the flames, impressing the hell out of the seniors. When I go to get some wood I pass close to them, and hear them invite Heitman to spend the night in their tent. He smokes his cigarette and smiles at them all, one at a time.

Sometime that night he parts the flaps to my tent. His underwear is gone. I have been awake, expecting him, lying on my back and gripping the sides of my cot. I've been expecting him because I did not hear him howl.

"Come on out, Bergman," he says. "Let's go explore."

I say nothing. I lie stiff, not moving, watching him under my eyelids. He crouches in the doorway, one knee up and the other down.

"Berrr-gie," he whispers, "Bergie, Bergie, Bergie . . ." I hold my chest tight, trying not to breathe. After a moment the tent flaps fall closed and Heitman is gone. His footsteps blend into the crickets and the bullfrogs and the sound of Old Willy's television. I lie awake and listen for him but he doesn't come back.

When I wake up Friday morning Heitman is still gone. Disappeared. He is still missing at breakfast. By lunch Casper is cussing and Old Willy is passing out trail maps to the seniors. Chadwell tosses his in the breakfast fire and laughs, but stops when Casper sticks another one in his chest. "Find him," he says, "or don't come back." He snatches the feathers from Chadwell's hair. "And get that shit out of here."

The seniors take me with them, almost running down the trail. A quarter mile from camp they stop as if on signal and sit on some rocks, begin smoking cigarettes. Garcia offers me one of my own but I say no. After about ten minutes they set off again, slower, and tromp as much around the path as on it. Nobody makes any effort to call out Heitman's name, or look away from the path. Chadwell walks along breaking off branches and Garcia strips leaves from everything he touches. What did you dare him to do this time, I wonder. Did you send him off into the wilderness alone, looking for himself as a man? Their backs don't answer me, and we walk on and on.

Two hours later we're back, running the last few hundred yards into the camp. It is abandoned except for Old Willy, who is asleep under the TV tarp. When Casper returns with a ranger he is rigid with anger; throughout dinner he is dead silent. Some whisper that the seniors took Heitman out into the woods during the night and abandoned him; others think he just ran away. By nightfall it becomes possible to believe the boy is dead. We wait in our tents for the call to the Indian ceremony; I leave the flap open for Heitman but he doesn't come.

The woods are black beyond the light thrown by the line of torches. There is no moon and the wind makes the trees brush up against each other in waves. Our line marches down the side of a ravine. The path is pebbly and some of the boys slip, reaching out to the man in front, sometimes bringing them both down. On the ground they are kicked by the Indians until they get up. If they try to brush their clothes they are struck on the shoulders with wooden lances. Porter starts to cry and two Indians whisk him out of line. Nobody turns to see what happens to him.

At the end of the path, at the bottom of the ravine, is a bonfire and in front of it stands a lone Indian, his arms folded. It is obviously Casper, in leather pants and striped makeup. In the light of the fire his tattoos seem to dance up one arm and down the other. His eyes are closed. We line up in front of him and the bonfire. The other troop is lined up on the far side of the fire, standing quietly. Unlike us they are in full uniform—their scoutmaster is also in uniform, and stands to the right of them. They blink and their eyes shift; one of them raises a hand to wipe his nose. I expect an Indian to rush up and knock the boy to the ground, but nothing happens. Suddenly my head is grabbed from behind and jerked side to side. "Eyes front," someone hisses in my ear. I smell cigarettes; I know it's Garcia, and I stand as still as I can.

Casper opens his eyes. He picks up a feathered pole and walks the line of the other troop. He stops and shakes the pole in front of a boy, and one of the other Indians steps up and taps the boy on the chest with his flattened hand, once, then twice. The boy steps forward and the Indian leads him up to the fire, hands him an arrow. The boy's face is cold and he stands with his arms folded, facing his old friends across the clearing, the arrow held diagonally across his chest.

Casper has two more boys tapped from the other troop, then starts with us, at the far side from me. My heart begins throbbing and my body starts to itch, but I can hear the crunch of footsteps behind me, and I can smell Garcia as he passes. I feel my pulse in my fingertips and in my shrunken stomach and I want to race back to camp where Old Willy is running the generator and watching television. I listen to the progress of Garcia from one end and Casper from the other, one in back and the other in front.

Casper shakes his pole and one of our own is tapped out, one of the older boys. The Indian hits him hard in the chest, much harder than the other troop, but he is ready, one foot slightly back, and the sound of flesh on flesh is so loud it echoes off the trees around us. The troop across the clearing sways in line at the sound, their eyes widening. Our boy walks forward and stands in front of us, his back to the fire. He stares over our heads.

Casper taps out one more, then two. He moves down the line and then stops dead in front of me. My heart clenches in my chest and my breath starts to catch in my throat. I am sure he sees me crying. He looks me in the eye and his face is too dark to see clearly, but I can see his eyes. They look crazy; the moisture in them reflects the beating of the bonfire. He stands there, staring at me, his chest rising and falling. He seems to stand there forever. Please, I say to myself, please. I want you to. Then he smiles, but in a bad way, the way Heitman smiles at fat Porter. I close my hot eyes when his feet crunch away from me.

He reaches the end of the line without again shaking the pole. The Indian behind him takes his place next to the three boys, and Casper walks to the bonfire and turns to face the rest of us—the small ones, the ones left over. He raises his arms high up from his sides, eyes squeezed nearly shut, and his chest starts to swell, getting ready to shout at the treetops. Because he is like this, he doesn't see Heitman walk slowly into the light of the clearing. When he opens his eyes and sees him, whatever he was thinking of shouting comes out instead as a kind of twisted yelp. His arms fall to his sides like shot birds.

Heitman is naked, smeared with mud in streaks across his sides. There is blood on his legs and what looks like shit in his hair. He carries something in his arms; a big mess of blood and bone and feathers sticking out this way and that. He is naked, but he walks with his skinny shoulders back, up on the balls of his feet. The way he moves makes the Indians look like schoolkids lost in the woods in their pajamas. They stare at him—next to them one of the chosen boys drops his arrow in the dirt. Casper, like a deflating balloon, sits down right where he was standing.

Heitman has caught a wild turkey, and killed it. Heitman has caught a wild turkey with his bare hands. He doesn't say anything, he just stands and faces us, the turkey in his arms. He looks exhausted; he looks done in. We glance at each other and we start to move and shuffle in our places, and just then fat Porter goes and does it. He starts in and after a second everybody joins him. We stand there, the small ones, all in a line in front of Heitman and the bonfire and the Indians, and we howl. We howl and we howl, and Heitman smiles down the line at us all, one at a time. When he gets to me his eyes rest only for a second, then drift on past to the next boy. My heart clenches again, but it is too late; now we are all Heitman's girlfriend.

Drinking Songs and Other Worthwhile Summer Pursuits

Dan Zanes

There's no question in my mind that summer camp changed me. I had spent the early years of my musical life listening to records; the songs were thrilling and the people singing them were mysterious and inspiring but it wasn't until I went away to summer camp as a twelve-year-old in 1973 that I realized what it meant to actually make music with other people.

I must have done some singing in school but I can't remember a single song. I started playing guitar around the age of eight but recollections of that solitary pursuit are vague at best. I know that I sat on the edge of my bed and struggled with "Swing Low, Sweet Chariot" and "Down in the Valley," although I'm sure I would have rather been out playing street hockey. I loved listening to Pete Seeger and the Beatles and Leadbelly but I wasn't really putting it all together until the day that my cousin Trigger picked up a guitar and played the opening riff from The Who's "Pinball Wizard." That made an impact. Here was a guy I had known my whole ten years of life and all of a sudden he was playing this incredibly wild song on an acoustic guitar!

When I landed at camp with my younger brother and sister that first summer, I knew only one thing: When the month was over we would be returning to a different house in our town of Concord, New Hampshire. My mother and stepfather had found a way, with generous financial assistance, to spare us the gory weeks of the move. What I didn't realize was that I would be singing songs I came to love with people I also came to love, every day for a month. These songs brought us together and helped shape us as a community. They were our common currency when we gathered together in the mornings and evenings, and they were also our window into other cultures and emotions.

It's easy for me to talk about communal music-making because I know what it feels like and I know how it affected me and helped me at a point in my life when very little else made sense. It wasn't that I was a particularly troubled child; I was just in the process of figuring things out, trying to find my place in it all. These days I play music for kids and families, and I'm constantly drawing on the incredible sense of belonging that I had when singing at camp. Everyone has a voice. There's always a way into a song. I didn't know this until I went to camp but I know that the lessons I learned in that environment apply to the world outside. They may be harder to convey, but they all apply.

I don't know what makes a good camp song but I know the

ones that stayed with me. My greatest hits of the seventies, as I knew them. Maybe if I go song by song I can begin to give some idea of what was happening that made this experience so meaningful to me.

"Wild Mountain Thyme"

Is this Irish or Scottish? It seems to depend on whom you ask. The melody is flowing and filled with emotion but it's the lyrics, particularly in the chorus, that never fail to move me.

WILD MOUNTAIN THYME

Oh, the summertime is coming,
And the trees are sweetly blooming,
And the wild mountain thyme
Grows around the purple heather
Will you go, lassie, go

And we'll all go together to pull wild mountain thyme
All around the blooming heather.
Will you go, lassie, go

I will build my love a bower
By yon pure and crystal fountain
And on it I will pile
All the flowers of the mountain.
Will you go, lassie, go

And we'll all go together . . .

I will build my love a shelter
On yon high mountain green
My love shall be the fairest
That the summer sun has seen
Will you go, lassie, go

And we'll all go together . . .

That said it all. As I became connected to the people I was sharing a cabin with, eating meals with, or sitting with at morning meetings I sensed that we were actually on some sort of trip together. Why not picking thyme? That was as good an analogy as I needed and it still is.

"Wild Mountain Thyme" is a grand air under any circumstance but there is a power in the sound of many voices singing together about *being* together that gives this song a life of its own that transcends any gathering.

"The Rattlin' Bog"

I was talking about singing, earlier this year, with Richard Herman, the man who started the Windsor Mountain Camp (back then it was called "Interlocken Summer Camp") almost forty-five years ago. I wanted to know if it was becoming harder to get young people to throw themselves into songs. As I expected, he said it was more of a challenge, but he went on to say something else that has stayed with me: "It's got to be fun."

I know that singing is good for us and that these traditional songs are an important connection to our heritage but Richard reminded me that if it's not enjoyable it's going to be a constant struggle to get people to join in, to engage. Everyone's idea of fun is a little different but "The Rattlin' Bog" and many other cumulative-type songs are an invitation for abandon and very often near chaos. And that can really be fun.

THE RATTLIN' BOG

Hi ho the rattlin' bog! The bog down in the valley-o
Hi ho the rattlin' bog! The bog down in the valley-o
And in that bog there was a tree
Rare tree a rattlin' tree
Tree in the bog and bog down in the valley-o

And on that tree, there was a limb
Rare limb, rattlin' limb
Limb on the tree, tree in the bog
And the bog down in the valley-o

High ho the rattlin' bog . . .

And on the limb there's a nest, and maybe an egg but maybe an elephant. Sometimes there's logic and sometimes there's just stacking. Perhaps the elephant is wearing a hat. There might be a truck on the hat. Or a snail. Or a magazine; who knows? Maybe people have memories that are finely tuned (young people seem to, older people are much less reliable) and the song will go on for a very long time, picking up speed with each refrain. Maybe, if things are in full swing, there are people who will act out the different things that appear on the branch. This song is totally open-ended and always cracks me up.

"Fathom the Bowl" and "The Barley Mow"

Although I took them for granted at the time, I realize now how lucky we all were to have English folk singers John Roberts and Tony Barrand make annual trips to our camp. Thinking back on their contributions tells me a few things. First, that one or two people armed with great songs and big personalities can have an enormous impact on the musical culture of a camp. The songs will continue to be sung year after year, long after the song leaders have filled their summers with other commitments (musical commitments, I always hope). My recent trips back to Windsor Mountain confirm this. The other thing I realize is that whenever songs are sung in the relaxed atmosphere of camp (and to be fair, in many, many other situations—school, parties, car trips, etc.), seeds are planted. The songs and all of the information that comes with them can linger inside people's minds for a very long time before taking hold. In the case of John and Tony, I thought that I was just hanging around, having fun singing and dancing but twenty years later I became mysteriously drawn to old English music hall songs, sea songs, and seasonal celebration songs, all of which I had been exposed to as a teenager in camp. And did I mention my strange fascination with drinking songs?

At that time, I had never been drunk but I would occasionally see other people elevated by spirits so I had some vague sense of what these songs were talking about. "Fathom the Bowl" and "The Barley Mow" are perfect songs to sing with gusto. We sang them loud and with humor. To me, they had very little to do with the actual ingesting of alcohol and a lot to do with rambunctious people celebrating each other's company. In other words, these songs were a harmless and joyous vision of merrymaking that I had not previously known, which filled me with a sense of life's social possibilities. These days there's nothing I enjoy more than leading a rousing drinking song at a neighborhood gathering. It's one of the many musical seeds planted at camp. They seem to sprout at different times and when they do, it can be powerful.

FATHOM THE BOWL

Come all you bold heroes give an ear to me song
I will sing in the praise of good brandy and rum
There's a clear crystal fountain near England shall roll
Give me the punch ladle I'll fathom the bowl

I'll fathom the bowl I'll fathom the bowl
Give me the punch ladle I'll fathom the bowl

From France we do get brandy from Jamaica comes rum
Sweet oranges and apples from Portugal come

But stout and strong cider are England's control
Give me the punch ladle I'll fathom the bowl

I'll fathom the bowl . . .

My wife she do disturb me when I'm laid at my ease
For she does as she likes and she says as she please
My wife she's a devil she's black as the coal
Give me the punch ladle I'll fathom the bowl

I'll fathom the bowl . . .

My father he do lie in the depths of the sea
With no stone at his head by what matters for he
There's a clear crystal fountain near England shall roll
Give me the punch ladle I'll fathom the bowl

I'll fathom the bowl . . .

And if that's not festive enough with everyone singing at the top of their lungs, how about this cumulative song, "The Barley Mow," a celebratory toast to the barley harvest.

THE BARLEY MOW

Here's good luck to the pint pot,
Good luck to the barley mow

Jolly good luck to the pint pot,
Good luck to the barley mow
Here's the pint pot, half a pint, gill pot, half a gill,
Nipper kin, and the brown bowl,
Here's good luck, good luck to the barley mow

Each verse toasts another aspect of the celebration building up to a list that includes the quart pot, the half-gallon, the gallon, the half-barrel, the barrel, the landlord, the landlady, the daughter, the brewer, the drayer, and finally the company.

I vividly remember a bunch of crazed (and, naturally, sober) teenagers being led through these songs by a couple of incredibly charismatic musical Englishmen. It made all the sense in the world to be howling these ancient melodies through the pine trees and up into the evening sky.

"Strike the Bell"

The ringing of a bell signaled the beginning and the end of the various activity periods at my camp. Most of my years there were spent working in the dining hall and so I was the guy doing a lot of this bell ringing. The sound of a bell also divided the watches on board ships during the Glory Days of Sail. "Strike the Bell" is a song that was sung on some of those ships and was also sung in camp.

I made a return visit to Windsor Mountain this year and was happy to hear "Strike the Bell" again. Even though I've recorded it and play it often at concerts, it was emotional to hear it sung fervently by a huge group of kids at an evening gathering. It confirmed my belief that good songs will live on as long as people take the time to teach them to each other.

STRIKE THE BELL

Aft on the poop deck, and walkin' all about,
There's the second mate, so steady and so stout.
What he's a-thinkin', he knows not himself,
We're wishin' he would hurry up and strike, strike the bell.

Strike the bell, second mate, let us go below,
Look you well to windward you can see it's going to blow!
Look at the glass, you can see that it has fell,
We wish that you would hurry up and strike, strike the bell!

Down on the main deck, workin' at the pumps,
There's the starboard watch, just a-longin' for their bunks.
Lookin' off to windward, they see a great swell,
They're wishin' that the second mate would strike, strike the bell.

Strike the bell second mate . . .

Aft at the wheel, poor Andersen stands,
Clutchin' at the spokes with his cold, mittened hands.
Lookin' at the compass head the course is true and well,
He's wishin' that the second mate would strike, strike the bell.

Strike the bell second mate . . .

For'ard at the fo'cs'le head, keepin' sharp lookout,
There's Johnny standin', a-ready for to shout,
The lights are burning' bright, sir, everything is well,
We're wishin' that the second mate would strike, strike the bell.

Strike the bell second mate . . .

Aft on the quarterdeck, our gallant captain stands,
Lookin' at the sea with a spyglass in his hand.
What he's a-thinkin', we all know very well,
He's thinkin' more of short'nin' sail than—strike the bell.

Strike the bell second mate . . .

"Friend of the Devil"

Thank god for the Grateful Dead! That's what I say. Their love of traditional folk, blues, jug band, bluegrass, and acoustic music was inspiring kids at my camp in the 1970s and it's still inspiring them today. I know because I was just there and was amazed at how many teenagers were interested in filling their songbags with old tunes. It became clear after hanging out for a while that most of these kids were largely turned on to this music by the Dead.

All songs that people enjoy have value but I think it's important that the old folk (using the word very loosely) songs survive. They tell us where we came from and how we got here and about the journeys of others. If we know several songs well enough to sing and teach others then we're rich with possibilities. If we don't know any we miss a glorious and soulful way to enjoy each other's company. The traditional songs provide an ideal common ground; they have time-tested melodies and are very often social by nature. But they don't just endure because they're good! Each generation needs to be inspired to fill their heads with these songs, and so I say hats off to the Grateful Dead for always giving a nod to train songs, work songs, West Indian songs, ballads, and sea songs, among others. Like Pete Seeger for the generations before, they make having a sense of musical history a very attractive proposition.

Many of the songs that we think of as traditional started their lives in a more formal sense; they were actually written by someone. Over time many of these songs have entered the oral tradition as they were passed from singer to singer. This process can happen at camp. Some may know "Friend of the Devil" as recorded by the Dead but if enough people like the way it sounds when two people sit under a tree singing it, before long it can become a staple of any musical gathering. In the absence of electronic media (a tradition that I hope is being upheld!) songs can take on a life of their own over the course of a summer. Songs of all types, when passed on from camper to camper can expand into the space that is usually occupied by radio, TV, CD players, and computers in the real world.

The Grateful Dead are wild and wooly messengers, helping to spread a love of old songs even as they have written dozens of classics of their own. "Friend of the Devil" easily leaves the realm of recorded music whenever people hang around to sing and play. I know that it's in all of my old camp songbooks right there with "The Cat Came Back" and "Deep Blue Sea."

Dan Zanes

FRIEND OF THE DEVIL
by Robert Hunter, Jerry Garcia, and John Dawson

I lit out from Reno, I was trailed by twenty hounds
Didn't get to sleep last night 'til the morning came around.

Set out runnin' but I take my time
A friend of the devil is a friend of mine
If I get home before daylight, I just might get some sleep tonight.

Ran into the devil, babe, he loaned me twenty bills
I spent the night in Utah in a cave up in the hills.

Set out runnin' but I take my time
A friend of the devil is a friend of mine
If I get home before daylight, I just might get some sleep tonight.

I ran down to the levee but the devil caught me there
He took my twenty-dollar bill and vanished in the air.

Set out runnin' but I take my time
A friend of the devil is a friend of mine
If I get home before daylight, I just might get some sleep tonight.

Got two reasons why I cry away each lonely night.
The first one's named Sweet Anne Marie, and she's my heart's delight.
The second one is prison, babe, the sheriff's on my trail,
And if he catches up with me, I'll spend my life in jail.

Got a wife in Chino, babe, and one in Cherokee
The first one says she's got my child, but it don't look like me.

Set out runnin' but I take my time
A friend of the devil is a friend of mine
If I get home before daylight, I just might get some sleep tonight.

Music and camp life is a hard subject for me to wrap up. There's so much that feels unsaid. Did I mention the incredible capacity of young people to absorb and appreciate the unfamiliar? Did I make it clear that one person armed with a full songbag can completely change the musical landscape of a camp? Or that music played live in a relaxed setting can mean more than a thousand downloads? Did I say that I wouldn't be doing what I do today if it weren't for my camp experiences? Did I ask how we could provide this type of experience for more and more people who struggle financially? Did I ask how these experiences and this type of learning under the guise of having fun could translate to the school setting? I love The Everly Brothers to an extreme degree but did I ask how it is that the two young camp counselors sitting on a bench in the shade of a tree playing acoustic guitars and singing in harmony for their own enjoyment on a July afternoon could inspire me more than the entire Everly's catalogue?

Life moves at a rapid clip for most of us in this twenty-first century of ours. There's no question that people are much more likely to buy music than to make it. Radio stations and CDs from anywhere in the world are at the fingertips of anyone with a computer.

You can sit on a couch in New Jersey and watch TV shows from China. DVDs are being released every day that have historic footage from the last century that most people didn't even know existed. There is a mind-boggling amount of cultural information available through the electronic media and yet I keep thinking about those pine trees. Sitting under those trees singing "Wild Mountain Thyme," I had a real sense of life's possibilities. With each chorus the rising voices would fill my mind and heart with the unmistakable thought that we were all on this crazy journey together, that I would always have friends I could count on, and that the world was ours for love and laughter. Then a bell would ring and I would dust off the seat of my pants and get ready to serve lunch.

I Like Guys

David Sedaris

Shortly before I graduated the eighth grade, it was announced that, come fall, our county school system would adopt a policy of racial integration by way of forced busing. My Spanish teacher broke the news in a way she hoped might lead us to a greater understanding of her beauty and generosity.

"I remember the time I was at the state fair, standing in line for a Sno-Kone," she said, fingering the kiss curls that framed her squat, compact face. "And a little colored girl ran up and tugged at my skirt, asking if she could touch my hair. 'Just once,' she said. 'Just one time for good luck.'

"Now, I don't know about the rest of you, but my hair means a lot to me." The members of my class nodded to signify that their hair meant a lot to them as well. They inched forward in their seats, eager to know where this story might be going. Perhaps the little Negro girl was holding a concealed razor blade. Maybe she was one of the troublemakers out for a fresh white scalp.

I sat marveling at their naïveté. Like all her previous anecdotes, this woman's story was headed straight up her ass.

"I checked to make sure she didn't have any candy on her hands, and then I bent down and let this little colored girl touch my hair." The teacher's eyes assumed the dewy, faraway look she reserved for such Hallmark moments. "Then this little fudge-colored girl put her hand on my cheek and said, 'Oh,' she said, 'I wish I could be white and pretty like you.'" She paused, positioning herself on the edge of the desk as though she were posing for a portrait the federal government might use on a stamp commemorating gallantry. "The thing to remember," she said, "is that more than anything in this world, those colored people wish they were white."

I wasn't buying it. This was the same teacher who when announcing her pregnancy said, "I just pray that my firstborn is a boy. I'll have a boy and then maybe later I'll have a girl, because when you do it the other way round, there's a good chance the boy will turn out to be funny."

"'Funny,' as in having no arms and legs?" I asked.

"That," the teacher said, "is far from funny. That is tragic, and you, sir, should have your lips sewn shut for saying such a cruel and ugly thing. When I say 'funny,' I mean funny as in . . ." She relaxed her wrist, allowing her hand to dangle and flop. "I mean 'funny' as in *that* kind of funny." She minced across the room, but it failed to illustrate her point, as this was more or less her natural walk, a series of gamboling little steps, her back held straight, giving the impression she was balancing something of value atop her empty head. My seventh-period math teacher did a much better version. Snatching a purse off the back of a student's chair, he would prance about the room, batting his eyes and blowing kisses at the boys seated in the front row. "So fairy nice to meet you," he'd say.

Fearful of drawing any attention to myself, I hooted and squawked along with the rest of the class, all the while thinking, *That's me he's talking about.* If I was going to make fun of people, I had to expect a little something in return, that seemed only fair. Still, though, it bothered me that they'd found such an easy way to get a laugh. As entertainers, these teachers were nothing, zero. They could barely impersonate themselves. "Look at you!" my second-period gym teacher would shout, his sneakers squealing against the basketball court. "You're a group of ladies, a pack of tap-dancing queers."

The other boys shrugged their shoulders or smiled down at their shoes. They reacted as if they had been called Buddhists or vampires; sure, it was an insult, but no one would ever mistake them for the real thing. Had they ever chanted in the privacy of their backyard temple or slept in a coffin, they would have felt the sting of recognition and shared my fear of discovery.

I had never done anything with another guy and literally prayed that I never would. As much as I fantasized about it, I understood that there could be nothing worse than making it official. You'd see them on television from time to time, the homosexuals, maybe on one of the afternoon talk shows. No one ever came out and called them queer, but you could just tell by their voices as they flattered the host and proclaimed great respect for their fellow guests. These were the celebrities never asked about their home life, the comedians running scarves beneath their toupees or framing their puffy faces with their open palms in an effort to eliminate the circles beneath their eyes. "The poor man's face-lift," my mother called it. Regardless of their natty attire, these men appeared sweaty and desperate, willing to play the fool in exchange for the studio applause they seemed to mistake for love and acceptance. I saw something of myself in their mock weary delivery, in the way they crossed their legs and laughed at their own jokes. I pictured their homes: the finicky placement of their throw rugs and sectional sofas, the magazines carefully fanned just so upon the coffee tables with no wives or children to disturb their order. I imagined the pornography hidden in their closets and envisioned them powerless and sobbing as the police led them away in shackles, past the teenage boy who stood bathed in the light of the television news camera and shouted, "That's him! He's the one who touched my hair!"

It was my hope to win a contest, cash in the prizes, and use the money to visit a psychiatrist who might cure me of having homosexual thoughts. Electroshock, brain surgery, hypnotism—I was willing to try anything. Under a doctor's supervision, I would buckle down and change, I swore I would.

My parents knew a couple whose son had killed a Presbyterian minister while driving drunk. They had friends whose eldest daughter had sprinkled a Bundt cake with Comet, and knew of a child who, high on spray paint, had set fire to the family's cocker spaniel. Yet, they spoke of no one whose son was a homosexual. The odds struck me as bizarre, but the message was the same: this was clearly the worst thing that could happen to a person. The day-to-day anxiety was bad enough without my instructors taking their feeble little potshots. If my math teacher were able to subtract the alcohol from his diet, he'd still be on the football field where he belonged; and my Spanish teacher's credentials were based on nothing more than a long weekend in Tijuana, as far as I could tell. I quit taking their tests and completing their homework assignments, accepting F's rather than delivering the grades I thought might promote their reputations as good teachers. It was a strategy that hurt only me, but I thought it cunning. We each had our self-defeating schemes, all the boys I had come to identify as homosexuals. Except for a few transfer students, I had known most of them since the third grade. We'd spent years gathered together in cinder-block offices as one speech therapist after another tried to cure us of our lisps. Had there been a walking specialist, we probably would have met there, too. These were the same boys who carried poorly forged notes to gym class and were the first to raise their hands when the English teacher asked for a volunteer to read from *The Yearling* or *Lord of the Flies*. We had long ago identified one another and understood that because of everything we had in common, we could never be friends. To socialize would have drawn too much attention to ourselves. We were members of a secret society founded on self-loathing. When a teacher or classmate made fun of a real homosexual, I made certain my laugh was louder than anyone else's. When a club member's clothing was thrown into the locker-room toilet, I was always the first to cheer. When it was my clothing, I watched as the faces of my fellows broke into recognizable expressions of relief. *Faggots*, I thought. *This should have been you.*

Several of my teachers, when discussing the upcoming school integration, would scratch at the damp stains beneath their arms, pulling back their lips to reveal every bit of tooth and gum. They made monkey noises, a manic succession of ohhs and ahhs meant to suggest that soon our school would be no different than a jungle. Had a genuine ape been seated in the room, I guessed he might have identified their calls as a cry of panic. Anything that caused them suffering brought me joy, but I doubted they would talk this way come fall. From everything I'd seen on television, the Negroes would never stand for such foolishness. As a people, they seemed to stick together. They knew how to fight, and I hoped that once they arrived, the battle might come down to the gladiators, leaving the rest of us alone.

At the end of the school year, my sister Lisa and I were excused from our volunteer jobs and sent to Greece to attend a month-long summer camp advertised as "the Crown Jewel of the Ionian Sea." The camp was reserved exclusively for Greek Americans and featured instruction in such topics as folk singing and something called "religious prayer and flag." I despised the idea of summer camp but longed to boast that I had been to Europe. "It changes people!" our neighbor had said. Following a visit to Saint-Tropez, she had marked her garden with a series of tissue-sized international flags. A once discreet and modest woman, she now paraded about her yard wearing nothing but clogs and a flame-stitched bikini. "Europe is the best thing that can happen to a person, especially if you like wine!"

I saw Europe as an opportunity to reinvent myself. I might still look and speak the same way, but having walked those cobblestoned streets, I would be identified as Continental. "He has a passport," my classmates would whisper. "Quick, let's run before he judges us!"

I told myself that I would find a girlfriend in Greece. She would be a French tourist wandering the beach with a loaf of bread beneath her arm. Lisette would prove that I wasn't a homosexual, but a man with refined tastes. I saw us holding hands against the silhouette of the Acropolis, the girl begging me to take her accordion as a memento of our love. "Silly you," I would say, brushing the tears from her eyes, "just give me the beret, that will be enough to hold you in my heart until the end of time."

In case no one believed me, I would have my sister as a witness. Lisa and I weren't getting along very well, but I hoped that the warm Mediterranean waters might melt the icicle she seemed to have mistaken for a rectal thermometer. Faced with a country of strangers, she would have no choice but to appreciate my company.

Our father accompanied us to New York, where we met our fellow campers for the charter flight to Athens. There were hundreds of them, each one confident and celebratory. They tossed their complimentary Aegean Airlines tote bags across the room, shouting and jostling one another. This would be the way I'd act once we'd finally returned from camp, but not one moment before. Were it an all-girls' camp, I would have been able to work up some enthusiasm. Had they sent me alone to pry leeches off the backs of blood-thirsty Pygmies, I might have gone bravely—but spending a month in a dormitory full of boys, that was asking too much. I'd tried to put it out of my mind, but faced with their boisterous presence, I found myself growing progressively more hysterical. My nervous tics shifted into their highest gear, and a small crowd gathered to watch what they believed to be an exotic folk dance. If my sister was anxious about our trip, she certainly didn't show it. Prying my fingers off her wrist, she crossed the room and introduced herself to a girl who stood picking salvageable butts out of the standing ashtray. This was a tough-looking Queens native named Stefani Heartattackus or Testicockules. I recall only that her last name had granted her a lifelong supply of resentment. Stefani wore mirrored aviator sunglasses and carried an oversized comb in the back pocket of her hiphugger jeans. Of all the girls in the room, she seemed the least likely candidate for my sister's friendship. They sat beside each other on the plane, and by the time we disembarked in Athens, Lisa was speaking in a very bad Queens accent. During the long flight, while I sat cowering beside a boy named Seamen, my sister had undergone a complete physical and cultural transformation. Her shoulder-length hair was now parted on the side, covering the left half of her face as if to conceal a nasty scar. She cursed and spat, scowling out the window of the chartered bus as if she'd come to Greece with the sole intention of kicking its dusty ass. "What a shithole," she yelled. "Jeez, if I'd knowed it was gonna be dis hot, I woulda stayed home wit my headdin da oven, right, girls!"

It shamed me to hear my sister struggle so hard with an accent that did nothing but demean her, yet I silently congratulated her on the attempt. I approached her once we reached the camp, a cluster of whitewashed buildings hugging the desolate coast, far from any neighboring village.

"Listen, asshole," she said, "as far as this place is concerned, I don't know you and you sure as shit don't know me, you got that?" She spoke as if she were auditioning for a touring company of *West Side Story*, one hand on her hip and the other fingering her pocket comb as if it were a switchblade.

"Hey, Carolina!" one of her new friends called.

"A righta ready," she brayed. "I'm comin', I'm comin'."

That was the last time we spoke before returning home. Lisa had adjusted with remarkable ease, but something deep in my stomach suggested I wouldn't thrive nearly as well. Camp lasted a month, during which time I never once had a bowel movement. I was used to having a semiprivate bathroom and could not bring myself to occupy one of the men's room stalls, fearful that someone might recognize my shoes or, even worse, not see my shoes at all and walk in on me. Sitting down three times a day for a heavy Greek meal became an exercise akin to packing a musket. I told myself I'd sneak off during one of our field trips, but those toilets were nothing more than a hole in the floor, a hole I could have filled with no problem whatsoever. I considered using the Ionian Sea, but for some unexplained reason, we were not allowed to swim in those waters. The camp had an Olympic-size pool that was fed from the sea and soon grew murky with stray bits of jelly-fish that had been pulverized by the pump. The tiny tentacles raised welts on the campers' skin, so shortly after arriving, it was announced that we could photograph both the pool *and* the ocean but could swim in neither. The Greeks had invented democracy, built the Acropolis, and then called it a day. Our swimming period was converted into "contemplation hour" for the girls and an extended soccer practice for the boys.

"I really think I'd be better off contemplating," I told the coach, massaging my distended stomach. "I've got a personal problem that's sort of weighing me down."

Because we were first and foremost Americans, the camp was basically an extension of junior high school except that here everyone had an excess of moles or a single eyebrow. The attractive sports-minded boys ran the show, currying favor from the staff and ruining our weekly outdoor movie with their inane heckling. From time to time the rented tour buses would carry us to view one of the country's many splendors, and we would raid the gift shops, stealing anything that wasn't chained to the shelf or locked in a guarded case. These were cheap, plated puzzle rings and pint-size vases, little pom-pommed shoes, and coffee mugs reading SPARTA IS FOR A LOVER. My shoplifting experience was the only thing that gave me an edge over the popular boys. "Hold it like this," I'd whisper. "Then swivel around and slip the statue of Diana down the back of your shorts, covering it with your T-shirt. Remember to back out the door while leaving and never forget to wave good-bye."

There was one boy at camp I felt I might get along with, a Detroit native named Jason who slept on the bunk beneath mine. Jason tended to look away when talking to the other boys, shifting his eyes as though he were studying the weather conditions. Like me, he used his free time to curl into a fetal position, staring at the bedside calendar upon which he'd x-ed out all the days he had endured so far. We were finishing our 7:15 to 7:45 wash-and-rinse segment one morning when our dormitory counselor arrived for inspection shouting, "What are you, a bunch of goddamned faggots who can't make your beds?"

I giggled out loud at his stupidity. If anyone knew how to make a bed, it was a faggot. It was the others he needed to worry about. I saw Jason laughing, too, and soon we took to mocking this counselor, referring to each other first as "faggots" and then as "stinking faggots." We were "lazy faggots" and "sunburned faggots" before we eventually became "faggoty faggots." We couldn't protest the word, as that would have meant acknowledging the truth of it. The most we could do was embrace it as a joke. Embodying the term in all its clichéd glory, we minced and pranced about the room for each other's entertainment when the others weren't looking. I found myself easily outperforming my teachers, who had failed to capture the proper spirit of loopy bravado inherent to the role. *Faggot*, as a word, was always delivered in a harsh, unforgiving tone befitting those weak or stupid enough to act upon their impulses. We used it as a joke, an accusation, and finally as a dare. Late at night I'd feel my bunk buck and sway, knowing that Jason was either masturbating or beating eggs for an omelette. *Is it me he's thinking about?* I'd follow his lead and wake the next morning to find our entire iron-frame unit had wandered a good eighteen inches away from the wall. Our love had the power to move bunks.

Having no willpower, we depended on circumstances to keep us apart. *This cannot happen* was accompanied by the sound of bedsprings whining, *Oh, but maybe just this once*. There came an afternoon when, running late for flag worship, we found ourselves alone in the dormitory. What started off as name-calling escalated into a series of mock angry slaps. We wrestled each other onto one of the lower bunks, both of us longing to be pinned. "You kids think you invented sex," my mother was fond of saying. But hadn't we? With no instruction manual or federally enforced training period, didn't we all come away feeling we'd discovered something unspeakably modern? What produced in others a feeling of exhilaration left Jason and me with a mortifying sense of guilt. We fled the room as if, in our fumblings, we had uncapped some virus we still might escape if we ran fast enough. Had one of the counselors not caught me scaling the fence, I felt certain I could have made it back to Raleigh by morning, skittering across the surface of the ocean like one of those lizards often featured on wildlife programs.

When discovered making out with one of the Greek bus drivers, a sixteen-year-old camper was forced to stand beside the flagpole dressed in long pants and thick sweaters. We watched her cook in the hot sun until, fully roasted, she crumpled to the pavement and passed out.

"That," the chief counselor said, "is what happens to people who play around."

If this was the punishment for a boy and a girl, I felt certain the penalty for two boys somehow involved barbed wire, a team of donkeys, and the nearest volcano. Nothing, however, could match the cruelty and humiliation Jason and I soon practiced upon each other. He started a rumor that I had stolen an athletic supporter from another camper and secretly wore it over my mouth like a surgical mask. I retaliated, claiming he had expressed a desire to become a dancer. "That's nothing," he said to the assembled crowd, "take a look at what I found on David's bed!" He reached into the pocket of his tennis shorts and withdrew a sheet of notebook paper upon which were written the words I LIKE GUYS. Presented as an indictment, the document was both pathetic and comic. Would I supposedly have written the note to remind myself of the fact, lest I forget? Had I intended to wear it taped to my back, advertising my preference the next time our rented buses carried us off to yet another swinging sexual playground?

I LIKE GUYS. He held the paper above his head, turning a slow circle so that everyone might get a chance to see. I supposed he had originally intended to plant the paper on my bunk for one of the counselors to find. Presenting it himself had foiled the note's intended effect. Rather than beating me with sticks and heavy shoes, the other boys simply groaned and looked away, wondering why he'd picked the thing up and carried it around in his pants pocket. He might as well have hoisted a glistening turd, shouting, "Look what he did!" Touching such a foul document made him suspect and guilty by association. In attempting to discredit each other, we wound up alienating ourselves even further.

Jason—even his name seemed affected. During meals I studied him from across the room. Here I was, sweating into my plate, my stomach knotted and cramped, when *he* was the one full of shit. Clearly he had tricked me, cast a spell or slipped something into my food. I watched as he befriended a girl named Theodora and held her hand during a screening of *A Lovely Way to Die*, one of the cave paintings the head counselor offered as a weekly movie.

She wasn't a bad person, Theodora. Someday the doctors might find a way to transplant a calf's brain into a human skull, and then she'd be just as lively and intelligent as he was. I tried to find a girlfriend of my own, but my one possible candidate was sent back home when she tumbled down the steps of the Parthenon, causing serious damage to her leg brace.

Jason looked convincing enough in the company of his girl-friend. They scrambled about the various ruins, snapping each other's pictures while I hung back fuming, watching them nuzzle and coo. My jealousy stemmed from the belief that he had been cured. One fistful of my flesh and he had lost all symptoms of the disease.

Camp ended and I flew home with my legs crossed, dropping my bag of stolen souvenirs and racing to the bathroom, where I spent the next several days sitting on the toilet and studying my face in the mirror. *I like guys*. The words had settled themselves into my features. I was a professional now, and it showed.

I returned to my volunteer job at the mental hospital, carrying harsh Greek cigarettes as an incentive to some of the more diffi-cult patients.

"Faggot!" a woman shouted, stooping to protect her collection of pinecones. "Get your faggoty hands away from my radio trans-mitters."

"Don't mind Mary Elizabeth," the orderly said. "She's crazy."

Maybe not, I thought, holding a pinecone up against my ear.

She's gotten the faggot part right, so maybe she was on to something.

The moment we boarded our return flight from Kennedy to Raleigh, Lisa rearranged her hair, dropped her accent, and turned to me saying, "Well, I thought that was very nice, how about you?" Over the course of five minutes, she had eliminated all traces of her reckless European self. Why couldn't I do the same?

In late August my class schedule arrived along with the news that I would not be bused. There had been violence in other towns and counties, trouble as far away as Boston; but in Raleigh the transition was peaceful. Not only students but many of the teachers had been shifted from one school to another. My new science teacher was a black man very adept at swishing his way across the room, mocking everyone from Albert Einstein to the dweebish host of a popular children's television program. Black and white, the teachers offered their ridicule as though it were an olive branch. "Here," they said, "this is something we each have in common, proof that we're all brothers under the skin."

Flipper

Kevin Canty

Something's gone wrong with the boy. It's easy to see: his face (once lovely, elfin) is cased in a block of suet now. Wings of fat droop over his belt, shiver when he moves. Eleven years old. Little fireplug, roly-poly, Mama's little fatty. When he bends to find his shoes, the rolls of flesh on his stomach meet in dolphin lips.

His mother said it and his sister overheard. Now it's just his name: Flipper.

Summer evenings, freeze tag, fireflies, War, lemonade and sleep before dark. At bedtime, the name of Flipper is called from child to child, through the alleys (creosote and new wood, the smell of fences, everything new and naked), the woods at the end of the road, all the way to the comics-and-candy store on Hudson Avenue where he is trying to make himself disappear. Baby Huey.

Then they are driving all the way to Pennsylvania, his mother, his father, and Flipper. His sisters have been left behind. No one should be forced to see the camp for fat children, none but the punished. A hundred Flippers! Spare the girls! He sits in the backseat, alone, watching the telephone wires gallop from pole to pole, trying to hypnotize himself. Grim necks of his parents. This is New Jersey, 1964, the cars of the Kennedy assassination. He doesn't dare speak. Flipper is hungry.

At camp, there is no common misery but a hundred separate ones, no two alike: Baby Huey, Little Lotta, Porky, Tubby, Flipper. They tip the canoes on impact. They stare at their dismal breakfast bowls: oatmeal, plain. They have swimming practice, like giant cabbages tumbled into the water, their noses fill and bleed with green lake. Harmonicas, campfires. In the absence of their everyday tormentors, they quickly organize themselves into bullies and victims, and fight over smuggled Milk Duds. Two boys are caught "fucking" and sent home. There are bed wetters. Flipper has the top bunk. When the counselor shuts the lights off, the room fills with quiet sobs, they sleep on damp pillows. Once in a while, the telltale rustle of wax paper. All ears alert.

One day Flipper goes for a walk in the forest. The counselors call it "hiking." Alone: The fat campers are solitary, each encased in each. Ridiculous in shorts, and knowing it—his legs are pink as pigskin despite weeks of sun—he clambers over logs, hops from rock to rock to cross the creek. He dreams that this path will lead him to a Rexall store, a place of comic books and candy, an hour of comfort. His soft and secret heart. He lies on the bank of the creek in the morning sun and feels the warm grass springing upright again, tickling his neck. Almost time to go back. He pictures his lunch: an orange dome of canned cling peach on top of white cottage cheese, like a mockery of a fried egg. Fried eggs! And dry toast, when all he dreams of is butter, butter and Heath bars and marshmallow Easter chicks. Bitter and small and hard. The idea takes shape in his brain, then, a wisp of smoke and then the hazy outline and then the idea: He is not going back.

Dead by the road. Anywhere. You'll be sorry.

He doesn't run, he *couldn't* run. The stumps and switchy branches reach to trip him, the smell of skunk cabbage fills the marshy bottoms like a gigantic fart racing after him. Poor Flipper! They will picture this escape when he's dead. They will see they were wrong. The emptiness inside him, the place where lunch ought to be and snacks, and the love of his mother, and softness, this empty place contracts and loosens around a burning core. Damaged organ. Unlovely wobbling. After half an hour he heaves himself over the last fence of the camp and into the forbidden world.

His skin is covered with a fine damp sheen of sweat and his thighs are starting to chafe, a little. Dying will be even worse. He fights back tears, girl-tears. The lumps of flesh on his chest, his father called them man-tits. A girl, an ugly girl, a fat girl. Flipper does not need a tormentor. He does not need help.

In an opening in the forest, not far from the lake, he comes across a girl who is also weeping. The terror of being looked at stops his own tears, the distant, longed-for call to heroism.

Are you lost? he asks, stepping out of the trees. She shakes her head, still nestled in her arms and her knees, won't give him anything. Her voice comes muffled through her dress: Go away!

I don't know where I am, he says.

Well, go away anyway!

He stands rooted in the meadow. She weeps again, head shaking, burrowing into her dress. It's checkered red-and-white, like a tablecloth. Screaming, splashing from the lake: other children having fun, the ones from the Baptist camp, the Boy Scout camp, the rich camp. Her hair is blond and cut abruptly at the neck, and on her neck are two small red spots, remains of pimples, so she's older. Is something wrong? he asks her.

This time she looks up, and her face is swollen and round and covered with pimples new and old, and she is enormously pregnant. How could she draw her knees up around that belly? The dress concealed her. Two years older than Flipper, maybe thirteen. Her belly rests between her legs like an enormous stone she has swallowed. I hurt my baby! she wails. I didn't mean to!

What?

Can't answer; not now. Buries her face in her dress again and weeps, head shaking, clasping her hands so tight that her fingernails make white half-moons in her palms. Can you do that? Flipper wonders. Can you make yourself bleed? Thirteen and pregnant. He's never thought about this. Opens her face to him again and says, You won't tell anyone?

No.

Opens her dress and a lapful of candy spills out, all chocolate, little Halloween bars of everything: Hersheys, Nestlés, Peter Paul

Mounds. He can't stop staring, though her lap is nothing he should be seeing—the primitive bulge under the silvery-brown candy. She says, They told me not to but I couldn't help it. I'm so bad. They told me not to for my baby!

The silence, wind in the trees and the splashing screaming happy children, voices torn into the wind like scattered paper. You're all right, he says. You didn't do anything bad.

Miranda!

The voice comes distantly through the forest, then closer, an adult voice, counselors, footprints breaking on the brittle leaves. Take these! she says, all frightened, pushing the candy into his hands, scooping the little silvery bits into his greedy hands. Flipper is rich! Ten or twenty little candies, they overstuff his pockets, he looks down and sees the tops of her breasts through the loose neck of her dress—blue-veined and milky white. Now go! she says, and Flipper goes.

Watches from the edge of the little clearing. A nun and then another nun come out, say something he can't hear. The full-dress model nun, with the hats and so on. Flipper squats, terrorized, Jesus will point him out, radio under the starched headdress, radar, they know—they have to know. Still he can't help following when they leave with her. A nun, the pregnant girl, another nun, like prisoners in a war movie. Pockets crammed with candy, he steals through the woods, following the white flash of the nuns and the red of her dress, a safe distance behind. Looking for what? He won't tell himself. Pizza face, preggy, the bulgy blue-veined skin. Not far from disgust, not far from himself. Pasty-white, fatty,

Baby Huey. White frame houses through the trees; he thrashes closer, breaking twigs. Nobody notices him.

Through the scrap and scrub at the edge of the forest, he sees green lawns, green shutters, porches, a swimming pool. Chaise longues on the lawn, a pregnant girl in a swimming suit in each, six or eight but he's not counting. Some kind of treatment? They aren't happy, they aren't talking. These are the two-piece kind of bathing suits, so their bellies shine like moons in the light. Flipper wants to cry. On the porches, on the lawns are pregnant girls, in bathing suits or tent dresses—one of those modeled after a sailor suit, navy blue with white piping . . . and the nuns like moving telephone booths, walking on invisible legs, keeping track. Guarding against pleasure or happiness.

They lead Miranda into one of the buildings and then, a few minutes later, lead her out again, this time wearing a bathing suit herself. They lead her to a longue and she lies, on her back, with her eyes closed but not sleeping. Not wanting to see. The blue veins stand out clearly on her breasts, the parts he can see, and on her thighs. Humiliation. He watches from the edge of the forest until he gets a feeling: She knows he is there, knows he is watching. Then turns, and starts back for the fat camp.

What kind of boy is Flipper? He hides his treasure in a hollow tree, a hundred yards from camp, though squirrels might find it. The little bars are soft from carrying them in the pocket of his shorts, almost melted from the damp heat of Flipper. He allows himself one, a Hershey, soft as velvet on his tongue. Leaves the lump of chocolate in his mouth, lets it melt to nothing. Bliss. He closes his eyes, feels the sunlight on his skin. A face in the darkness. Hair as soft and blond as a baby's, No More Tears. She was fucking, really fucking, there is no other explanation; the thought makes him tremble. She had outgrown the small sins of children. Someday soon, he thinks. No More Tears. Holding the chocolate in his mouth, not swallowing, until the last taste melts away, eyes closed, concentrating. Then licks the wrapper clean.

Tells the counselors that he fell asleep in the woods. Either they believe him or they don't care.

The counselors were never fat. The counselors have beautiful, tanned bodies; they watch each other, the children disappear. Lesser species. Burning ants with a magnifying glass.

Canned cling-peach halves for dessert, cold from the refrigerator, they taste like refrigerator.

I'm not supposed to, Miranda says. They say it makes my baby excited.

It can't hurt anything, Flipper says. It's just a little bit.

I don't want to do anything to hurt my baby.

You don't have to, Flipper says, if you don't want to.

This time it's Special Dark. Slowly he unwraps the paper, then the foil, and slips the little sharp-edged square into his mouth, still cool and hard from a night in the forest. This time he carried it in a bag so it wouldn't melt. Ten-thirty in the morning, hazy blue sky, the sun warming toward the dust and emptiness of the afternoon. He closes his eyes but she doesn't go away; and in a minute he hears the rustle of the bag, the snap of a paper wrapper opening. He brought three for himself and three for her. No hurry. They have all morning. The edges soften, bittersweet.

There! She says. You can feel him, there! She guides his hand to the lower curve of her belly, presses her own hand over his. Through the soft cotton of her dress, he can feel her taut skin, bulging, ready to burst. She smells of soap and milk and medicine. Suddenly he feels it, the soft bone turning deep inside her, the baby. Instinct tries to pull his hand away, but she presses down, holds it close, and this time he feels a stronger shove, an elbow or a knee, something alive in there! A person inside you, Flipper thinks. A person inside me. His hand on her belly, inches away from her breasts, inches away from where she pees from, where the baby will come spilling out not long from now. Disgust and fascination mixed. The sweets well up inside him, and still he can't take his hand away. She won't let him anyway.

He doesn't like it when I eat chocolate, Miranda says.

She's there again the next day, and the next.

At weigh-in Sunday morning, it turns out Flipper's lost three pounds, champion of the week. His cabin gets pizza that night. He dares to dream about her. Special Dark, he's been saving them: three for her and three for him. Flipper will lie next to her in the grass, eyes closed, both of them. Lying alone on his hard little bunk, he can feel the morning sunlight on his skin, tickle of damp grass. With his eyes closed, Flipper sees the milk-white and porcelain-blue of her breasts, she's careless with them. Once he saw her right down to the nipple. Two bunks away, a boy is sobbing in the darkness. The wind is churning the leaves of the trees outside, a sound like rain. Right down to the nipple. He opens his eyes to the darkness of the cabin, and imagines that she meant for him to see her.

In the morning it is raining. Two days until it will end. He stays away from the tree, to save the last of the Special Dark. When the third day comes up sunny, he barely finishes his breakfast. Miranda has been with him each night, growing inside him. He has dared to dream about her.

At the tree he finds a litter of foil and wrappers on the ground, nothing in the hollow. Another camper has been here.

Flipper shrinks again, pathetic. A cheap sound like a crying baby doll bubbles out of his thick stupid body, and scalding tears. Flipper is the fattest and the stupidest. Miranda has big zits all over her face. He can't go see her empty-handed, but the camp store sells only wholesome snacks, nothing she would love, nothing for them to share. The nearest real chocolate is in the country store, three or four miles away, the rumor says. It might as well be Mercury. He can feel her in the sunlight, how she would turn her face toward the sun, eyes closed, like some vine twisting toward the light. Gone and gone. Flipper is discarded, weeping trash bag.

Now Flipper is hurrying down the shoulder of the road. Now Flipper is running. Big trucks are driving by, inches from his feet. It doesn't matter what happens to him.

For love, he thinks, oh love. The word comes into his mind at an angle, like another language, because it's the wrong word. What he really wants is this: He wants her to look up at him when he comes into the clearing, he wants her to see the big bar of chocolate in his hands, wants her to know that he had gone especially for her, all the way to the country store, way out in the forbidden world, the dangerous world, and brought this back for her. He wants to see her eat as much as she wants. He wants the smear of melted chocolate on her lips.

Hero.

Now Flipper is trying not to cry again. The counselors caught up to him while he was in the country store, or maybe the bitch behind the counter called the camp on him. She has a hatchet face: bitch. They joke back and forth. This isn't the first time. While she's laughing, Flipper backs up to the candy counter, slips a book-size slab of Special Dark into underwear. No one will notice. His shorts are enormous. He can feel the waxy wrapper, cool against the skin of his ass, and then it melts and shapes itself to him.

Kid Galahad, the counselor says, driving back. She sees the crafty look in his pig eyes.

He's grounded for a week, confined to cabin. His parents are written. He carefully straightens the bar of Special Dark back into a rectangle during the hot afternoons alone, in the sunlight next to his cot. He can feel her in the sunlight, how she would turn her face toward the sun, eyes closed, like some vine twisting toward the light. He can feel her inside him. He practices in whispers, moving his lips: I brought this for you. I got this at the country store.

Now Flipper is standing alone in the little clearing. The sound of an outboard motor rings up from the lake, splashing, swimming, aluminum canoes. She isn't there.

He'll come again tomorrow, and the day after. He will come every week for the rest of the summer but she will not be there. Miranda's gone to have her baby.

Flipper knows this right away. The clearing is empty. Flipper is a big stupid baby.

He lies on his side in the grass. He sees himself from above, like he was already dead. Trash bag. He puts his hand on the bare skin of his own soft stomach, remembering the tigh-stretched skin under the thin cloth. He touches his tiny dick. He saw her once, right down to the nipple. He takes the chocolate bar out of the bag, unwraps the waxy paper and the foil, breaks off a little jagged triangle and slips it in his mouth, no hurry, he's got all afternoon, he's got the whole thing to himself. But the taste is wrong or the feel of it in his mouth, maybe from the melting and unmelting but it tastes like breakfast food or sawdust. She isn't coming. He eats the whole bar anyway, slowly, like it was his duty. Dust, sunlight, aluminum canoes, the grass against his neck. He finishes the chocolate and wads the wrapper up into a ball and stands up, a little dizzy from the sugar but the empty place inside him is still empty. He wants, he wants, he wants, an open mouth and nothing more. Flipper is still hungry.

Nuts

Gahan Wilson

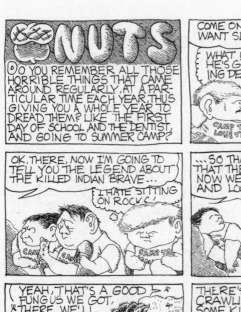

The Brief Summer of Amir and Ariella—An Allegory

Josh Lambert

Ariella steps down off the motorcoach, a reasonable facsimile of the five girl campers who have emerged before her: sweatpants cut to capri length, three-strap Naot sandals with gray wooly socks folded at the shin, a periwinkle tank from the Gap. Yet her hair— genetically as brown and ringlet-prone as the others'—gushes in honey-blond waves. Everyone has heard the stories about her father, the real-estate developer/multimillionaire. And her precocious fifteen-year-old breasts are better, hands-down, than any here at Camp Chalutzim.

Amir brandishes a clipboard and beholds the disembarking children. His skin is glazed a deep hazelnut tan. Short shorts and a size-M STAFF T-shirt exhibit the sharp definition of his calves, thighs, pecs, and arms. The other male counselors are a year or two out of high school, pale and nebbishy with bad posture. At twenty-four, Amir has already served his country as a soldier and an officer.

July in the Laurentian Mountains. Their gazes meet just long enough to establish the inevitability of an unnameable something to come. As if every time he squinted through dry-ice fog in makeshift kibbutz dance halls or the discos on Allenby Street in Tel Aviv, he was searching for her. As if every time she scanned a crowd of pimpled faces in science lab or at a bar mitzvah reception, she expected to discover him.

After this moment it is only a question of days, hours, and minutes.

Camp Chalutzim Staff Manual, page 7: #11. CAMPER STAFF RELA-TIONSHIPS. *Any relationship beyond friendship between staff and campers is expressly forbidden. Intimate relationships between a staff and a camper will result in the immediate termination of the staff member's contract.*

3:30–4:30 P.M., GENERAL SWIM. Since he does not have life-guard certification, Amir does not patrol the beach or police the swimmers. He dangles his legs off the edge of the floating dock near the girls who tread water for exercise. "Come in," she teases him, all tongue and batted eyelashes, "we're waiting." Other days, he dozes on the picnic table near the sunbathers, eyes concealed by mirrored sunglasses. She lets him get comfortable and then applies her sunscreen.

10:15–11:15 A.M., SPORTS ROTATION. Not being athletic, Ariella and her clique form a row on the paved sideline of the basketball court near the water fountain and ogle the camper-staff contests of 4-on-4. Amir doesn't know the game as well as the Canadians, but moves decisively through the key. He always plays for the skins and he visits the water fountain every five minutes, whether time has been called or not. "You are kipping score?" he asks her group, wiping sweat from his brow and arching over the faucet.

The program includes a brief service on the beach at sundown on Friday. Two hundred campers aged eight to fifteen close out the prayers with a listless *Adon Olam*. They rise, wipe grass off their bottoms, and begin to hug—everyone, campers and staff. Even the awkward and ugly kids find someone to hold. The male counselors have been warned during pre-camp: "Watch out. After prayers, the girls'll press their little tits into your stomach, rub up against you, try to give you a hard-on." On this first Friday night, as the camp gropes and feels, Amir waits for Ariella while his erection gradually solidifies.

She emerges from a melee of preteen fondling and flashes him the product of $5,000 of orthodontistry.

"*Gut shabbes*," she purrs, hurling herself into him. She links her hands near his tailbone and squeezes.

"*Shabbat shalom*," he replies, amused to hear an old Yiddish phrase emerge from the lips of this little Canadian. His arms hover awkwardly at his sides but he knows she can feel him where it counts.

She releases him and stares at the grass between his toes while he considers the golden crown of her head. Pivoting on her heels, she stalks off in the direction of her friends. He lowers a hand into his pockets, tucks his rigid dick into the elastic of his briefs, and strolls up the hill to the dining hall for challah and chicken soup.

In a letter to her friend Melissa at Camp Algonquin, a hundred kilometers away, she scrawls in loopy cursive.

> . . . & I know it sounds crazy but I have this thing for a counselor. & I think he likes me too!! His name is amir & he's from israel & he is _so!_ hot! He is so cut you would never believe he is jewish! Except that he looks like a soldier because he just got out of the army, he would kick the shit out of every single other guy here put together. Carly says that geoff z. & aaron & dan g. all want to go out with me but they are all so _lame._ I hope something happens but I dont know, don't worry Ill write you when it does. . .

In a letter to his friend Tzachi at Camp Hatikvah in Maryland, USA, he writes in blocky Hebrew script.

> . . . AND TZACH, THESE GIRLS! EACH ONE FATHER'S LITTLE PRINCESS, AND THEY ARE IN THE TENTS EXPERIMENTING, SUCKING AND TOUCHING WITH THE FIFTEEN-YEAR-OLD BOYS WHO ALMOST DON'T HAVE DICKS YET. AND NO ONE CARES. LET THEM, THE DIRECTOR SAYS. THAT'S WHAT THE PARENTS PAY FOR. IS IT LIKE THIS WHERE YOU ARE, TOO? THERE'S THIS ONE, RICH, BEAUTIFUL

BLONDE. NEVER ONCE ASKED WHAT UNIT I SERVED IN OR WHAT
TOWN I COME FROM, DOESN'T KNOW FROM THE SITUATION,
COULDN'T TELL LABOR FROM LIKUD. THESE THINGS DON'T EVEN
EXIST FOR HER . . . SHE KNOWS COMFORT AND PLEASURE AND
THAT'S ALL. IT'S QUITE BEAUTIFUL, ACTUALLY. BUT STRANGEST
OF ALL, TZACH, IS THAT SHE WANTS IT. FROM ME, I MEAN. I CAN
TELL FROM THE WAY SHE LOOKS ME UP AND DOWN WITH HER EYES
HALF CLOSED LIKE I'M ALREADY INSIDE HER . . .

Monday night, he strolls between the tents, reminding campers
that at 11:30 the program director will cut power to the electrical
outlets in the concrete bases of their tents. "Tur-teen minutes to
Lights Out," he bellows.

Returning from the bathrooms, she tracks him down among
the pegs and candy bar wrappers between #12 and #14. On either
side of them, the tents glow wan and orange like paper lanterns.
She wears a terrycloth bathrobe and swings a plastic bucket
loaded with skin cream and hair products.

"Hey," she says.

He lowers his flashlight. "Hello." Blood rushes to his cheeks:
under the terrycloth, she is naked.

"Can I tell you something?" She indicates his ear, raises herself
up on tiptoe. Warm breath tickles his earlobe and his body bucks
as if passing over a speed bump.

"I'm setting my alarm for three in the morning," she whispers.
"I'm going to wake up and go down to the beach to look at the stars."

"You are going to bich—" he repeats, and then he understands.

She bites her bottom lip, sucks it like a gummy worm.

"Emmmm—" he stammers, without a word to express his desire.

"Layla tov," Good night, she sings, and skips off to bed.

He waits for her on the grassy hill above the docks, contemplating the lake and the pinpricks of light on the far bank. Starlight reminds him of guard duty in the Golan and of quiet evenings torn up by barking dogs and the distant whine of a Katyusha. He wonders what it would be like to feel completely safe in the night without a weapon.

With no warning, hands slip over his eyes from behind. "Guess who?"

His heart bangs into his ribs. He restrains the impulse to pin her with his elbow over her throat. His breathing steadies.

She waits, her hands still covering his eyes. "Guess *who*."

"Miss America?" he guesses.

"This is Canada, stupid." Her fingertips slip down his cheeks, neck, and bare shoulders. He hefts her onto his lap. She weighs nothing, as if constructed of chicken wire and papier-mâché. "Emmmm—" he says, clawing through his vocabulary. The phrase he wants, if it exists, is stranded somewhere between two languages. He settles for: "I nid you."

"I know," she says, staring past him. Her eyes reflect a row of street lamps burning on Rue du Lac in the hamlet on the opposite shore.

"And you? You nid me?"

"Well, duh."

Enough talking: He cinches her head between his hands and pours his tongue into her mouth. She squirms backwards.

"Wait," she says, and wipes his spittle from her upper lip with the back of her hand. "Okay, now."

They begin again, knowing they have hours until sunrise. Grass teases their bare legs. He is surprised by how much she teaches him.

. . . Meliss it was really really good & I cant write about it but Ill tell you everything when we get back to the city . . .

. . . SHE'S LIKE ICE CREAM, SO SWEET AND SOFT, THIS ONE. I DON'T THINK UNTIL NOW I HAD ANY IDEA WHAT THE WORD PURE WAS SUPPOSED TO MEAN. THE GREATEST JOB ON THE PLANET, NO? I WOULD BE A CAMP COUNSELOR FOR THESE CANADIANS FOR THE REST OF MY LIFE . . .

The schedule contains more than enough time. Fifteen minutes here for MORNING SNACK. Thirty-five minutes there of REST PERIOD. They choose two clearings near the stream, where the constant tinkle of running water obscures the sounds of their movements.

9:30–10:00 A.M., MORNING DISCUSSION. He leans against the doorpost of the rec hall, maintaining his distance from the Canadians inside. Braying laughter follows jokes he can't parse. He notices, now, how they look at her when she raises her tiny wrist, waits to be called upon, and speaks.

The boys and young men seek her out with their eyes, their mouths slightly agape. She smiles into face after face, devastates each with her perfect teeth and brightly moves on to the next and the next. The girls and young women squint and study her from oblique angles. They observe her like a guard watching a fence: waiting for a breach, or, if there is none, with growing admiration for the unbroken strength. What she says doesn't matter because they praise and flatter her in any case. He realizes: One and all, they love her. For them, she is perfect.

That she absorbs their admiration, all of it, without effort, is to him irresistible. She is theirs—and they are hers—as he will never be.

10:15–11:15 A.M., SPORTS ROTATION. He dribbles straight for the basket with no thought of passing and plows through anyone unlucky enough to stand between him and the hoop. On defense, he sends opposing players tripping over themselves to the concrete. Ariella can't stand blood and feels nauseous when he breaks the skin of one of the boys she has known since Grade One. Still, her mind drifts from the game and she envisions him pummeling the math teacher from last year who stared down her shirt, and then mounting her on one of the high school's cafeteria tables.

3:30–4:30 P.M., GENERAL SWIM. Ariella and her friends gossip and leaf through *Cosmo*. Stretched across the splintery wood of the picnic bench, pretending to read a legal thriller, he listens. She spreads cruel half-truths about a girl in the unit, a former friend who gained weight. She can't choose between a Jeep and a Mini for her sixteenth birthday. Amir tries to forget his room in his parents' three-bedroom apartment in Ashkelon, and how he had to ask two days in advance to borrow his mother's Corsica. He fantasizes about railing Ariella in the many plush beds of her parents' mansion, on a chaise longue next to her pool, on the soft leather upholstery of her mother's Mercedes and her father's Lexus.

They convene in the hiding spots, communicate by signals, observe schedules. They avoid awkward silences by not talking at all, groping for each other immediately and disappearing back into the woods when they finish.

. . . Meliss I don't know things are weird. Hes so quiet & doesnt talk & doesnt know anything about any of the bands we listen to or anything. He said he doesnt even go to temple on yom kippur or whatever even though hes from israel. I wish he would open up & say something cause I really really like him but I feel kind of bad about not hanging out with the other guys so much. . .

. . . I CAN'T UNDRESTAND IT, TZACH. THESE KIDS LIVE IN A WORLD THAT SIMPLY DOESN'T EXIST. THEY PLEASURE THEMSELVES WITHOUT CONSEQUENCE AND ACT AS IF THE LITTLE INTRIGUES OF WHO WORE WHAT AND WHO KISSED WHO AND WHO SAID WHAT ABOUT WHO ARE THE BEGINNING AND END OF THE UNIVERSE. MINE, THE BLONDE, IS THE SAME. IT'S TRULY UNBELIEVABLE. SOMETIMES I WONDER IF SHE HAS EVER REALLY FELT PAIN, ANY REAL PAIN WHATSOEVER . . .

Late one Friday night, Amir waits three hours in their clearing behind the tennis courts under a nearly invisible ribbon of moon. He dozes off and starts awake, furious and clammy with dew, only fifteen minutes before morning assembly.

At breakfast he looms over her table and blows his nose. This signals a meeting after the meal in the far clearing. She rolls her eyes at him as if he is her father demanding that she tidy her room. He blows his nose desperately, wipes his nostrils raw against a scrap of brown paper towel.

She shows up fifteen minutes late.

"Where have you bin?" he says. "Where were you last night, tell me."

"Don't yell, jeez. Relax."

"Relax?"

"Chill, okay? Don't be so selfish." One of her tentmates has broken up with a boyfriend. The girl was bawling all night—a crisis. "She really loves him, okay? It's a big deal. I had to be there for her."

"Big dil?" It's typical. There are eleven nights left in the summer and for this, another teenage soap opera, he has forfeited one of them? "It is a child romance, no? She will forget."

"She's my friend. Don't say that. It's serious."

He laughs. Does she know what serious is?

"She's not a child. We're not *children*."

"Oh, no?" He shakes his head. She is. They all are. "Each and every one," he mutters aloud in Hebrew.

"What?"

"Nothing"

She glares at him.

He growls: "Nothing. Nothing!"

She scrunches up her face as if disgusted. "Who do you think you *are*, anyway? *You're* the child. *You're* the one who doesn't understand anything. You think you're so fucking cool, but you're not. You're not! No one here even knows who you are. No one even cares." She is crying now.

He tries to be soft. "If we have a meeting, you come on time. Understand?" But the words spurt out sharper than he'd like, a command.

She laughs. "Or what? What are you going to do?" She wipes her face and backs away from him in the direction of the tentsite. "Leave me alone," she says.

She surrounds herself with friends while he hides out in the staff lounge, struggling through English paperbacks. The camper yentas inform him she is with Brad Mandel. She hears the rumors of his rough sex with Amy, the A&C instructor.

Only a few days remain in the session. Almost everyone manifests symptoms of homesickness or sinus infection or lice.

The final morning. A September chill is in the breeze. The luggage truck is loaded, the buses idle. Campers bawl and scream, as always, "Best summer ever!" Time for one last round of hugs. She approaches him, her eyes red-streaked and cheeks puffy, and loops her slender arms around his torso.

He squeezes her, pouring everything he can't express—the simultaneity of his desire and revulsion—into the force of his grip.

"It was a great, great summer," she says.

"Okay." He peers down at her: she is the most perfect, the most perfectly impossible girl he will ever hold. Their gazes meet and the inevitability of their separation overcomes them. How did he not see it from the start?

"I'll miss you so, so much. Will you write me?"

"Yeah."

"I'll write you. You have to write to me."

"Okay."

The director shouts, "On the buses. Move it or lose it!"

"Goodbye," he says.

"Bye."

She squeezes him one last time and joins her friends in front of Bus 3. He crouches on his haunches and listens as the motor-coaches rev up to haul these children back to bright and large Canadian homes he can't even imagine, homes in which he will never have a place.

In her high school years Ariella flirts with all types of boys and men. The only ones as big and strong as Amir are non-Jews she has to lie to her parents about, guys who play hockey in the middle of the night in Scarborough, alcoholics, bullies whom she can never trust. At university, she prefers premed students. Sometimes, when she is held, she remembers Amir: No man makes her feel as safe and protected as she remembers having felt with him.

At law school in Tel Aviv, Amir encounters other North American girls. Some of them are very pretty, but none as pretty as the Ariella he remembers or as rich, none as content or sure of themselves. He remembers her body when he's with women for the rest of his life. When he buys a jacket or a pair of shoes, he often stares at a more expensive item he can't afford and wonders what might have been. As he ages he begins to doubt there ever was such a girl, or that he could have been a part of her life.

They live without each other, half a world apart, almost unaware of a longing for those brief moments when, in each other's arms, their lives made sense.

Cello, Goodbye

Lev Grossman

My musical career reached its peak in 1986, the spring of my junior year in high school, though I didn't know it at the time. That was the year I was appointed principal cellist of the Massachusetts All-State Orchestra.

The All-State Orchestra was an ensemble made up of musicians from each of Massachusetts's four regional high school orchestras, which drew in turn on dozens of individual high school orchestras. If you didn't play in your high school orchestra, you weren't eligible for the regional level—a constraint that, I knew in my heart of hearts, eliminated the very best players, the ones who were too cool to bother with their school orchestras. But I didn't worry about what was in my heart of hearts. I was the principal cellist of the Massachusetts All-State Orchestra. I gave the head cues. I assigned the bowings. We played Mussorgsky's "Night on Bald Mountain"—you may recall the disco version from the *Saturday Night Fever* sound track—and it was awesome.

I had no idea at the time that I had reached the pinnacle of my career as a cellist, and that I was about to begin a slow but ever more rapidly accelerating spiral downward. I had it all, cellistically speaking, and I was just going to get more. Beyond my strong showing at All-State, I was the principal cellist of my high school orchestra. I had a respectable seat in the All-Eastern Orchestra—that's one rung up from All-State, don't you know—and a spot in the senior division of the Greater Boston Youth Symphony Orchestra (or GBYSO; pronounced, dyslexically, "JIB-so"), which I was planning to ditch the following year for a spot in the even more prestigious Youth Philharmonic Orchestra, which was associated with the New England Conservatory.

What's more, I had been accepted at a highly competitive, really rather exclusive summer music camp. Let's call it, oh, say, Greenmeadow.

I took up the cello in the fifth grade, late by the standards of most adolescent hotshots. Why would a fifth grader take up an earnest, technically demanding, inconveniently large instrument like the cello? I chose it because my elementary school didn't offer guitar lessons, and the two looked alike. I must have been nine or ten at the time, and my musical universe consisted of the Beatles, the Bee Gees, and Kiss, plus a record of Allen Ginsberg singing Blake poems in a barn, which my parents played with inexplicable frequency.

I've had some experience with prodigies in my life. In college

I once escorted the fourteen-year-old violinist Midori around campus for a day—this was shortly after her famous debut at Tanglewood with the BSO, when she broke two E strings playing Leonard Bernstein's *Serenade after Plato's Symposium* and still brought the house down. So I can say with some confidence that I was definitely not a prodigy.

I was, however, one of those diligent children who plugged away at things, and cello was one of the things I plugged away at. I was a scrubber: solid technique, 100 percent enthusiasm, no panache. I was also a small kid, and skinny, and the cello was more or less the same size as I was. I couldn't carry it more than a few hundred yards without switching hands.

My hands were one of my few natural advantages: they were large, strong, well-proportioned hands, with limber, muscular fingers. The first time one of my teachers saw me he seized them and exclaimed, to nobody in particular, "He has Feuermann's hands!" Feuermann being Emanuel Feuermann, one of the great cello virtuosos of the twentieth century.

By the spring of my junior year in high school I had come to terms with some of the cello's less technically challenging masterpieces. I could get through Haydn's Concerto in C major, Bach's Suite no. 3 in C major—cellists know it as "the easy one"—and Brahms's brooding E minor sonata. I had already spent two summers at a small music camp in southern Switzerland, halfway up the side of an Alp, where I ate chocolate for breakfast and exchanged clumsy, furtive kisses with an older, college-bound pianist. I spent those summers practicing five hours a day, building the foundation of a rough but functional cello technique. I was ready for Greenmeadow.

Greenmeadow is located in the northwest corner of Massachusetts, the one defined by Vermont to the north and upstate New York to the west. It's a dead quiet, deeply rural pocket of land, occupied mostly by farmers, liberal arts colleges, bed and breakfasts, and other summer camps. Greenmeadow isn't unique: it's one of an incestuous little gulag archipelago of highly competitive New England music camps. A goodly fraction of America's precocious young classical musicians audition for them—I had tried the year before and had been turned down—and quite a few of those who get in go on to distinguished performing careers. Itzhak Perlman came up through the Massachusetts system. So did Pinchas Zukerman and Yo-Yo Ma.

At the beginning of July, my parents drove me the three hours from Boston to Greenmeadow's campus, which is situated on what's left of a rambling former dairy farm now gone to seed, at the dead end of a dirt road. It was and is a good-sized tract of land, eighty acres or so, covered in trees and meadows and crisscrossed by wandering stone walls. As there was absolutely nowhere else to go, the campus took on the character of a tiny self-contained universe for its inmates. The main building was an old farmhouse known universally as the House, as if there were only one of its kind in the world. The faculty, staff, and most important, the girls lived in the House. There was also a cabin called the Cabin, which contained more girls. The Hutch was a ramshackle shed where the younger boys lived. The older boys, myself included, slept in the Barn.

The Barn and the Hutch were at one end of the campus, the House and the Cabin at the other, and between them were arranged Greenmeadow's sparse amenities. There were tiny practice cabins and rehearsal spaces scattered around the grounds. There was an elegant but small and punishingly chilly swimming pool, and a lumpy, weedy clay tennis court. The campus was bordered on all sides by working farms, so the air was always full of dust and pollen and the smell of manure. Taken as a whole it probably had a certain lumpy, Robert Frosty New England charm, although I, as a teenager who had spent most of his short life in suburban New England, was completely immune to it.

There must have been fifty or sixty of us there that summer, ranging in age from thirteen to eighteen. Greenmeadow was primarily a string camp: we were violinists, violists, and cellists, along with a handful of pianists (though the piano is, as any pedant will tell you, technically a member of the percussion family). It's tempting to imagine us as a refined, patrician lot, but in fact we were a strikingly ordinary cross-section of middle-class American adolescence. There were hopeless nerds, leggy blond private school girls, beefy specimens who could have passed for jocks, and the occasional pale distracted aesthete, as well as a large, undifferentiated mass of ordinary-looking kids who just happened to play classical instruments unusually well.

We played and socialized together on what appeared to be a more or less equal basis, but that sense of equality was purely an illusion, and a temporary one. Greenmeadow was a test, designed to establish whether or not we had a true vocation: Some of us were talented amateurs, and some of us were future professionals, gifted with that little extra something. The former had yet to be weeded out from the latter, but that summer the difference would be made clear. For the mediocre among us, time was running short.

Life at Greenmeadow revolved around chamber music. Every week the faculty would reshuffle and reconfigure us into a new set of trios, quartets, quintets, sextets (no giggling, please), up to and including the occasional octet. On Mondays after breakfast we would rush to the wall where the weekly groupings were posted. We would spend the rest of the week rehearsing our newly assigned pieces with our newly assigned colleagues, and at the end of the week we would perform for the other students.

For people who are supposedly practitioners of an aesthetic discipline, musicians are abnormally obsessed with rankings and hierarchy, and the chamber music assignments posted on Mondays provided fodder for a full week's worth of petty and malicious gossip. The faculty never explained why anybody was placed with anybody else, and their silence left us free to engage in endless, ornate speculation. Why did they put X with Y? Don't they know they broke up just before camp? And Y doesn't have the *sound* for Ravel. And why is Z doing double duty in the Mendelssohn *and* the Schubert? You really shouldn't play Schubert on a cheap violin like his. And all Q got is the Dvořák! And she had that exact same movement *last* summer! And she *still* can't hit the harmonic at the end!

These weekly groupings and regroupings gave life at Greenmeadow its rhythm and its structure. Every Monday morning we would sit down with our new collaborators for our first rehearsal, still reeling from the fresh reorganization of our tiny universe, scooching our chairs together in whatever rural outbuilding we'd been assigned to, tightening and rosining our bows, tuning to the A from somebody's pocket metronome. I would stab around on the floorboards for a suitable crack in which to lodge the endpin of my cello. Everybody was either elated or terrified or pissed-off to be there, depending on whether they felt flattered or intimidated or grievously insulted by the company in which they found themselves. A complicated skein of glances would fly back and forth over the music stands.

Chamber music was the focus at Greenmeadow, but we also had a mandatory choir and an all-string orchestra, although nobody took them seriously. If the faculty could spare the time they would throw the occasional solo lesson our way, but nobody paid any attention to those either—we all had long, fraught histories with our regular year-round teachers, and there was no point in letting an outsider meddle with your technique; you'd only have to undo the changes again in the fall. My teacher at Greenmeadow was a tall, horsey woman who held a seat in the Boston Symphony Orchestra, which is no easy feat, but our sessions had almost no effect on me whatsoever. They were frequently interrupted by the wasps that constantly invaded our practice cabin. My teacher wouldn't allow me to swat at them because she was a Christian Scientist, and the wasps, she insisted, were "God's Creatures."

Every Sunday the camp would assemble for the weekly recital, which took place in the Barn. The concerts were informal occasions, and the appropriate attitude toward them, I quickly learned, was amused cynicism, although the younger campers would get excited, and a few townsfolk might wander in to listen out of curiosity. The older boys would watch from the hayloft and greet the end of each piece with lusty shouts of *bravissimo, bravississimo*, and *bravississississimo*.

We were required to dress entirely in white, which, apart from a few grass stains, we did. It gave the concerts a pleasant, Edenic feel—there was something otherworldly about a bunch of adolescents playing classical music in a barn in the deep countryside, arrayed in garments of purest samite, with crickets chirping in the background and motes and seeds floating in the air.

In my first week at Greenmeadow I was placed in a string quartet. As it was my first summer there, I had no particular expectations of my colleagues, though I studied them with avid curiosity. We had been assigned a movement from a quartet by the Hungarian composer Ernö Dohnányi, a lovely, lush, dreamy, summery little scrap of music. I remember very little about the Dohnányi now, except that distinct but distant impression of its loveliness. I can remember the feelings the melody evoked, but not the melody itself.

Some kids meditated before the recital. Some did curls with dumbbells. Others, especially the private-school set, took furtive puffs of marijuana. A few kids dusted their hands with talcum powder. I thought I'd give that a try: I'd been having problems with my left hand in the hot weather. My fingers got sweaty and tended to slip and slide on my cello's smooth ebony fingerboard. I thought the talcum powder would give me a little extra traction.

How wrong I was. When I got out on stage, under the hot, bug-swarmed lights, I discovered that the talcum powder had the opposite effect. Whereas before my fingers were slippery, now they were completely frictionless. The strings felt as thick as cables, and my fingers skated up and down them uncontrollably. Vibrato was an impossibility. Pitch, never my strong suit, was a distant memory. Every shift was a trombone slide. I tried to silently convey to the rest of the quartet that yes, I shared their horror at my grotesque performance, but my mortified glances were met only with contempt. I haven't heard the Dohnányi since then, but I feel sure that one day I'll bump into it accidentally—strolling past an outdoor concert, maybe, or as the background music in a movie—and break down crying with remorse.

Talcum powder aside, I was never a good performer anyway. I had a hard time relaxing into the moment—onstage I suffered bouts of adolescent self-doubt and Sartrean nausea. In fact, the only performances at Greenmeadow that I remember with any real pleasure involved what we called zilching. I don't know the origin of the word, or whether it has any currency elsewhere—Google suggests not. But at Greenmeadow zilching meant sightreading a piece of chamber music with as much brio and zeal as possible, and usually as fast as possible.

Zilching was never scheduled; it only occurred spontaneously. Once the sheet music was produced, whoever happened to be loafing nearby was press-ganged into service to fill out the necessary configuration. Lush, passionate composers were preferred: Schubert and Ravel, and the demonic Belgian virtuoso Eugene Ysaÿe. Tempos were generally extreme: Zilchers hurtled through their material at full throttle. Any prior preparation was forbidden. Technical mistakes were jeered at in passing and then forgotten. The summer nights were hot, and sweat would fly from the foreheads of the players. Horsehair snapped. Rosin dust floated up toward the rafters on the humid air. A peanut gallery would assemble around the frantically sawing musicians. Turnover was high: between movements members of the crowd would sub in and out, as they would in a pickup basketball game.

Criticism, commentary, and trash talk were offered freely, both by onlookers and by the performers, even in mid-performance—players would chatter back and forth at each other as they played. Extemporization, embellishment, and even unscheduled cadenzas were not necessarily frowned upon. It was bad music, but there was something pure about it. It was music made for the musicians, not for the listeners.

The daily schedule at Greenmeadow never varied: breakfast at eight, followed by chorus or orchestra rehearsal, chamber music or private lessons, lunch, practice and more rehearsals, goofing-off time, then dinner and an evening orchestra session if there hadn't been one that morning. Naturally we were starved for nonmusical recreation. Like a prison inmate, I ran laps around a long, looping local road, paced by a lanky violinist. Ping-Pong tournaments were organized: the faculty felt the game encouraged a sense of rhythm. Once somebody managed to get a softball game going, but it ended after half an inning when it became clear that none of the fielders was willing to come within ten feet of the ball until it had completely come to rest, for fear of spraining their long, limber fingers.

We staged the usual summer-camp pranks—nothing very

original. The residents of the Barn and the Cabin spent a day dressed up as each other, which was mildly amusing, though in retrospect I think I probably queened it up a little too much. Two of the younger counselors borrowed a chicken from a local farmer and let it loose in the Cabin around dawn. By the time they recaptured the chicken, an hour later, the joke had long stopped being funny.

The only other recreation at Greenmeadow was the opposite sex. To be clear: to the best of my knowledge there wasn't a whole lot of actual sex going on. Most of the kids had come up through the New England Conservatory's Extension Division together. They'd known each other since they were in grade school, had gone to private school together, had played together in orchestras and chamber groups, taken music theory and solfège together, toured together, and of course gone to summer camp together. They'd been hooking up with each other for years, and they were bored. The list of possible couplings had been all but exhausted.

To them I was exotic: I studied with an independent local teacher, and I played on the rough-and-tumble public school circuit. I was a novelty. The first week a rumor went around linking me with the Dohnányi quartet's first violinist, a deeply tanned young woman with auburn ringlets and a Roman nose. She was as baffled by the idea as I was. It turned out that she had unwisely remarked within someone else's hearing that I looked a little like Luke Skywalker, on account of my feathered blond hair—this being 1986—and the tale grew in the telling.

After several unsuccessful flirtations, I did eventually acquire a girlfriend. In my second week I was placed in a piano quintet—we were given Franck's lugubrious Quintet in F minor—and I started going out with the pianist, a bubbly Korean girl a year younger than I. Several times a week, for the rest of the summer, we arranged to sneak out of our respective dorms after lights-out and meet in the mosquito-swarmed darkness. For some reason the traditional venue for late-night trysts was a large boulder out in front of the House. It was known as the Rock, and it was brutally uncomfortable to make out on.

One night three older girls snuck out of the House, snuck into the Barn, and woke me up and two other guys. This came as a shock: it seemed all out of proportion to my modest popularity and my limited capacity for hijinks, which was well known, but they must have been desperate. We crept out of the building, all six of us, at around three in the morning.

We wandered around the camp in the dark, somewhat at a loss as to what to do with our nocturnal freedom. We stripped to our underwear and swam in the freezing cold pool until we got foot cramps. We slid down the Barn's hay chute, which we were strictly forbidden to slide down. We sat on a stone wall (known as the Wall) that overlooked a scenic prospect. At dawn we found ourselves in a pasture belonging to a neighboring farmer, petting a sleepy brown horse.

A strange thing happened to me as my summer at Greenmeadow wore on. Every week, when the new chamber group listings were posted, my partners got younger. Not only that, the music I was assigned got easier. In my third week I was given a remedial Beethoven trio that sounded like an ice-cream truck jingle. In my fourth week I was paired with two eighth-grade violinists and an older violist who was a known hack. Nobody said anything, but they didn't have to. The message was clear: whatever secret rankings the faculty kept, I was falling in them. Whatever expectations they may have had for me, I wasn't meeting them.

It was a revelation that dawned on me slowly, the way all truly terrible revelations do. We were being sorted into the gifted and the giftless, and I was in the latter category. I had come close, by dint of perseverance or Feuermann's hands or some combination of the two, but the spark was missing. I was not a top-flight cellist, and I never would be. I'm not sure now whether I ever really wanted a brilliant, glamorous career as a classical musician, but I'm sure I would have at least liked to walk away from one.

At the end of Greenmeadow's session that year, awards were handed out to virtually every camper. I received the award for Best Waiter. People say that going to camp is about growing up and learning who you are. I never learned who I was at Greenmeadow, but I learned something almost as valuable, which is who I was not: a genius.

My romance with the Korean pianist survived a bare three weeks after camp ended. She invited me to visit her at her house in an immaculate Boston suburb. I met her family, who didn't take kindly to their daughter running around with a white boy. They very politely fed me painfully spicy kimchee, and when I left that night I discovered that the rear window of my car—my mother's Toyota Corolla station wagon, which was parked in their driveway—had been smashed in. I took the hint.

My romance with the cello ended less suddenly but just as decisively. My senior year of high school I performed the first movement of Shostakovich's Concerto in E minor with my school orchestra. I played in my college orchestras, but only when I thought there was a chance we would tour somewhere interesting. Later I played cello in a Brit-pop band called Monterey. We cut a single album, to which I have never listened. Since then my cello case has languished virtually unopened, and my fingers have grown stiff and clumsy. I have been known to noodle on the guitar.

Not long ago, at a dinner party, I was a little disconcerted to find myself sitting next to a fellow Greenmeadow alum. Her name was Natasha, though she went by Tasha back in the day, and she was and still is a cellist. She was at Greenmeadow with me that summer, and she was also present at my moment of glory: When I was principal of the Massachusetts All-State Orchestra, leading the charge up Bald Mountain, she was the assistant principal, sitting right beside me.

Neither of us knew back then that I was at the height of my powers as a cellist. Nor did we realize—or at least I didn't—that Tasha was at the very beginning of her own vertiginous upswing. Whatever it was I was missing, she had. When I asked her what she'd been up to since I'd seen her last, she explained—with faultless modesty—that after Greenmeadow she had gone on to the Curtis Institute in Philadelphia, the most exclusive conservatory in the country, which accepts one cellist per year. She has performed as a soloist in any number of major European cities, and, she concluded, was recently made assistant principal of a major symphony orchestra.

When I told her what I'd been doing since Greenmeadow, she regarded me with mingled pity and contempt.

Queechy Girls

Cynthia Kaplan

There was always one girl at camp whom everyone hated. It had nothing to do with cliques or teams or personal dislikes, and it was not even that everyone had discussed it and a consensus had been raised based upon certain irrefutable evidence. It was just like everyone hated lima beans and the color brown. It was obvious and it was universal, so it didn't require organization.

Everyone at Queechy Lake Camp hated Lisa Hope Mermen. There were no reasons why and there were a million reasons why. Her breasts were too large and her hair was limp. She had probably had her period since she was ten. She was a *very* mediocre athlete. She was not nor ever would be considered coltish. She was nice to everyone, and some people hate that. She had no friends and some people took that as a sign. She had two first names and insisted on using both. At best, she was ignored. At worst, she was teased and bullied and shoved into the lake. Tricks were played on her, food stolen from her, intimate articles of clothing, particularly her brassiere and large to-the-waist panties, were raised on the flagpole in the morning just before assembly. There they were buffeted unkindly by the Maine breeze, these colors of the enemy territory, to be saluted by smirking, suntanned cuties.

Why was she still here, Lisa Hope Mermen? Why did she return summer after summer to a camp where a philosophy of equality symbolized by a de rigueur camp uniform of simple white midi blouses and navy shorts still failed to work in her favor because *her* midi blouse required darts? Why didn't her parents switch her to music camp or send her to Europe where everyone had limp hair?

Queechy Lake Camp was certainly the most beautiful girls' camp in Maine. It was situated on a tree-topped hill which gracefully sloped down to the edge of the lake, clear blue-black and serene. At the high end of the camp the bunks formed a large circle around a perfectly manicured blanket of grass, unlike the bunks at Pine Forest and Bluebird Lake, which were dotted willy-nilly throughout the woods. At the center of the circle was the aforementioned flagpole. As night fell, this happy configuration of lodgings, their lights winking in the dusk, resembled nothing so much as a shoreline of exclusive summer cottages; the darkening courtyard, a navy lake. Paradise.

Then, a little lower down, there was Queechy House, an enormous green Adirondack affair standing exactly as it had for almost one hundred years, its plaque-covered walls a testament to the overachievements of past Queechy girls: Best Field Hockey, Best Basketball, Best Waterskiing. The Archery Award. The Craft Award. The Queechy Spirit Prize. On one side of Queechy House there were the living room and the commissary and the mail room and on the other side were the dining room and the kitchen (which no one ever saw except on Cinnamon Toast Nights, when everyone in your bunk got to go in and eat as much cinnamon toast as they could. The record, set by Rose Bunn-swanger in 1957, was something like forty-nine pieces). Behind Queechy House was a gathering of humongous old pine trees and beneath the trees were twenty or so Adirondack chairs, painted dark green. This spot was called Beneath the Pines, without sarcasm. Team rallies happened here, and Friday night services. If you were friends, one of you sat in the seat and one of you perched on the wide armrest, so you were connected, so there was no mistaking it.

Every building had a name. Please Come Inn and Nellie's Nest and The Barn and Hill House and Mildred, *just* Mildred, after an English lacrosse counselor who perished in the bombing of Dresden. She had gone there with false papers to search for two elderly cousins who were believed to have been in hiding. There was a hockey field and a lacrosse field and two softball fields and there were tennis courts and volleyball courts and basketball courts and sailing and canoeing and waterskiing. And there was kickball and newcome for the younger girls. The field hockey and lacrosse counselors came from England, like Mildred, because the English know those sports best.

There were no socials or dances with boys' camps because

Queechy girls were renown for their winning combination of athletic ability, teamwork, and pep, and pitting them against each other for the attentions of pimply faced, perpetually engorged (that's Deb Edelstein's word, not mine) boys from, say, Camp Tonkahanni, might undermine the confidence of even the most spirited, talented Queechy girl, not to mention threaten many deep friendships. I, for one, was perfectly happy not to have to deal with some dopey tennis nerd trying to guess my bra size. There were male counselors, of course, but it was not the same because they were all over eighteen. There was Bill Ski and Mark Ski and Jamie Canoe and Jack Tennis and Bill Tennis and Chris Swim and Mike Softball. There was Somebody Riding whose name I never remembered because I hated riding. And there was Corey Silver Shop whom everyone assumed was gay even though most of us had no idea what we were talking about.

There was a theater called Marion's Tent, though no one remembered Marion and there was no tent. My theatrical career at Queechy Lake Camp was distinguished by many memorable performances as the second lead; a girl named Wanda Massey always got the starring role. For seven summers, I was the male half to nearly every romantic coupling written for the musical theater. I was Oscar to her Charity, Captain Von Trapp to her Maria, Tony to her Maria. She was, metaphorically speaking, *always* Maria.

The very moment parts were posted and scripts handed out each of us would rush to the edge of some grassy slope to count our lines. The more lines, the bigger the part. Plot development and character were irrelevant. This summer we were doing *The Miracle Worker*. Wanda Massey was Annie Sullivan and I was Helen

Keller. When I opened the script and saw that I had only one line for the entire first half of the play, and that line consisted of one word, "wawa," I nearly went beserk.

Once a summer the Story of Queechy Lake Camp was retold by Aunt Jeanne, the camp director. The entire camp gathered Beneath the Pines, a tangle of interlocked arms and legs, with much tickling of forearms and backs and braiding of hair, to hear how during World War One the camp planted its playing fields with navy beans. Girls as young as nine years old pushed the seeds into the soil and two months later plucked the beans from the leafy vines. They sewed shirts and knitted socks. They were industrious and patriotic and occasionally had air raid rehearsals. They wore baggy bloomers and smocks and maybe in those days it didn't matter if you were bad at sports or had a large bosom. Some of these girls were the grand-mothers and mothers and aunts of future Queechy girls. Katie Co-hen was a legacy and so was Beth Reingold and so was Deb Edelstein. Tessie Green's grandmother won the spirit prize twice in a row and she was completely deaf in one ear. Joan Grobman's mother lost half her middle finger in a rock-climbing accident in 1968, the summer she was fifteen, and came back to camp as soon as she was out of the hospital. That's what Queechy girls did. When the story was over everyone sang Queechy Lake songs: "Spirit of Queechy," "Far Above Dear Queechy Waters," "Queechy Friends Forever."

Surely Lisa Hope Mermen was not the only girl whose bathing suit, with its built-in brassiere, remained dry on the front follow-ing the backstroke race at swim meets. Surely she was not the only girl without a lilting voice or curly ringlets. And surely a lilting voice and curly ringlets were not the only prerequisites of a successful adolescence. Although who was I to say since I had a reasonably lilting voice and decent head of curly ringlets?

But did Lisa Hope Mermen really look all that unhappy? She cheered from the benches at softball and field hockey games, gave her ineffectual all on the "B" basketball squad, sang her heart out in the chorus of *Call Me Madam*. She befriended younger girls who either didn't know any better or were similarly ill-suited to the demands of popularity. Counselors were sympathetic. I was bewildered almost out of my complacency. Almost.

I'd had too many s'mores. I had a weakness for them. I liked the marshmallows to catch fire and burn the entire outside black. I liked the Hershey's chocolate to still be hard, even a little cold; it had to hold its own dually against the heat of the marshmallow and the firm crunch of the graham cracker. If you ate a s'more during a lunchtime campfire, chances were the chocolate bar would be melty from sitting in the sun. Then it melted even more when it came into contact with the marshmallow, and suddenly the graham cracker dominated. I hated that. I'd just as soon skip it if that was how it was going to be. At night, though, on the beach, when everything cooled down, the grains of sand a silver trickle between your toes, when the lake met the sky, when hooded sweatshirts were in order, *that* was the time to gorge yourself into oblivion on s'mores.

I'd had seven, which as anyone knows is four too many. And actually I was feeling all right until the camper-counselor game of duck duck goose. A few woozy moments after I'd chased Karen

Basketball two loops around the circle, I felt the s'mores rising up. I felt a revolution of s'mores. I ran up the beach and gave them their freedom behind the sailing hut. I looked down to inspect the damage (everyone looks at their vomit, everyone) and catch my breath. Running and then vomiting is harder than just vomiting. I leaned against the side of the hut. My breath was loud in my ears. Too loud. And there was a funny humming noise. *Mmmmm. Mmmmm.* It took me a minute to realize it wasn't coming from me. I inched forward, careful not to step in my pile of ex-s'mores, and moved around the corner of the sailing hut until I was crouching beneath its one open window, just next to the door.

At first I thought it was, I don't even know, just this big thing, this moving shadow, it was so dark in there. *Oh, God, it's a bear. Shit, fuck, shit.* But then, *then*—in that way you can see people in the movies when there are scenes in the dark, like there's an illogical light source but you accept it because it's the movies and you really want to see what's going on—*then*, I saw her. Years later I realized the moon must have broken through some clouds.

Lisa Hope Mermen lay all but naked on a pile of sails. Her brassiere was wrapped like a bandage around one arm, her dark blue camp shorts scrunched between her legs. Her white body, all breasts and belly and thighs, was aglow. She was breathing heavily; her face looked . . . I didn't know. Like she was constipated but happy about it. What was she doing? My legs, already vomit-wobbly, were starting to ache from crouching at the window, but I couldn't tear my eyes away. I was watching the Lisa Hope Mermen Movie. The humming got louder. Why was she lying there, naked, humming? *Why?* It wasn't even a song. Then, suddenly, the dark shorts between her legs were moving and I saw that they weren't her shorts. It was like realizing a piece of mud stuck to your ankle is really a leech. The thing between Lisa Hope Mermen's legs rose up and smiled. A glistening, mustached smile.

Mark Ski.

He moved out of the shadows, naked, his back to me, and stretched his neck to both sides. She said, "That was yummy." He said, "Good." There was a rushing noise in my ears. He lowered his whole body onto Lisa Hope Mermen very, very slowly. I saw his penis. My legs collapsed beneath me. I dropped onto the sand. *Poomf.*

When I returned to the beach everyone was sitting Indian style in a big circle around the fire and singing "Leaving on a Jet Plane." Joan Grobman and Deena Saks made a place for me between them. I guess I sang along.

A substantive discussion of What I Saw did not commence until after the campfire died and everyone more or less headed off to bed. It lasted until well after two and included my own eyewitness testimony, followed by a question-and-answer period and concluding with a sort of fake, sort of real hypnosis session, in case there was something I was repressing. Then we tried to levitate Beth Reingold.

We slept in pairs in canvas tents on the sand. Lying in my sleeping bag beside Deb Edelstein, her soft asthmatic wheezing keeping time in the dark, I realized this would be the last time. In the morning we would have blueberry pancakes and hot chocolate and go skinny-dipping in the glassy, dawn-cold lake, and then head off up the hill to our various scheduled activities—lacrosse or archery or pottery. But this was the last senior overnight. The last campfire on the beach. And there was only one more swim meet to go and one more day trip to Acadia National Park and maybe one more pajama breakfast, if we were lucky. There was only the counselor show, *Man of La Mancha*, left to see. All the craft projects would have to be finished in the next week, all the bunk food eaten, all the lost things found. Suddenly it would be the very last night, the night of the Senior Serenade, when we would go by flashlight from bunk to bunk, like carolers, singing the old songs. I was not going to come back the next summer as a junior counselor because my parents wanted me to do a summer session at Andover. And anyway it wouldn't have been the same. When something's over, it's over.

The Performance of Drowning

Terry Galloway

When I was twelve I tried to drown myself during a swimming competition at the Texas Lion's Camp for Crippled Children. I was racing a blind girl and a one-legged girl for an ugly, plastic two-handled cup with the word "Best" lettered across its middle. The race for Best Swimmer was confined to just the three of us because we were the only children among the many dozens at the camp for cripples who were allowed to swim in the deep end of the pool.

We were allowed to swim there, to compete among ourselves, because we'd lucked out. We had the muscle to lift up our heads, the coordination to get a fork full of food to our mouths, the sensation to know when we had to shit or pee and enough physical control to hold it until we could. These skills marked us as separate from our peers. For our mastery of these skills we were granted the boon of racing a half-hour each day from one end of the deep pool to the other, using a variety of strokes taught to us by the Deep End Instructor.

There was just one Deep End Instructor. She was tall, tan, accomplished and wholly ours. After our half-hour sessions she'd treat us to one of her own perfect splashless dives. We loved her for her body alone, the beauty of it as it knifed through the water. So unremarkable, so unmemorable, so very normal with nothing to distinguish it but the grace with which it moved. Our hearts throbbed with her every stroke.

I don't remember my heart throbbing for any of the Shallow End Instructors. I suppose they were too busy to display their accomplishments or even to have any. They spent their time looking out for the other kids in the camp—the kids who couldn't feed themselves, couldn't hold it, couldn't turn their heads or lift a finger.

Those women always worked in pairs, floating their charges in large lazy circles at the shallow end. They talked incessantly, telling those children, who were always made anxious in the water, to relax, to expand their lungs just a little more, just enough to pull in an extra bit of air. I would watch those other little girls from the floating line that separated deep from shallow, us from them. I was fascinated when one of them would take in a breath, turn her face into the water, and with that extra push of air create a ripple across the surface.

Watching that effort made me uneasy. It frightened me to see those children struggle so. And for what? That was always the question—about them, about crippled children generally; and about the three of us, of course. Even though we would have scoffed at the idea. We were, after all, the favored.

Competition among the favored was fierce. And at the deep end of the pool, competition was scored not just by effort but by results. In our daily races my compatriots and I were already unquestioning little capitalists. We understood the basic math. Accumulate the most daily races, win the ugly plastic cup. But we were most anxious to claim the unspoken dividend of winning that ugly cup—the attention of the Deep End Instructor herself.

At the gala end-of-the-summer awards ceremony it would be she who would bend her pale-eyed gaze on the most deserving one of us, she who would pass that cup like a torch, proof that here was one little girl, crippled though she might be, who was unarguably worth the effort it might take to keep her alive.

I simply had to win that thing.

For years I thought it was the depth of my desire that had propelled me past my competition because I usually did win the races. Only recently has it occurred to me that maybe the one-legged girl still hadn't quite figured out how to get the necessary ballast to push her lopsided weight through the pool and that was, perhaps, why she'd end up swimming in circles; or that the blind girl, newly blind, might have been freaked out by the clueless texture of the water, and maybe that was why she'd bonk her head against the side of the pool.

But I was a kid. I didn't care about complexities. I just cared about winning. And truthfully, I felt entitled to win. Of all the bodies in that camp, my own body—once I'd junked the thick glasses and the Walkman-sized hearing aids—looked the closest to normal.

So long as I won and kept on winning, the tactics I employed to win remained entirely honorable. But then fate took a downturn. And when it did, my winning tactic became to drown.

There were a couple of extenuating circumstances. Usually, at the start of the race, the Deep End Instructor would stand at the opposite end of the pool in her vivid red bathing suit, which always got and held my attention. Then, after a suspenseful pause, she'd chop her arm down like an ax while screeching, "Go!" The chop was for my benefit; the screech for the blind girl. But this day we had begged for the privilege of doing the ready-set-going among ourselves.

First dibs had gone to the one-legged girl who, in addition to having just one leg, had a mild speech impediment (which, as an aside, was in no way connected to the accident that had deprived her of her leg).

But even if she had had the necessary crispness of enunciation, the fullness of volume, the perfectly modulated emphasis that would have left no doubt that "gloah" did indeed signify "go," it wouldn't have mattered. The distinction was still too subtle for me to get. I was expecting an unmistakable sweeping chop of air and all I was getting was a slurring blur of lips. I knew that somewhere within that blur all that was being said was "Ready, Set, Go," but I just couldn't bring myself to trust my own crude perception, even though I knew, crude as it was, it could still steer me right, get me out of the chute in time.

At least that's what I told myself. But in truth, my mind wasn't really being befuddled—it was being snotty. It wasn't going to accept any information given to it by a moving blur. And in that instant of hesitation when my mind chose to be a stickler in its stubborn insistence on perfection of form over a shrugging, ragged, intuitive leap, the race was lost.

Now I'd lost races before. And this wasn't going to be a particularly humiliating loss. Not with the honorable competition swimming in circles and bonking their heads. But it had been a long day. And I'd been berating myself for even being at this sorry excuse of a camp. Camp was supposed to be the place where I'd finally come into my own, shed this fleshy misinterpretation of my soul, and be transformed into the beauty I knew I was meant to be. And instead there I was, my own tubby, ill-favored, deaf, near-sighted little self in messy competition with two other cripples who were going to beat me in a pathetic water race for a two-handled plastic cup.

In that chill moment I realized life was ruthless. Just as ruthless as the one-legged or the blind girl would be if I suddenly stopped swimming, and called back the race by claiming the truth—that I didn't hear the word "go" and that's why I wasn't going to win.

I knew how those two would react to that. The same way I would have. The blind girl wouldn't even bother, maybe wouldn't know how, to hide her visible contempt. And the one-legged girl would swirl her stump around in the water and flick a look back at the shallow end of the pool—it, like her stump, a reminder that far greater, far more visible tragedies than mine existed.

And that is when I slipped into my dark water epiphany. No matter what excuse I offered, there was no excuse. The rest of the world was going to look on me the way I looked on the shallow-enders. In the context of a good hard race, they were a joke. So what if they were working just as hard—no, harder than I would ever work in my life for the dubious pleasure of blowing a few fucking bubbles in the water. No one would ever call that winning, would they? Not in this world, not in the larger context, where the push was always toward beautiful completion, flawless efficiency, perfection of form or, at the very least, some kind of solid utilitarian usefulness. All those words words words we cripples could never hope to embody. Words that we knew, even then, young as we were, would determine who lived well and who didn't; or even simply who lived.

I knew then that the lives of all the children in the pool were destined for the ash heap of history. And I? Oh, why bother with first-person singular in a place where even the deep end of the pool signifies nothing? Of course I didn't articulate it like that then. I was just a kid. But I felt it. A whirling, terrible loss of heart. So I took the only action I could against that sea of troubles. I drowned.

Drowning on cue is not as easy a thing to do as you might think. Forcing yourself to drown, willing yourself to sink. But I did it. I sank. I dropped an inch under the water and then my natural buoyancy bobbed me right back up. The Deep End Instructor had already seen me go under. I could feel her eyes the moment I decided to let go. So by the time I bobbed back up to the surface, my pretense (if it was a pretense) was already long out of hand.

We were a camp for "Crippled Kids." Everything that surrounded us was viewed as a potential danger. Many of us needed the simplest things just to keep us alive, keep us breathing. In a camp like that a cry for help was always and only the real thing.

I had no choice. I had to choke and flail and keep on drowning. It seemed infinitely preferable to drown rather than admit I was faking a crisis because I couldn't see a real victory through. And I didn't have the skill, the power, the language to explain that I had suddenly (some might say opportunely) found it impossible to believe that such a thing as a "real victory" actually existed. I had to carry out my performance of drowning to the bloody, chest-compressed end. And it was an excellent, convincing performance if I do say so myself.

I knew the mechanics for drowning from TV. How the body is snatched down, then shoots up again spluttering, three times in a row. But I knew, again from TV, that the act wasn't quite that clean, that clear.

The real act of drowning is all about the deprivation of air. I knew that from watching the kids at the shallow end. I had learned from them how to make my fight for breath seem desperate and real; how to make myself actually fear that my last suck, my last gasp was the one I had already taken the breath before. And I knew from my own overwhelming moment of existential despair how to give up, give in, be perfectly drawn down. And I knew, I'm not sure how, that on my way up I ought to gulp in great gouts of liquid, as if the pathetic victim I was making of myself had tragically mistaken the killing element of water for the saving grace of air.

I came as close to drowning as I possibly could to make my act ring true, look real, be worthy of rescue. I was so perfectly convincing that my audience was taken in. Blind girl, one-legged girl, shallow-enders all—their lives were brought to a halt by the realism of my performance of drowning.

And they were completely enthralled when, with perfect verisimilitude, the Deep End Instructor joined me in my act, dived in to play out her own role of savior. She cut through the churning water, reached down, and lifted my head up to face the flat blue sky above us; and then, with perfect strokes (exactly as she'd rehearsed every day that she'd trained) she pulled me away from the beckoning deep and hauled my ass out of the water.

On the hot concrete where she laid me, we made an elegant duo. She would push my chest and I would let the watery froth come rolling out of my mouth as if it had been lodged in my lungs and not merely held near the back of my throat. And when finally I thought the timing right, I gagged, spluttered, opened my eyes. And she, looking into my perfectly mimicked daze, unknowing/all-knowing gaze of someone who has eyeballed death in the water (as, ah yes, I had)—she pulled me to her and held me tight against the wet, panting, perfect body that I loved.

So I was saved. It was such a sincere, driven act of rescue. And given the excruciatingly sexual culmination, how could I bear the shame of revealing to the object of my desire that I'd been faking it? Even if I had been faking out of real despair. Even if what I had been performing was the invisible damage of a damaged body.

No. I had to take my punishment. Awards Night.

I'm not sure what I expected from Awards Night but early on I began to realize that there were awards for both real and, shall we say, fictive accomplishments. By the time the little girl with MS (whom the rest of us knew to be a fatuous brownnoser) was given Most Cheerful, the jig was definitely up. So when the girl in the wheelchair next to me grabbed the box speaker of my hearing aid and shouted, "You won!" I couldn't help but roll my eyes. Was this the Almost Drowned sympathy vote? Had I really perfected the art of swimming or had I just beaten the other cripples out? And who cared anyway? I no longer needed some chintzy bit of plastic to forge a bond with the Deep End Instructor. I'd been intimate with the woman for god's sake. And art, not competitiveness, had won me that embrace. A single dramatic performance had propelled me miles beyond where any dinky old swimming award could have taken me.

Late that night, the last night of camp, I stayed awake on my cot brooding over my ill-gotten knowledge. I might as well have had a cigarette dangling from my lips. Once when I was five and on my way home from school I'd fixed my white cotton sweater to look like a sling and told the bus driver that I'd broken my arm. He'd known I was lying. The memory of his sorrowful gaze that day had bothered me for years. And this was a much more serious breach. I knew that, on the strength of her passionate rescue of me, I could get up from my cot, go down the hall to the Deep End Instructor's room and knock at her door. And even if all I did was stand there beseechingly, she would have a hard time turning me away. She might even let me under the covers with her, maybe even stroke my back until I slept or just passed out from the sexual tension. But I didn't dare.

Because I had a secret: None of what had so intimately passed between us in the water that summer day had been remotely real.

The award she had so innocently presented to me was not for Best Swimmer but Best Actress. And that was a secret we could never share. Long before I discovered Shakespeare I knew what he was about. All the world's a stage. And my guilt and exhilaration in using it as such would throw me straight into the arms of theater.

Apple Pie

Thisbe Nissen

At camp, when you are nine, there is a floppy-breasted Birdie-section counselor named Mary-Allison who gives you piggyback rides to the dining hall. But when you come back the next summer you've gotten too big to carry and too awkward to be cute. Mary-Allison finds littler Birdies to carry on her shoulder across the big field. Sometimes you still get to walk alongside them and hold Mary-Allison's hand. Also: she braids your hair once before a social at the boys' camp, loans you her lifeguard whistle on camper-counselor switch day, and lets you sit in her lap while she paints a daisy on your cheek at the county fair.

On Visiting Day you can't find her *forever*, and you ask Bobbie, the nurse, who says Mary-Allison is running swim down at the waterfront so you drag your mom and dad down the piney hill and stand behind the do-not-cross line by the buddy-board and shout to Mary-Allison at the other end of the dock: "Mally! Mally! These are my parents!"

Mary-Allison turns for a second, startled. When she sees you, she calls to your parents, "It's nice to meet you!" waving with one hand and pulling down the bottom elastic on her orange bathing suit with the other before she turns back to the swimmers and rings the buddy bell.

"BUDDIES!" the lifeguard counselors shout from the docks as bathing-capped girls try to grab hands with their swim partners. You want to run out onto the dock and hold Mary-Allison's hand, but you can't because it's a buddy check and besides, nobody would understand. You watch as the other girls tread water, holding their clasped fists in the air, gasping, waiting to be counted.

"She seems very nice," your mother says diplomatically as you trudge back up the needled slope. On the waterfront you can hear Mary-Allison calling for the buddy counts.

"Cindy?"

"Twenty-two deep, fourteen shallow, four on the raft!"

"Sooze?"

"Four, twenty-two, fourteen!"

You have to pinch your eyes shut not to cry. When you stumble into his leg, your dad says, "Hey kiddo, *faites attention!*" and gives your shoulders a love-squeeze right where your sunburn is.

You and Vivian are leaving. You've been scooping ice cream at Charlie's ever since you were tall enough to reach into the freezer and pull yourself back out; Vivian makes a shitload caddying at the country club. Your brother Lance has a '79 Ford Econoline van, banana yellow, and if you start saving now, when you and Viv are both seventeen and have your licenses, you'll be able to buy it off him. You live on a tiny island where, once the summer renters go home to New York City, everyone knows everything about everyone else and nothing ever changes year after year after year. Tourists call it "close-knit" and "traditional." You call it suffocating. You plan your escape for five years from now, just after the Fourth of July. Independence Day seems appropriate.

The way you imagine it, your parents will drop you off at the high school where buses will be waiting to cart you upstate to basketball camp. The Banana Van will be parked out behind the gym. You and Vivian won't ever get on the bus. Camp won't miss you; you will have withdrawn your registrations months before. You'll have a friend on the bus bound for All-Star Camp Mohawk, armed with a collection of postcards and letters addressed to your parents and to Vivian's. She'll mail one every so often and it will arrive at your island homes bearing a Lake Placid postmark, news of the game against Camp Starlight, and horror stories of poison ivy. This friend will be thrilled to be in on your diabolical plan, giddy with the importance of being the only one who knows what you're really doing: sneaking off to some boy's house or running away to New York City to become stars. Your friend will think it's the coolest thing anyone at Island High has ever tried to get away with. You won't disagree.

On the Fourth, everyone will be in town, sitting on the curbs eating saltwater taffy and tossing their sticky pastel wrappers into the street like confetti as they watch the parade: three sparkling firetrucks, all buffed up for the display; Mrs. Robeson's Girl Scout troops, knee socks and pageant sashes drooping in the heat; grandfathers strutting slowly in sherbet-colored walking shorts, a perfect fez perched firmly atop each bald head.

That night you'll all go down to the beach for corn-on-the-cob and hot dogs and watermelon, and as the Catherine wheels and Roman candles shower sparks into the blackened sound, you and Vivian will watch from under the docks, tucked in the darkness, cornsilk stuck between your teeth, lips sticky from apple pie, until the last flare dies—*whizbang!*—on the horizon and parents try to out-shout each other, calling their children's names into the salty night.

You'll ride home in the back of Viv's mother's Subaru wagon, tasting of baked apples and sea air and Vivian. If you make it, that will be the last time you ever watch the fireworks from this beach, on this island, in this stifling, seagull-ridden sound.

Once in eighth grade you and Vivian are standing in line at the vending machine in the cafeteria behind Stacy Weintraub, a junior. Stacy gets the last apple pie. You stare through the glass down the long, empty aisle where silver coils disappear into the depths of the machine, turn to Viv, and say, "Bummer, no more apple."

Stacy is by the trash can and she hears you. "Hey," she says, pulling one pie-pocket from the wrapper, "do you want the other?"

Stacy Weintraub has never talked to you before. "Oh, no," you stammer. "I didn't mean you had to . . ."

She cuts you off. "Seriously, take it." She waggles the pie

toward you. You try not to watch how her breast jiggles under the thin, white cotton of her T-shirt.

"Really?" you say.

"Like I need another pie!" Stacy presses the package into your hands.

"Thanks," you say. "Like *I* really need an apple pie . . ." you add, whacking yourself in the stomach.

"Oh, hush," Stacy says. "You've got nothing in the world to worry about." She takes a bite and clomps off into the cafeteria crowd, her Doc Martens—steel-toed, twelve eyelets, in oxblood—squeeching against the lunchroom floor.

Viv pulls her sack of Skittles from the mouth of the vending machine, then turns back, eyebrows raised to you. You bite into your pie.

When you are a freshman and they are seniors, Stacy Weintraub goes to the prom with Naomi Bentner. The morning after the dance, all you underclassmen go down to Charlie's Grill and wait for the seniors to show up for their postprom breakfast. They come in: the girls stockingless, dangling broken-heeled dyed-to-match pumps from manicured fingers, stiff hair pulled back in makeshift buns held in place with Class of '86 elastic garterbelts. The cuffs of the guys' tux pants dribble sand from the beach where they've been since midnight when the official prom ended. They've gotten drunk on Smirnoff, felt up their dates, and finally watched the sunrise.

Naomi and Stacy haven't rented a limo like the others.

Naomi's older sister Janna, who used to date your brother Lance, is home from college and chauffeurs the girls in Lance's gigantic Banana Van: a queen-size mattress in back and a rainbow of teddy bears dancing across the rear windshield. You watch through the window of Charlie's as Janna wrenches the door handle and slides open the yellow carriage. Stacy emerges first, her silver pumps gleaming in the sun like glass slippers. She has on a shimmery stretch-velvet tank dress you've seen in the Victoria's Secret catalog. Naomi is wearing a suit. It's vintage, from one of those cool places in the City, not another rented penguin suit making its annual trip to the Island High prom. Naomi even has a cummerbund. Her bowtie—you can see as they pass, arm in arm, and disappear into the ladies' room—is tied around Stacy's ponytail.

In the late fall of eleventh grade, Vivian's dad gets a job offer in California, three thousand miles away. There is nothing anyone can do. They leave on a gray day between Christmas and New Year's, and you say good-bye to Vivian out by the woodpile her dad chopped and stacked all summer and fall and now will never burn. Vivian has on her red parka. Her nose is red and her cheeks and ears, too.

"We can write," you say.

"Swear you will," she says.

"Swear."

"Me too."

You hug her there by the woodpile, wishing you could stay like that forever, never lift your face from the damp nylon collar of Vivian's coat. All you want—more than anything in the world—is to stay there long enough to get up the courage to do what you've wanted to do for as long as you can remember.

When their station wagon pulls out of sight, you walk home in the cold, relieved by how much it hurts. On the table in the hall there's a note from your mom: she and Dad have gone to rent a movie and are bringing back pizza, so if you're hungry . . . In your room, on your bed, your fingers are so numb you can't hold the pen to write. You watch your parents' minivan pull into the drive-way, get up, and lock your bedroom door. You draft four different versions of the same letter. You flush each one down the toilet, watch the notebook confetti disappear in a porcelain whirlpool, everything spiraling down.

Weeks pass. You feel as if there is a cloudy scrim between you and the rest of the world. You are clumsy. You forget things. Your tongue is too big for your mouth.

When a letter finally comes, you can't feel it between your fin-gertips, as if they are frostbitten again. You slice a papercut in your thumb as you tear into the envelope, but still you don't feel any-thing. The words on the page are big and happy and make your mouth go to glue. *California is awesome*, she writes. *Even school is good—there are more kids in my homeroom than in all of I. High. I swear. I met a guy! Craig. I'm scared to say too much and jinx it. I'll tell you details later. I like him, I think. Really like him. I can't handle it that I get a boyfriend and you're not here! I don't know how I'll sur-vive not talking to you every ten minutes. This is so unfair! Are you go-ing to come visit? Come spring break, but not if it's the week of Easter because Craig'll be away and you have to meet him.* There is more, about her dad and his job, and her teachers, and classes, and more about Craig because in the end she just can't resist telling you all the details. No one will ever be her best friend like you are, she writes. You will be best friends forever.

You try to write back. Really. There just isn't anything to say.

By spring you get a boyfriend too. Eli. I. High Tribune Photography editor/Yearbook staff/Environmental Club. You meet him on the Earth Day celebration planning committee, which you only joined in the first place because Chloe Storfer is committee chair. Chloe Storfer looks like a cross between Michelle Pfeiffer and Melissa Etheridge and has a voice so throaty it sounds like she's seducing the cafeteria workers when she orders the lunch special with fries.

Chloe Storfer looks nothing like Vivian.

Chloe Storfer dates Peter Sanchez, who is in your algebra class. Sometimes you and he lend each other the homework. Usually you sit together, and on especially boring days you play Dots or Tic-Tac-Toe, passing the papers back and forth beneath your desks. One day while Mrs. Fiorello is putting up the "Do Now" problems on the board Peter passes you a note: *I know somebody that likes you.*

Who? you write back.

Eli Pressman.

You're such a liar, you scrawl.

Ask Chloe, he challenges.

You would never pass up an excuse to talk to Chloe.

Chloe grins at you, her eyes twinkling like a merry matchmaker. She arranges it so you and he work the sound board together, piping R.E.M. and Carly Simon over the PA system, so you wind up spending Earth Day smushed into the sound booth with Eli Pressman. He's pretty nice and sort of cute and kind of still boylike and not all big-sweaty-manly, which makes him a lot easier to deal with. You bond over a secret devotion to Billy Joel and confess to weeping during "While the Night Is Still Young" when he sang it at the Meadowlands concert last year.

When Earth Day is over and you and Eli are outside the booth coiling wires and sorting records, Chloe skips over, flushed with the success of the celebration.

"Hey you two . . . ice cream or whatever at Charlie's . . . club fund's paying . . ."

You and Eli split a sundae: pistachio with strawberry sauce. Chloe makes gagging noises. "You guys belong together," she groans.

By Monday, you are "going out" with Eli Pressman.

Your parents think Eli is the greatest thing since sliced bread. Eli appears to think you are the greatest thing since "Uptown Girl." You go away to basketball camp the summer before twelfth grade and meet Layla, who strikes you as being the greatest thing *ever* and about whom you cannot conceive of evoking descriptions of food products or pop medleys.

"Nice shot," a voice says behind you.

You turn. "Thanks," you say.

"I'm Layla," she tells you.

"Isn't that a song?" you ask.

"You've got me on my knees . . ."

"Huh?"

"My folks like Clapton," she tells you.

"Pretty hip folks." Your parents like Bach.

"They're pretty cool," she admits.

You're at a loss for words. Layla sets up a shot. She's tall—5' 9",
5' 10"—with long straight blond hair and biceps that flicker like
heartbeats under her skin when she shoots. It goes through. "Are
they coming for Visiting Day?" you ask, feeling like a moron.

"Nah, too long a drive." She sinks another.

"You can come out with me and my folks," you spurt out, far
too quickly.

She doesn't look at you funny, just cocks her head to the side.
"Thanks." She smiles, but it's a smile with a question imbedded in
it somewhere. "That's really nice of you to say."

You are disarmed. "Where are you from?" you manage to ask.

"New York," she tells you.

"New York where?"

"City," she says like she forgot there were other parts of New
York State. "How 'bout you?"

"Long Island," you say, careful to enunciate and to pause between the g and the I. "Way out, off the eastern shore. A really little island."

"Wow," she says, trying to grasp that.

"Not really," you say. "There's not really anything 'wow' about
it in the slightest."

You both laugh.

The two of you are inseparable for the rest of the summer. Layla is
loud and sarcastic and fond of lapsing into a phony Brooklyn ac-

cent to tell bad jokes. You are in awe of most things about her: her basketball game (All-State champ), her wardrobe (she's from New York City after all), her breasts (low-slung and mature and utterly fascinating to 34A perhaps-you'd-like-one-with-a-bit-of-padding you), and the way she takes up space in a room. You get weird and nervous around her and live in terror of falling into a Long Island drawl. This does not stop you from wanting to spend every minute of the day with her. Somehow, miraculously, she seems to want to spend every minute of the day with you too. You make each other lanyard bracelets, on Candy Store days you get Skittles and she gets M&Ms and you share, and you save seats on your blankets for each other at Campfire Sings. You think you have never been so happy in your entire life.

Spring break, senior year, your parents invite Eli to join the family on a road trip down to Western Kentucky for your grandma Flo's seventy-fifth birthday bash. They even let him drive their minivan, which they never let *you* drive. You sit in the passenger seat; Mom and Dad play Twenty Questions in back. "How big *is* a bread box?" Eli asks coyly, catching your mother's eye in the rearview mirror. She laughs far too loudly. On the highway, when you pass signs for Big Bone Lick State Park, you tell Eli he has to pull off so you can buy a hat, or something, for Layla.

"That's ridiculous," your mother says. Eli looks torn between loyalties. Finally, in the exit lane, he says, "It might be good to get out and stretch, don't you think, Mrs. R.? Use the facilities, and get a bite to eat." He is stiff, waiting for her response. You are fuming at what an ass-kissing pansy he can be. A smile breaks across your mother's face. "Good thinking," she says. You know that in your mother's world, a man who caters to her daughter—no matter how absurd her daughter may be—is a good prospective son-in-law. You want to gag.

Chloe is going to the prom with Peter. You're going with Eli. One day in calc, you slip Peter a note you wrote out last night at home but pretend to scrawl right there in class so it doesn't look premeditated.

You guys want to share a limo with me and Eli? it says.

Sure, his note answers, *that'd be good.*

Excellent, you write.

Did Chloe tell you? he asks.

You feel a little scared. You're not sure why. *Tell me what?*

We set a date, his note says. *October 16th.*

You write so hard you break your pencil point midsentence and have to switch to pen. *You're getting MARRIED?!?!*

Peter turns to you, nodding like a thirsty puppy.

After graduation you convince Lance to lend you the Banana Van, which you've never succeeded in buying from him. You and Eli and Layla are going to drive across the country to see the Pacific Ocean, which you think eighteen years is too long to have gone without seeing. You haven't talked to Vivian in longer than you can remember and don't plan on calling when you get there. You just want to see California. Since the day she left you standing at the woodpile, the state itself has taken on epic proportions in your mind.

The morning you set out is so sunny it hurts. You pick up Layla in Manhattan, and she takes the driver's seat to maneuver out of the city. The Banana Mobile has a three-foot-long gear shift shooting out of the floor, more phallic than the pigs-in-a-blanket they served at your Sweet Sixteen and more unwieldy than Eli's penis, which you find to be ridiculously unwieldy and try to tangle with as infrequently as possible. Layla drives with the window rolled down, her hair whipping around her face and neck. From behind her seat you rein it all into a ponytail for her and tuck it through the back of the *Big Bone Lick* baseball cap you got her, which, she's told you, she adores and wears everywhere.

At a rest stop in Pennsylvania while Layla is in the bathroom, Eli pulls your elbow to him and whispers: "She's kind of a ditz, huh?"

You give him a look that you hope says *die* and pretend to knee him in the balls. You walk over to the vending machines and buy M&Ms. Eli's allergic to chocolate.

As Layla drives Eli keeps peering over her shoulder at the speedometer so that it looks like he's blowing in her ear, which makes you wonder if what he meant when he called her a ditz is that he thinks she's sexy.

"You're worse than my grandmother," you say to Eli, tugging at his shirt. Your grandmother is a back-seat driver prone to blatantly obvious instructions: *there's a traffic light coming up here on the corner and if it's red you'll need to stop*. Eli backs off and sulks. He picks up Layla's camera and starts taking pictures out the window. You get mad that he's wasting Layla's film without even asking her and say, "This green blur is Indiana, oh yes, and this green blur, this is Iowa. See that smudge of white? That's a cow." Eli starts to remind you just who *is* and who *is not* photo editor of the yearbook, but you do a Grandma Flo impersonation, pointing at your ears and saying, "Honey, I don't hear." Eli, who has adopted all of your mother's views of your family and thinks your grandmother is a saint, looks at you disparagingly. You turn away and stare out the window. You have vowed to stop fighting with Eli; it isn't worth it. It's only a matter of time anyway before you have to tell him. And everyone else.

The first night on the road you stay with friends of Layla's parents, professors at a little college in Ohio. They have a big, expensive house, and you each get your own room.

The second night on the road you stay in Iowa City at the Christian Community Youth Hostel even though all three of you are Jewish. To your delight there are separate dorm rooms for men and women, and you get to share with Layla while Eli has to sleep with a squawking soccer team from Des Moines. The girls' room is turquoise and green, with Sunday school drawings taped to the walls: Crayola renditions of biblical scenes titled in preschool penmanship. JOHN's *N* is backward, Ezekiel's *E* has seven prongs instead of three. The floor is covered with a gritty shag rug, swirled in shades of aquamarine and infested with fleas. You and Layla spend the night on a foam-rubber mattress, also riddled with fleas. You don't sleep much for the itching. Once, when you wake up, Layla isn't next to you. You raise your head and twist around to find her sitting by the window: the silhouette of a girl. Without turning, she speaks like she knows you're listening. We could stay, she says to the sky. Get to California and never go back. Just us. We could.

You realize you are nodding. You nod yourself to sleep.

The next day Eli drives. You and Layla sprawl in the back eating Funyun Rings and Skweez-Cheez and singing every song from every Broadway musical you've ever known. Eli threatens to pull over if you don't stop. Layla gets out her Walkman and the Red Hot Chili Peppers, clips the headphones over Eli's ears, and cranks the volume. The two of you pick up "I'm Gonna Wash That Man Right outta My Hair" right where you left off.

In Cheyenne you stay with Layla's aunt and uncle and their new baby, Fred, who sticks his fingers in Eli's ears and yells, "MAMA!" Aunt Gayle and Uncle Jim put you to sleep in their basement-turned-rec-room in sleeping bags on the floor. You sleep in between Layla and Eli and have a dream in which you are walking through a snowstorm with Layla on one side and Eli on the other. You go into a jewelry store where Eli buys a cheap mood ring and proposes to you on bended knee. Layla turns into a butterfly and flies away. You pierce your nose with the ring and walk back out into the snow alone. You wake up with a sleep-dent in your nose from lying facedown on a zipper.

You pull an all-nighter through Nevada, impatient to get to the ocean and willing to forgo the sights of Elko and Winnemucca in the name of speed. You hit San Francisco at sunrise and buy groceries from a supermarket called Lucky, because you never know: it could be. Highway 1 takes you down the coast, a stream of annoyed Porsches at your tail. The Banana Van was not designed for skinny, curvy, cliff-side roads. Eli pulls off at a scenic overlook and lets the traffic pass.

The Pacific Ocean is breathtaking. The water is the bluest

thing you've ever seen and you cannot take your eyes from it, waves cresting stark white and crashing into the rocks with a force you are sure will imminently erode the cliff on which you are standing. Eli says he is exhausted and climbs into the back, heaves himself onto the mattress, and falls asleep nearly immediately, a little puddle of drool forming on the sweatshirt he's using as a pillow. You and Layla are not so much sleepy as ravenous. Layla reaches into your Lucky grocery bag and pulls out the day-old apple crumb pie you bought for a dollar ninety-nine. You've got a quart of milk in the Playmate chest your mother made you bring along "for perishables." You bought the milk at a gas-mart near Reno in the middle of the night to lighten Eli's coffee. He said he'd puke if he consumed any more nondairy creamer. You didn't really blame him.

You and Layla go up front, trying not to disturb Eli but knowing that he could sleep through an earthquake. The way you've been to him this trip, he's probably glad to leave you two alone. You think he probably won't put up with you for much longer.

Layla is curled on the passenger seat, balancing the pie between the gear shift and the open ashtray. You take the driver's seat, passing the milk between you in a Dunkin Donuts mug you find in the glove compartment. Layla eats the pie crust, making her way around the circumference, then nudging aside the apples to excavate the bottom. You pick at the crumb topping, dribbling it across the seat and through your hair on the way to your mouth. (Eli always says: Why can't you just take a whole piece of pie and eat it, like normal people? It doesn't taste as good, you tell him. You like to pick.) You hold up a sticky hand, laughing silently.

Layla grins and reaches out for it. She puts your sugary fingers into her mouth and, one by one, licks them clean. There are piecrust crumbs in Layla's hair and you straddle the gear shift and climb over into her lap to pick them out. Then you kiss her. You've always expected Layla's teeth would be somehow soft, like cooked apples. Instead, they are slick and hard, like porcelain. Eating apple pie and kissing Layla is like licking the bottom of a cereal bowl. It's like Apple Jacks.

When you join Eli on the mattress, you spoon around Layla. She snuggles backward into your arms, and you fall asleep like that, Eli's snores notwithstanding. Pie innards lie in a gelatinous heap in the box, still open on the front seat. Breakfast for Eli, you figure. When he wakes up.

You realize you haven't saved him any milk.

Summer Memories of Egghead Camps

James Atlas

July 17, 1964

Dear parents:

Today we read "The Trial" and it was so terrific—devastating: tomorrow is our two-hour panel discussion on modern poets. Also, they included two of mine. I've been writing madly. And also, the state of girls up here is amazing—beautiful girls wandering about the grounds with long hair and guitars. I've been writing ballads, which this girl puts to music and sings. They've come out with some measure of success. Sunday we are going to Stratford, Connecticut, for the Shakespeare festival, and tonight is Duke Ellington and the Boston Pops at Tanglewood, tomorrow Three Sisters by Chekhov at Williamstown, Culture! I can't take it anymore; send comic books—anything.

—James

The camp near Stockbridge, Massachusetts, where I found myself in the 15th summer of this life, was a far cry from Camp Willahwagen, where I had spent the previous three summers. It was fine for a boy of 12 or 13 to while away two months in a barracks-like, sports-obsessed institution near Drummond, Wisconsin, but I had lately discovered music, literature, poetry—what were known in my family as "the finer things in life"—and cared more for art than archery.

Besides, I had had enough of the authoritarian tactics of Camp Willahwagen, where I was once ordered to finish my cottage cheese before leaving the table, and sat from lunch until dinner in the canteen—as it was called, in keeping with the camp's military tenor—in defiance of what I told the director was "dietary fascism." The following spring, I studied the classified pages of *Saturday Review*, in the hope of finding a camp more congenial to my delicate, overwrought sensibility (and one that stressed arts more than crafts; I had braided enough lanyards on rainy days the summer before to distribute to our entire family, cousins included). After a flurry of correspondence and the completion of an application—"I never heard of a camp that required a transcript," my father complained—I settled on a camp in the Berkshires.

Campers—if we could still be classified as such—were advised to bring, instead of flashlights and 6-12, a notebook and several Bic pens. Instead of a list of rules and regulations, we were sent a reading list to work through before we arrived: *Dubliners*, *Of Mice and Men*, *Rhinoceros*, *Winesburg, Ohio* and *Heart of Darkness*. Rather than activities, we were to choose "electives"—from "Fiction in the Modern World" to "The Appreciation of Poetry," from

"Drama, Old and New" to "The Novel in America." And, of course, there were seminars in creative writing—why else the Bic pens? How different from Camp Willahwagen, where I had once labored for a whole summer over a tie rack in the shape of a dog.

I arrived on campus, as it were, the last week in June, and was reassured to find solid cinder-block dorms rather than the flimsy wooden cabins I had endured the previous three summers—and there wasn't a canoe on the premises. Wandering about the grounds were campers who in no way resembled the lithe, muscular bullies Camp Willahwagen attracted. Pale and bespectacled, they sat under the trees with books open on their laps. No one tossed a baseball around—no one had even brought a mitt—and the tennis courts were deserted.

After registering, I was assigned a room in the boys' dorm—the camp was coed—and walked in to find my roommate studying at his desk. As I entered, he stood up, a tall, awkward, long-limbed boy in a short-sleeved white shirt with a plastic penholder clipped to the pocket. "Hi, I'm Larry Grossbart," he announced. "Bronx High School of Science."

"Jim Atlas," I murmured—then, supposing it only polite to give my affiliation: "Evanston Township High School."

"I've just been looking over this new collection of wit twisters," Larry said, holding up a brochure. "There're some really good problems here—for instance, if a boat going 20 knots in a 10-knot wind is passed by a boat going 32 knots, how many knots ahead will the faster boat be in an hour's time?"

"Uh, I don't know really," I said. "I'm not too good at math."

"No? I got 800 on my math S.A.T."

I began to wonder if I hadn't been better off last summer putting up with Ollie Gunderson, a cruel, gigantic boy who wore a T-shirt with the legend "WANNA MAKE SOMETHING OF IT?" emblazoned across the front and who used to shine his flashlight in my eyes all night.

"By the way," Larry said. "Do you know what Mensa is?" I shook my head. "It's a club for people with I.Q.'s in the 98th percentile or above. Would you like to join? I could arrange for you to take the test."

"I'm not sure my I.Q. is that high."

"Well, there's only one way to find out," he said, returning to his wit twisters. "Nothing ventured, nothing gained."

The following day, I registered for classes: "Creative Writing: Poetry" and "The Art of the Short Story." My poetry instructor was a sad-faced man with thinning hair who wore an ascot and was said to be going through a divorce. He liked to read aloud from Yeats in a delicate, musical voice. Whenever he was particularly moved by a poem, he would look from the volume in his hand— *The Oxford Book of English Verse*—and say, "Now, if anyone here could write like that, I'd be happy." Still, he was polite about our work, though seldom effusive—a measured response, given the self-indulgent confessions we were turning out. Often, as I sat by the window listening to the incessant chirp and whir of crickets in the summer fields while some girl with a strained look on her face read aloud a poem laden with adolescent misery, I longed to be back in Wisconsin playing Capture the Flag.

My other class, the short-story seminar, was conducted by a

tense, enthusiastic high-school teacher from Long Island. Running a hand through his thick, curly hair, he would expatiate on matters we were scarcely old enough to grasp: the thwarted passion of von Aschenbach in Thomas Mann's "Death in Venice," the fanatical jealousy of Gabriel Conroy in James Joyce's "The Dead." "God, that is a beautiful story," he would exclaim, while we sat, numb with confusion, chewing our Bic pens. "Wait—it'll happen to you some day."

Afternoons were reserved, as they had been at Camp Willahwagen, for "free time." None of my campmates had even the slightest interest in athletics; most of them were from New York and, far from being fascinated by the lovely mountains that surrounded the school, the woods and meadows behind our dorm, they tended to gather in the lounge and talk. Early on, the directors made some halfhearted efforts to organize baseball games, but nearly every boy was of the type known in my gym classes back home as a "spaz." Bridge was their game.

Across a wide lawn were the guitar-toting girls, who sat beneath a huge elm combing one another's hair and writing letters to their boyfriends in New York. They were relentlessly artistic; they danced, wrote songs, knew French, painted watercolors. They were spoiled and demanding. "Can you believe this place doesn't have a darkroom?" wailed a girl who had arrived with several thousand dollars' worth of camera equipment.

In the evenings, after dinner in the big house, we mingled uneasily on the porch, flirting and establishing intense, short-lived romances. Late at night, when the talk turned to Steinbeck and Theodore Roethke and the suntanned girls in their summer dresses seemed radiant, I remembered with contempt nights spent sitting around the campfire at Willahwagen, scorching my tongue on a charred cinder of marshmallow congealed on the end of a stick as we sang, "It's a treat to beat your feet on Willahwagen mud." It was only when I returned to my room to find Larry at his desk, unknotting some wit twister, that I found myself longing for the inane rituals of my old camp.

Having seen the greater world of intellectual summer camp, I turned once again the following spring to the pages of *Saturday Review*, where I noticed an advertisement for Blithedale Farm Workshop—"an intense program of recreation and study for the highly motivated." No one was more motivated than I—to get away from home, if not to have a profound educational experience. So it was that I found myself, one mild evening in late June the next summer, debarking from a turboprop in Bangor, Maine. As I wandered down the corridor to collect my baggage, a girl in granny glasses and suspended blue jeans came up to me and said, "You're not on your way to Blithedale Farm, are you?"

"I am," I said. "How did you know?"

"I could just tell. You had that earnest look."

It was true, I suppose, that my madras jacket, my Harvard-style bookbag and the paperback copy of *A Portrait of the Artist as a Young Man* clutched in my hand made it unlikely that I would be headed for Outward Bound. Together we found the car from Blithedale Farm, a beat-up Ford station wagon, and, half an hour later, pulled up before a weathered old farmhouse on a knoll. On the grounds nearby were an equally weathered barn and a trim clapboard building that turned out to be the girls' dorm; the boys' was in a far corner of the cornfield, a desolate clearing at the edge of a thick forest.

I dragged my Olivetti and duffel bag crammed with Signet paperbacks through the cornfield, pulled back the tent flap and discovered within, stretched on a bunk and reading a paperback copy of *No Exit,* a long-haired boy in a corduroy suit. His name was Peter, he informed me; he "prepped" at Hotchkiss, lived with his widowed mother on East 62nd Street and wrote poetry. I showed him a few of my own poems, only to be told they were "derivative"—an objection, I thought wistfully, Ollie Gunderson had never made.

There were fourteen of us at Blithedale Farm Workshop— seven boys and seven girls—and the curriculum made the camp in Stockbridge seem like a remedial-reading school. Our counselor, a courtly Southerner who was working toward a Ph.D. in history at Harvard, had laid in a store of thin blue paperbacks that contained the classics of English philosophical thought: Bentham on utilitarianism, Godwin's "Enquiry Concerning Political Justice," John Stuart Mill's "On Liberty." These were the texts we discussed every morning in the old barn—followed by "creative writing" with the hardy-looking, pipe-smoking director of the farm; modern poetry with his wife; and music, taught by a prim young woman from Mississippi who wore diaphanous white dresses and led us in austere church hymns.

After lunch on the porch, we rehearsed for the annual summer performance of a Greek play; this year's offering to the townspeople of Rumford was to be the "Electra" of Euripides. I had the part of a long-winded messenger who bears bad news, and I studied my lines far into the night, crouching with a flashlight in my sleeping bag. But to no avail: I couldn't learn them, and by the second week I had wearied of the rigors of Blithedale Farm. "Mom," I complained tearfully over the phone, "all anyone ever does here is read. The only athletic event we've had so far was a sack race."

A week later, my parents arrived and took me away, while the camp director and faculty stood in the driveway, glowering like the Furies in Euripides' play. The following summer, I stayed home and hung out in the back booths of Rexall's Drugstore.

How to Make It to the Promised Land

Ellen Umansky

Here is the game they want us to play. Bobby Z., the camp director, explains it to us the night before. First, he reads us the names: Treblinka, Birkenau, Terezin, Auschwitz. "This is what happened to so many of the Jews of Europe," he says, as if we didn't know. "But what about the ones who got away?" He asks this, and then he splits us up. We are no longer the three dozen fifteen-year-olds attending Camp Shalom in the summer of 1991. Tomorrow will be November 1, 1940, and we will be in Lodz, which was invaded by the Nazis last September. Two-thirds of us are Polish Jews, living in the ghetto. The remaining third are "officials"—Polish, German, or SS guards. The challenge, for the Jews, is to escape deportation.

We are handed yellow stars and strands of plastic beads that will double as currency. We are given purple, ink-smudged maps of camp on which everything has been renamed. All the Hebrew names are gone: my bunk, formerly called Machon, is the Polish Passport Agency. Bunk Alonim is the bank. The kitchen is the town's desecrated synagogue and is entirely off-limits. The old canyon fire road is the Polish border. We are also given ID cards. I am not Lizzie Lenthem, fifteen, of Topanga, California, but Anya Ossevsheva, twenty-one, of Lodz. I have four kids. I have a long aquiline nose and a hard unsmiling mouth. I look nothing like me.

We are told: "You will have to make it across the Polish border by sundown." We are advised to try the official routes first. A very few of us are lucky, our names already on visa lists. But most of us are not; we will try to trade our pathetic beads, acquire visas, meet up with relatives and friends who are better off, masquerade as goys, charm guards into letting us stow away on a train to Zurich or a boat to Buenos Aires. How will we do this? Who among us has money? Who doesn't? Bobby Z. won't tell us. "Go to the bank. Try the passport office," he says. "You will see."

We are told: "The wood between the girls' and boys' camps is Central Europe; the goal is to move beyond it, past the fire road, to the old tennis courts, to America. The guards will try to prevent this—the soccer field will be used for roundups—but if you have the proper papers, there is nothing they can do." Bobby Z. says: "Do not enter the synagogue; do not try to trade real goods or real money; and do not, I repeat, do not try any funny business, or you'll never leave this camp, let alone Poland." Any of these rules can change at any time, we are warned. We are told all this, and the next morning we are sent on our way.

Except I don't go on my way. What do I know? I am the newcomer. When I was a kid, I once asked an old woman on a Santa Monica beach if the numbers tattooed on her arm were her phone number. I spent last Yom Kippur with my Filipino boyfriend, making out in the parking lot of the Wendy's on Pico, eating double bacon cheeseburgers. The only reason I'm here is that my mother (Israeli, atheist) wants to piss off my father (Bostonian, Presbyterian), who is six months behind on child support. She sent me here so she could "rejuvenate," she said. Where's the rejuvenation in steaming off wallpaper and installing new bathroom tiles? That's all she seems to do these days. I haven't answered a single one of her letters since I've been here. But one thing I do know is this: Malibu in 1991 just isn't Lodz during the war. And I'm not going to pretend otherwise.

We are forced up and out of our bunks before the summer sun has warmed the air or dried the dew on the clumps of yellowing grass, and the basketball court we assemble in is buzzing in the bluish morning light.

A small group settles down on the blacktop, just inches away from Bobby Z., all anxious and excited. They're kids like Leslie Epstein and David Margolis, who are always offering to lead one of the million prayers that I still don't know, sending those stupid Shabbat-o-grams back and forth to one another, or saying, "You haven't been bat-mitzvahed?" as if I'm some kind of alien. They cup their IDs in their hands. They have already pinned on their stars.

Then there are the boys in loose flannels throwing mock layups into the sagging basketball net, and a knot of languid lip-glossed girls in little white shorts and tanks, who don't seem to notice the cold, stretching out their legs, exchanging looks. A girl with a great smear of purple eyeshadow is braiding Jill Simon's long lush hair; Jill is drawing a bunch of daisies on her knee. In front of them, in a bright pile of shifting colors, are their IDs and stars. There's no way they're going to put them on until they have to.

This is the difference between cool and not cool here: who wears the stars and who doesn't. And this is just one of many reasons I can't stand this Jew-camp hell, which everyone else has been coming to since they were fetuses. I am sitting behind the basketball net, away from everyone else, just as I've been doing all summer. In order not to look for Rafi, whom I look for far too often, I am staring at the distant hay-colored hills. Rafi is a *madreich*, a counselor for the little kids, a guitar-playing junior from Santa Cruz, with sleepy silvery eyes and a mass of jet-black curls, who hitched around the Golan Heights last summer. You'd think everyone else would be after him too, that all those lip-glossed girls would try to sidle up to him during meals, and the fact that they don't just proves what I've known since I first set foot in this camp: They know nothing.

"You'll have an hour here in the 'town square,'" Bobby Z. tells us, slicing his fingers through the air to form quotation marks. "You can trade items with one another, you can look for family members—it will be easier to get across as a unit than alone." His wide bearded face breaks into a grin; nothing in his look lets on that his camp is on its way down, that parents now prefer Ramah or Wilshire Boulevard camps to Shalom. "You must wear your star and ID at all times. Failure to do so will jeopardize your chances of obtaining a visa."

"Fascist," I hear a low voice say. It is Kron, with her crazy red hair and dozens of black rubber bracelets wallpapering her pale wrists, the closest thing I have to a friend in this place.

"You're lucky to be here in America. All of us are. For just one day we'd like you to pretend otherwise," Bobby Z. concludes.

Names are being called out: "Rosie Glass, Wolfe Gootman, Lev Levy." People are milling about, searching for family, grabbing their friends. I am doing none of this. I am not interested in finding Anya's husband. In my family (my real family, my only family, that is), marriage is a burden, not a boon, and one that the women of every generation have worked hard to shake off.

A boy with a moon face comes by. "Have you seen Helen Markowitz?" he asks. I study him for a moment. He should be at the other end of the basketball court, where people really care about this stupid game, where counselors are pointing out wives and distributing extra safety pins and tips on how to make it to the promised land.

"Helen is dead," I say.

His face shifts colors, from pink to purplish red—I see it happen. "Dead?"

For a second, I feel bad—I don't even know him—but I continue. "Of course, she's dead. You're dead, she's dead, Anya Ossevsheva is dead, too," I say, thrusting my ID in his face. "It's only a game."

He looks at me and scowls. "Thanks a lot."

I smile. "You're welcome."

"Bitch."

"Asshole."

He leaves. I look at the ID in my hand. I stare until the photograph of Anya no longer looks like a face. It becomes something else: a fingerprint, maybe, or a scattering of sand, or an oil stain. It looks like everything and nothing at the same time. I fold it up and stick it in my back pocket.

"The bank and Passport Control are opening up," Bobby Z. says, getting excited. "Get moving."

The weak sun is now casting a pale glare. The basketball court clears out. Clutching their plastic beads, kids file past the red-painted iron sculpture that looks like dueling tampons. I see them line up in front of Bunk Machon, then circle back to Alonim.

Bobby Z. and the couple of counselors who didn't take the younger kids to the water slides in San Marino are walking around, sweeping the place. "Time to get going," Orna Lewis says. "No dilly-dallying in Poland."

"If this is Poland, how come we're not speaking Polish?"

She just scowls at me. "Let's go," she says. "There's KP duty in Poland, too."

I head down the slope toward the dining hall, acting as if I know where I'm going. Kron appears by my side. Her red hair is wild, each curl going off in its own direction, disobeying the laws of gravity. She looks at me and says, serious, "How are we supposed to remember what we never knew in the first place?"

It's a good question. Kron occupies the only single bed in our bunk; no other girl wanted to be near the black netting she draped over her bed, the weird atonal music she plays. She and I started hanging out a couple of weeks ago, eating at those empty tables in the back of the dining hall; still, I don't know much about her. The counselors call her Karen, but she insists that her name is Kron, that she was born on the planet of Lamu. She moves her bracelets up and down her wrist, following my eyes.

I don't know what makes me say it: her bracelets, her sad serious face, or mine? "Let's get out of here," I say.

I lead the way through a raggedy stand of pines and up a back path that I like to take to the dining hall. If you climb far enough up this hill, you can sometimes spot a glint of metal—cars streaming up and down the Pacific Coast Highway, heading north to Santa Barbara or south to L.A.

Somehow we manage to reach the kitchen without running into any guards. You'd think there'd be someone here to acknowledge the building's transformation into a desecrated synagogue, but in a way I'm not surprised. My mother had told me stories about her uncle Avi, a fat, black-hatted father of eight with disarmingly pale blue eyes and a sour-pickle smell; he refused to join the army, railing against the godless Israeli state and his heathen relatives, while he ripped off his business partner and cheated on his wife. The more pious they look, the more hypocritical they are, she'd say. She thinks this and yet she still sent me here?

I rattle the screen door and call Yarden's name. Yarden is from Honduras and has skin the color of milky tea. Sometimes when I'm supposed to be at swimming or archery I sneak in here and plant myself on the counter, helping him to peel potatoes until they form a pyramid. He tells me about the importance of breathing through the diaphragm, his long fingers resting on his ribs, or he tells me about the mangroves back home. I am beautiful and smart, he says, but I shouldn't be so down on makeup. "A girl should never be afraid to wear a little color," he says firmly as he chops onions, the tip of his knife gleaming.

"Yarden?" I hiss again. No answer. Kron stays several feet back, on patrol.

"It's better that he's not around," I say. "We'll just pop off the screen window, and you'll crawl in."

I give her a leg up, guide her to the loose part of the screen. She is as light as a bird. I am loving this. We are misfits, we are outlaws. We won't be around for deportation. If we were in Poland, we would be the ones to survive.

"This is a bad idea," Kron whispers.

I boost her up even higher. "It's the best idea I've had all summer," I say.

She twists around. "I don't think—"

"That's right," I say. "Don't think at all." That had been my policy all summer: not thinking, trying to forget, trying to imagine that the person stuck here with a freak as her only friend is someone else, that it's someone else standing under the weak shower spray, tears mixing with the lukewarm water, wondering, why me?

Finally, Kron gets the screen off and slips through the window. A minute later, she is at the back door, opening it for me.

"I bet you they're all inbred," I say, inside the dark narrow kitchen with its cracked linoleum. "They probably have those weird diseases, like the Amish or the English royal family."

We are discussing the girls in our bunk, or rather, I'm discussing them. Kron isn't nearly as interested as I am in Jill Simon's breeding. There's only the scratch of her pencil as she sits on the floor, drawing.

I lean over. On the yellow cardboard face of her star, she's sketching a disk with radiating spokes. It's creepy, but kind of cool too. I'm wondering what it's supposed to represent, when Kron, in her small, flat voice, says, "It's not so bad in here."

"No, it's not," I say, thinking that we could stay here for days, weeks even. Yarden would come back and the two of us could help him in the kitchen, hanging out in this sanctuary of warmth, away from the onslaught of activity after activity performed in the name of "camp spirit" and "Jewish community." "If they wanted to make sure the Holocaust never happens again," I say, "they'd be teaching us stuff so we don't end up like them."

Kron snorts. "What kind of stuff?"

I'm thinking of my mother's two years in the army. "Stuff so we could kick ass, so no one could push us around."

Kron doesn't say anything but she doesn't laugh either. A minute or two pass with the sound of her scratchings, Then she says, "If we get caught—"

"We're not going to get caught."

"If we do," Kron says again, flatly, "we meet at the canteen at three. No one will bother us there."

"Okay." I sit back, grateful that she's taking charge. "Tell me about Lamu," I say. Kron gives me a look. I shrug. "What's the weather like? Who lives there?"

"Some things are better left unsaid," she says beneath the curtain of her hair. "You know, Anne Frank survived years in an attic, barely talking above a whisper."

"Good for Anne Frank," I say. I pluck a pan off a hook above the industrial chrome stove and stare into it. The surface is all scratched up, but I can just make out my face. An old-looking face I've been told ("classic," my mother says)—the hard jaw, the formerly blond hair that has settled into a harmless and unexciting shade of brown, the tiny nose and light-blue eyes that I'm told are dead ringers for my father's. Not that I see him often enough to know. It's an okay face, not great, not terrible. I say, "I'm surprised they didn't make me a guard or a Nazi or something."

Kron looks up.

"Are there Jews on Lamu?" I try. "Jews who look like me?"

"Lamu does not host organized religions," she says after a pause. "We don't believe in them."

"That's good," I say, softly.

I am looking out the window to see if I can spot Rafi but I see only Bunk Machon. A couple of girls are sitting back to back, their chins upturned to the sun. Some guys are playing tic-tac-toe with sticks in the dirt. Nobody looks anxious. Nobody looks Polish. Nobody cares about anyone but themselves.

I hear footsteps behind me. "Kron?" I say.

"Whatsa matter, Lizzie?" a voice says. "You afraid of being a Jew?"

I turn around. Orna Lewis taps her fingers against the clipboard she clutches to her chest and flicks a strand of stringy blond hair behind her ear. "Game over," she says impatiently. "Let's go."

"The game's over?" I say slowly. She could send us to the soccer field for deportation, if she wanted to. "We can go back to the bunk now?"

She bangs her clipboard against the counter. "You have to get your papers and get out of Poland. Now! Let's go! Both of you!"

I start to move, but Kron doesn't. She's sprawled out, lying prostrate on the dirty linoleum, her pale birdlike arms at her sides, her hair spreading around her. Orna nudges her foot against Kron's butt. "Karen! I'm serious!" she says, but Kron doesn't respond. Her eyes flutter open. She looks at Orna, she looks at me. She smiles, and out flies pale-colored vomit from her mouth—elegantly, in an arc, it flies up and shoots down on Orna's woven open-toed sandals.

"Oh," Kron says.

Orna shrieks and stomps around, light brown drops flinging around like wet paint. I freeze. I live in fear of throwing up. The last time I did I was in the fifth grade. It was a rainy Wednesday, and I was having dinner with my father at a restaurant. I twirled great masses of spaghetti and clams around my fork, my eyes fixed on the Dodger game on the TV set above the bar. He talked about his new office, the great view he had of the Hudson.

"You mean, New Jersey," I said.

His eyes crinkled blue. "How did you know that?"

"Geography," I said, my voice filled with exasperation. "We learned that in fourth grade."

On the way back to my mother's, not knowing when I would see him again, I threw up in his rental car. I am remembering his "Jesus! Jesus!" when I hear Orna yell, "She needs to go to the infirmary!"

"Orna," I moan, clutching my stomach, "the chicken, I think it was . . ." But I am two beats too late.

"Don't even try it!" she says. "You're going to Machon. Now."

Orna stomps across the linoleum. Kron turns around, raises her sharp eyebrows. "Canteen at three," she mouths to me.

The sun is on full blast. We pass the empty basketball court, its black asphalt glittering in the heat, and a ring of campers standing around with clipboards like Orna's. They watch as she marches me to the Machon line. I stare right back at them and wave, just to let them know that I'm still around, but I'm feeling a little nervous with Kron gone. Orna deposits me at the back of the line, where the rumors are flying. "You don't even need a visa." "No one is getting across." "Kids are disappearing; no one's seen Leslie Epstein for hours." "Bobby Z. is standing at the gates, making you pay real money; it's all a front so he can make a little extra cash." But they don't stray from the line.

I am not here, I tell myself. I am not here at all. If I concentrate hard enough, I can put myself behind the counter at Häagen-Dazs on Seventeenth Street, where I should be, scooping shivery happiness for anyone with $1.49.

Jill Simon, the premier girlie girl of my bunk, saunters up to the line with her boyfriend, Jesse, a short guy with thick hair who acts inches taller than he is.

"We could be at Zuma right now," Jesse says. "Out there, in the water." He traces the line of skin between Jill's shorts and her top.

"You can't go surfing," Jill says. "We have visas to worry about." She guides his hand to her navel, laughs lightly, as if no one were around for miles.

I cough, loudly.

"What?" she says, as if interested in my response, but there is a hitch to her tone that tells me everything. "What are you looking at?"

"Nothing," I say. "Nothing at all."

"Let her watch all she wants," Jesse says. "If that's how she gets her kicks." He flings an arm over Jill's shoulders.

"Yes, you're splendid entertainment."

"You don't think I could entertain you?" Jesse says in a voice knitted with sweetness. I feel his eyes travel up my body. I know what he's looking at. Earlier this year, my body took off without me; this was the year that my mother and I spent too many hours at Bullock's shopping for bras. Last week, Jesse came up to me in the dining hall and leered at my chest as I held a glass under the soda machine's spigot. "Go bother your Barbie doll of a girlfriend," I said, but that did nothing to wipe the smirk off. Now his lips curve into a smile.

I cross my arms. "In your dreams."

But it is as if I've said nothing at all. And I do what I've been doing all summer, I concentrate so hard that a hum starts up in my ears and light wavers in front of my eyes. I pull my ID out of my back pocket, and I stare again at Anya's face. Thick eyebrows set far apart, a narrow bridge of a nose, dark hair that hangs down heavy over her cheeks. It's a strange look, but not unattractive. I wonder what her life was like. Did she really have four kids? What happened to them? What happened to her? Was she one of the people they were talking about last night? I think of those train tracks, skin stretched thin over bones, and those in my family who never made it out. I won't let that happen to me.

It takes close to an hour, but when I finally get inside, the bunk is cool and dark. The fans click. As my eyes adjust and the shadowy shapes sharpen, my heart does a dance. I should've come here hours ago.

Someone has pushed all the bunk beds against the far wall, their metal legs peeking out beneath the mint-green sheets they're using as curtains. In front, sitting, resplendent, as if on some kind of stage, is Rafi, beautiful Rafi. He is in charge of passports. He is in control.

A rectangle of butcher paper is covered with a grid of names, X's and O's marching down in columns. In front of me, a fat girl in orange hightops is arguing with a short, sallow-skinned boy whose name I also don't know. "I'm not selling the painting just to get across," she hisses.

Rafi waves them over. They hand their papers to him. Rafi's fingers fly. They waltz across the keys of the adding machine, they flip through the IDs. They are long and limber with a life of their own. They could be anywhere, those hands—tapping on a glass-topped table in Paris, unbuttoning an Israeli Army jacket, caught in the tangle of my hair. I can't say if it is minutes or seconds later—time is a slippery, iridescent glaze—but soon Rafi stamps their cards and is calling to me.

"Hey," he says, folding his hands in front of him. "Look who we have here." He is smiling. Tiny holes ring the neck of his worn T-shirt, which reads, "Once Is Never Enough."

I breathe. "Hey," I say and smile back.

He brushes hair out of his eyes, clears his throat. He asks for my papers.

"You're married," he says, "with four kids." He tells me this like he's telling me: You can stay out all night.

I bite my lip. "I've been busy," I say.

He laughs. "Clearly," he says. And I laugh, too.

He swivels around, checking names on the paper behind him. I stare at the curve of his tanned neck, the point at which his curls stop and the knob of his spine appears. There is a dime-sized patch of peeling skin, and I resist the urge to reach out and tear it off. Maybe he'll give me a train pass for later this afternoon; maybe I'll get to wait here for hours with him.

Rafi turns back around, places his hands flat on the table. Can he tell that I've been with older guys before? That I'm not just some silly fifteen-year-old who doesn't know anything?

"I can't let you through."

"What?" Stupidly, I smile some more.

He leans closer; his lips are a little chapped. His skin smells like clean laundry. "I can't give you a stamp."

"What do you mean?" I say, and I badly need to swallow. "You can let me through. I know you can."

He shrugs. "Sorry."

I hate myself for what happens next. It's just a game. But the tears well up anyway. "I don't understand," I say, and my voice is a pathetic whisper. "Please."

"You'll be fine." He tips his chair back on its hind legs, gives me what I'm sure he thinks is an encouraging nod. "See you on the other side."

The sky is too blue, hard with color and cleared of any clouds. The basketball court is a ghost town. The back door to the kitchen is padlocked shut; the window Kron and I crawled through is now covered with yellow caution tape. There is the soft hum of a generator, and an oceany rush that I know is the flow of cars on the PCH.

I peek through the back window of the infirmary, but all the beds are empty. Where is Kron? Why didn't she warn me she was going to throw up? I would have told her that I couldn't do it. Maybe she knew that; maybe she wanted to get rid of me and go over to the other side. Maybe everyone will make it but me. I lean against the stuccoed wall of the dining hall. I'll do what I should have done in the first place, what I should have done that first week of camp. I'll hike down to the cars careering up and down the highway, and I'll hitch a ride north to Santa Barbara or Los Ojos. I'll learn to waitress, to balance plates on my arm and know what people want before they ask. I unlace my sneakers, easing my sticky heels out of the canvas. The smell is so strong, so deep and purely rank that for a second I breathe in, impressed. I close my eyes and daydream about Topanga and my mother; her hard freckled shoulders and her cigarettes and the orangy-brown lip-stick she's been wearing since I was four. She'd probably hate this game, even more than I do, and I'm thinking about how the summer will be over in three weeks and maybe I should write her back when I feel something brush against my foot. I slit my eyes open.

Standing above me is a boy I recognize from archery. He has a wide, sun-dusted face, and the stiffest hair I've ever seen, sand-colored hair that must add two inches to his height. Larry, Gary? He is cooing "who, who" at me.

"Hey." I blink.

"Hello, Jew." He toes his right sneaker in the dirt, pointing it into the ground and making a hole. "Jew, let's see your papers."

I can't even speak. His eyes are dark, water-slicked rocks. "Jew, where's your star?"

Jew? "Bullshit," I feel like spitting. I want to say: No, I'm not. Not in real life. But I am and I know it and I just stare. None of this can be happening. None of it at all.

"Get out of here." He taps the words out against my bare leg with his dirt-encrusted toe. "You should be long gone."

He could haul me in; he could march me down to the soccer field and collect whatever stupid reward they're handing out. This should make me hold my tongue, but I don't. "Why don't you go bother a midget your own size?"

He kicks my ankle. "Because I can bother you, Jew."

Tears spring to my eyes. "Fuck you," I say, and grab his leg with both my hands. I throw him off-balance, and he spins around, hopping. I give it a furious yank, and he falls. "You're a Jew, too."

"Not now I'm not." We're both in the dirt, and he's grabbing me, clutching my mouth, my throat. He pins my arms back so far; I swear something inside of me crests and breaks.

"Okay, okay!" I start laughing. "Please, stop, please."

He moves his mouth to my ear. "Why should I?"

"Because I'm asking you nicely. Please."

His fingers are still around my collarbone. He speaks in almost a pleasant tone. "Okay. Get the fuck out of here."

And I do.

He has my shoes. The bastard has my sneakers. I run hard anyway, wincing as I step on sharp rocks, twigs that scrape against the softness of my soles. I try to tell myself that I don't care, that it's good for me. My feet need to toughen up anyway. But I do care, I do.

I head up the incline, fast. There is the shallow rhythm of my breathing, the sound of leaves and twigs cracking beneath my feet. My forehead is covered in a fine light mist. This fucked-up game isn't funny anymore. I'm almost at the top of the hill when I hear a tangle of noises. I reach one of the stone arches that leads into the amphitheater. The noise is now a steady hum. An orange banner hangs limply at the entrance, a remnant of the color wars held last week. I was picked second to last for green and spent most of the time on the sidelines, cheering for blue.

My feet hurt. I am hot and tired and I can't imagine the noises being anything good. Why should I go inside? I wonder this and it's as if the wondering is my answer. Stepping gingerly on the balls of my sore feet, I pass under the orange flag.

The amphitheater is ours. Hot damp bodies crowd the stage. They throng the makeshift aisles, stepping over piles of clothing, pools of brightly colored plastic beads, bins of sneakers and flip-flops, pyramids of baseball caps. There are Walkmans and headless Barbies and Gameboys galore. There are dozens of voices braiding together, high- and low-pitched throbs that vibrate long past the words. All are clamoring for attention. Nothing is for sale.

"A pass for a dozen beads. Get your passage here!"

"Exit for exchanges."

"Music for cash!"

It is a quick business. People don't linger. They file out like a steady stream. They want to get to the other side.

I hang back, stunned. Has this been going on all day? Has everyone known about it but me? I notice that Jill and Jesse have beat me here, and I watch as they hand over a fistful of beads and a Lakers cap for sweat-stained visas.

Everyone is going to the other side. Why can't I?

"What do you have?"

I turn. "Excuse me?"

He is pale and rail-thin. Sam, if I remember right. A really good tennis player who practices all day long. You can hear the thwack, catch the gleam of the moving ball, as you leave the dining hall in the falling darkness. Secretly I like him for that, for the way he avoids everyone and everything for the only thing he cares about.

"Hi," I say, smiling at him now.

"Hello." His amber-colored eyes slide over the surface of my face. His oxford shirt, the kind everyone else saves for Shabbat, is tucked neatly into his khakis, and his topsiders are polish-bright. He reaches out, brushes his hand against my cheek.

"Hey!" My hands fly up.

"What do you want for the earrings?"

"Nothing," I say, touching the small braided hoops that I'd forgotten I was wearing. They were my paternal grandmother's, and except for a dark-blue fraternity tie that my mother used to hang on our refrigerator door as a joke, the earrings are the only thing I have from my father's side of the family. I step back, almost trip over a wicker basket.

He grabs my elbow. "Watch yourself," he says.

"I'm just fine," I say.

Behind him, a tall girl with legs like a stork hands over a box of jujubes; a freckled boy readjusts his Dodgers cap and screams, "Two hours! We've got two hours to get out of here!"

"I could get you to America in no time with those," he says, his eyes on my ears.

"We are in America," I say.

"Right," he says, smiling. "Do we have a trade or not?"

"I can't sell the earrings," I explain.

"Fine," he says, annoyed, and begins scanning the crowd for the next prospect.

"Sam—" I blurt out his name and touch his sleeve; I'm that desperate. "There's got to be something else you'd want."

"From you?" He raises his eyebrows, looking me up and down.

I flush, embarrassed. Who is he to do this to me? Who are any of these people? I look down at his diver's watch; the digits glow 2:38 P.M. I want out so badly. I feel as if I'm peering over the edge of a cliff when I say, "What if I have information on a fugitive?"

"Look around you," he says, looking bored. "They're everywhere."

237

"It's Kron." I say it and wind whistles in my ears. "I know where you can find her."

"Kron from Lamu?" He says it quickly. "Now that's a different story."

I nod, tired.

"Where is she?"

"Visa first," I say.

This time, when I cut through no-man's-land, through the stand of eucalyptus trees where the ground is freckled by shadows, I walk more slowly. I feel a little sick, but I tell myself that Kron is fine, that she never showed up to the canteen, that she is worlds away.

"We've made it," I say to Anya, and I'm surprised to hear my voice out loud. I pass the creek, which is little more than a trickle. The rocks lie gleaming, dry, white, and smooth as calcified bones. A lizard skitters from one to another. Its head is enormous and ugly, weighted down by a spiky, prehistoric-looking crown. I stop as it leaps closer to me, its tail wiping the rock. It is more graceful than anything I've ever seen. I lean over, holding my finger out. The lizard's body goes rigid. Except for the slight quiver of skin hanging beneath its chin, you wouldn't know it's alive. I think: I could hurt it, if I wanted to. I could.

"Hello, Mr. Lizard," I say, softly. "I won't hurt you."

"Hello."

I jump and the lizard darts off. Jesse is behind me. He is perched on a rock, his tanned legs dangling down, the bare soles of his feet flashing.

For a moment, neither of us says a word. Finally, he speaks. "You crossing?"

I take a step back. "Where's Jill?"

He jerks his head around. "Around. Somewhere." He hops off the rock, takes a step toward me. The air shifts—it becomes heavier somehow—but I don't look away. "I haven't seen her in a while. Everyone seems to be disappearing. Where's your freaky double?"

"Around," I say carefully.

He nods, moves even closer. "What about your papers?" He asks this easily, smiling. But before I can stop him, he reaches around me and pulls my ID and visa out of my back pocket.

"Hey!"

He backs away, laughing and shaking his head. He lets out a low whistle. "This is funny, you know. You and I."

"Funny?"

"Just—well, you are my wife."

I stare. "Your wife?"

He pulls a green square out of his back pocket. "Moishe," he reads. "I'm Moishe Ossevsheva. You're Anya."

He can't do that. I don't care if it's just a game. I feel a force pressing down against my temples. He has no right to me. He has no right to Anya.

"I heard we got a divorce."

"Really?" He folds his arms and looks down at my chest with a little smile as if my body is telling him something else. "Why would we want that? If we're married, I can help you get across. I hear you'll do lots of things to get across." Still smiling, he puts my visa and ID in his back pocket. "Why are you shaking, Anya?" He moves his mouth close to mine. "It's only a game."

"Don't touch me," I hear myself say. "Don't you dare."

"Oh, please," he says. "As if this isn't what you've wanted all along."

And his lips are on mine and he's right but oh so wrong and I feel both small and large, beautiful and grotesque, so unlike myself that I'm not sure I'm even there. He pulls me down to the rocky ground and wraps his legs around mine. And I don't want to think about Kron and Anya, but they're all I see. I'm horrible and I'll do anything and his elbow is digging into my ribs and his hands are everywhere and mine are too. It's probably only seconds but it feels like centuries later when we both hear it—a sharp noise, a crackling somewhere in the distance.

"Shit," he says. He twists around fast and scrambles to his feet. "Where did that come from?" I get up too, pulling my shirt back down. "Jill?" He scans the wall of trees, brushing his fingers through his hair.

"It's not her," I say, and somehow I manage to reach over, grab the papers fanning out of his pocket.

"What are you doing?" Jesse twists around, blinking—his eyes are strangely lidded, thin and opaque—just like the lizard's.

"You don't even have a visa, Jew. This isn't going to get you far." My voice trembles. I feel an unbearable urge to pee. "You thought you were going to touch me? You and your dirty Jewish ways?"

I'm shivering as I rip up his ID, letting the pieces fall through my fingers like glitter. "Jew," I practically coo. "Now why would I ever have married a Jew like you?"

"Freak."

"Fuck you."

"You'd like that, wouldn't you?" Jesse gives me a withering look and turns and lumbers away.

Now I'm shivering even more. I feel my way over to a boulder still warm with sun and I flatten my hands against it. I look at my own ID one last time, at that face, those eyes, so familiar, staring back at me, and I am dizzy with recognition. Carefully, I tear the green slip of paper apart. Anya's face becomes speckles on the rocks in the drying creek. As much as I wish it were otherwise, the speckles remain; there isn't enough stream to carry them away.

The Girls of Camp Lenore

Diana Trilling

"And what do you do in the arts, Mr. Trilling?" Mrs. Spectorsky greeted Lionel in her splendid contralto.

Lionel had often heard me speak of the directress—I was twenty-three and, after all, the many summers I had spent at her camp in the Berkshires, whether as camper or counsellor, constituted a considerable portion of my youthful experience of life. Now that we were about to be married I had at last brought him to meet her.

No doubt Lionel was about to reply that he was a graduate student at Columbia, working for his Ph.D., when I broke in recklessly, "He's an Apache dancer, Mrs. Spectorsky. He throws me around all day—that's why I'm so thin."

I had never before teased the directress and I was startled by my temerity. As I saw Mrs. Spectorsky glancing uneasily from Lionel's face to mine, I began to laugh in order to indicate that what I had said was only a joke. The directress visibly relaxed. In her long years of association with the young, she had learned to accommodate their strange humors.

The fact that Mrs. Spectorsky greeted Lionel with so prompt a reference to the arts was scarcely a surprise to me, and even Lionel had to have been prepared for it: describing Camp Lenore to him, I must surely have made plain to him the special role of art at Mrs. Spectorsky's institution and the important difference that this represented between Mrs. Spectorsky's venture and the other girls' camps which in these early years of the century were beginning to dot the Adirondacks and the Berkshires. Although Lenore, like other such enterprises, had its required quota of athletic activities—swimming and canoeing, baseball, basketball, tennis, track—unlike its competitors it was not merely a place to which parents sent their young daughters during their school vacations so that they might live healthily outdoors and be instructed in sports. Mrs. Spectorsky's camp was a place of spiritual aspiration and dedication before it was a place for the development of our physical competences. It was an aesthetic rather than an athletic camp. Indeed, it was at Lenore that, at the age of thirteen, fourteen, fifteen, my pores open to whatever might come to me either by chance or by adult design, I first discovered this new and wider dimension of life, the dimension of art, a range of emotion and perception that had previously not been accessible to me.

Our camp day began at Lenore with morning Assembly, and regularly the directress took advantage of this gathering of her young charges to remind us of what it was that distinguished us from other summer camps for girls and in what way we were the beneficiaries of this difference. It was not that the body was neglected at Mrs. Spectorsky's camp. "*Mens sana in corpore sano*—a healthy mind in a healthy body," the directress translated with even emphasis. Not only did we have a superior kitchen at Camp Lenore, presided over by the directress's niece, a trained nutritionist. We also had a full corps of athletic instructors, including a special riding counsellor for those of us whose parents afforded us this addition to an already complete athletic program. But mind was in command, and mind, for Mrs. Spectorsky, was a state of grace most readily attained to by love of the arts.

Art had not been without its place in my childhood home. My parents had a music box with a wide assortment of tinkling musical disks. We also had a Victrola with records by Caruso and Kubelík and Fritz Kreisler, and a piano. From an early age, all three of us children had music lessons from Professor Steinmetz, the one-man musical conservatory who performed his feats of instruction in our Westchester community. And we had books. From a door-to-door salesman my father had bought a library that substantially filled a six-shelf glass-fronted bookcase with the works of Mark Twain, Balzac, George Eliot, Molière, Dumas, and Victor Hugo, all of them in rich leather bindings stamped in gold. Unhappily, my intimacy with this parade of immortal talent was much limited by the fact that we children were not allowed to approach the costly volumes without first washing our hands, and that each time I removed a book from its shelf I was freshly cautioned against dog-earing it or injuring its spine by laying it facedown on a table.

Art was not put at this forbidding distance from us at Camp Lenore; at Mrs. Spectorsky's camp it made the very fabric of our lives. We were a hundred and forty campers and between thirty and forty counsellors. And at least half of our counsellors were chosen for their skill in dance or drama or the crafts. In addition, Mrs. Spectorsky engaged a trio of musicians—a pianist, a violinst, and a cellist—to perform for us each afternoon. The pianist was the hardest worked of the three. She had not only to play for us during Music Hour each afternoon but also to accompany our many dance classes and to assist as needed in the preparation of our pageants and musical revues. In good weather, dance classes at Lenore were held on the softly rolling lawn in front of the Lodge, the rambling stone cottage in which Mrs. Spectorsky had her office and living quarters. In bad weather, they met in the Assembly Hall.

It was at these afternoon concerts provided for us by Mrs. Spectorsky's trio, all of them aspirants to professional careers, that there was confirmed in me what was undoubtedly a native love of music; it was sufficiently strong to have withstood even the teachings of Professor Steinmetz. The concerts took place at five each afternoon in the camp Assembly Hall and they were entirely devoted to classical music: Brahms and Tchaikovsky, Schubert, Dvořák, Fauré. The Assembly Hall was a bare wooden structure with movable benches and a slight elevation at one end, which we used as a stage. When the hall was used for morning assemblies or for indoor theatricals, the benches would be set up in row after backless row, the front rows reserved for our smallest campers, the Bluebirds, as they were called, with behind them the Intermediates, then the Seniors and the P.C.s, the latter the handful of older girls, Privileged Campers, who were in line to become junior counsellors. I had myself started at Lenore at the age of thirteen, one of its younger Seniors. On the outside of the Assembly Hall, facing the distant line of Berkshire hills, ran a narrow veranda. Music Hour was not compulsory, but I never failed to attend. The weather permitting, I listened outdoors, sitting on the veranda floor with my back against the rough shingles. As I sat gazing toward the surrounding hills, the music would drift out to me and my heart would swell with longing. From my earliest years, longing was always my secret companion.

Mrs. Spectorsky had ruled against ballet at Lenore. She said it was against nature to bind our poor little feet in tight silk slippers and to try to raise ourselves on our toes. At Lenore we danced in Grecian tunics, barefoot and bare-legged, in the manner of Isadora Duncan. Was it not the superb Duncan herself who had recorded the horror with which she had observed the bleeding feet of Pavlova, the famed Russian ballerina, after but a few hours of practice or performance? No art could be art, said the directress, if it entailed suffering. Art was joy and love, art was transcendence.

I was the readiest of Mrs. Spectorsky's youthful adherents and I very much wanted to achieve transcendence, but I was too self-conscious to dance. I had come to Lenore with the sad knowledge that aspiring though I might be in mind, I was sorely lacking in physical grace, and to this dispiriting self-assessment had been added the appraisal of my bunkmates. Their judgment was final. My legs were too thin and my knees too bumpy to merit careless exposure. I must find other means of participating in the pageants that were so notable a feature of our dramatic program.

Like our dance classes, our pageants took place on the lawn in front of the Lodge. They were a composite of narrative and dance. Sometimes the drama counsellor, more often Mrs. Spectorsky herself, acted as narrator. Majestic, classical, the directress would stand on the steps of the Lodge and with vibrant voice call upon the ancient religious mysteries to reenact themselves.

"With fruits and flowers we deck thy altars," Mrs. Spectorsky's wonderful contralto rang out to the surrounding hills, while to the accompaniment of this and other similarly broad-metered sentiments a dozen barefoot little dancers, virgin priestesses in the Temple of Aphrodite, disported themselves on the wide green lawn in front of the Lodge. They bore baskets of crêpe-paper offerings that had been fashioned for them during the previous week in our arts-and-crafts classes. One summer—it must have been during my second or third season at Lenore—I was given a special part to play in one of our outdoor spectacles. I was made to arrive at the steps of the Lodge on horseback. Puccini's Girl of the Golden West had come to the rescue of the maidens of Greece.

Mrs. Spectorsky seldom sang for us, but I loved her voice, even in speech. As a young woman in Paris, she had studied with the great operatic tenor Jean de Reszke. It was seldom discussed but we older campers plainly understood that it was the directress's marriage that had defeated her operatic ambitions, or perhaps not the marriage in itself but her choice of Mr. Spectorsky as her husband.

"Spec!" Addressing Mr. Spectorsky, the directress's usually modulated voice became hard and biting. It was plain that Mrs. Spectorsky had little love or regard for her husband; he was not a respected partner in the management of Lenore. Lenore was Mrs.

Spectorsky's lone venture. The life of the camp flowed from her alone. He was a striking-looking man, tall, thin, straight-backed, with very black hair that had begun to gray and a short pointed beard that was also graying. His eyes were disconcertingly small and intense—or so they seemed to me. I knew virtually nothing of his or Mrs. Spectorsky's life before the start of Lenore. I assumed that they had been born in Russia and had met as students in Paris.

At Lenore, in addition to pageants, we put on one-act plays—I remember the whimsical "Six Who Pass While the Lentils Boil"—and musical revues, especially evenings of Russian folk dances and songs. I had a clear and appealing soprano voice, and when there was solo singing to be done I would be called upon to perform. For our Russian evenings, I was costumed and made up like a Russian nesting doll. "*Spi malyutka, moy prekrasny . . .*" In phonetic Russian taught me by Davy, one of our arts-and-crafts counsellors, I sang the lullaby of an unknown country—it was as if the River Volga lapped at my feet. The Volga was a familiar river to us at Lenore, far more so than the Mississippi or even the Hudson.

Through many summers, Mrs. Horn (I invent her name as I do several others which I no longer reliably remember) was in charge of our camp dramatics. She was both of our camp staff and independent of it. While not only the campers but all our other counsellors lived in groups of four in "bunks"—little wooden cabins with canvas flaps instead of walls and windows—Mrs. Horn lived alone at a small distance past the Senior campus, at the edge of the woods that separated us from the lake. She had been a Shakespearean actress and was a cherished friend of Mrs. Spectorsky. If there had ever been a Mr. Horn, he was well out of mind. Although she was technically a member of the staff, she shared none of its duties: she had no campers in her charge, nor did she eat like the rest of us in the Mess Hall. She had but one responsibility: to assist us with our pageants and other dramatic presentations. When she narrated a pageant or was otherwise onstage, she stood with her head slightly thrown back and with her left hand cupping her left breast.

As far as I could make out, Mrs. Horn never ate. But I sometimes saw her, swift and lithe, carrying a large jug of milk from the kitchen to her cabin. Did milk alone sustain her impressive energies? I never saw her at the Senior washhouse, where we older girls had our washbasins and toilets. The camp had another washroom, too, at the rear of the Lodge, where Auntie Ella, the camp disciplinarian, was in command, but I never saw Mrs. Horn at that washhouse, either. In private, she no doubt took her bar of soap to the lake, as we girls did. I once caught a glimpse of her alone at the lake. I saw her dive from the high diving board, birdlike, effortless. It awed me that anyone of her age—how old *was* she? forty? fifty?—could dive as Mrs. Horn did.

We older girls were fascinated by Mrs. Horn, but none of us had crushes on her as we had crushes on Hermit or Red or Billy. But if Mrs. Horn was out of the reach of our fantasies we weren't out of the reach of hers. I was a Senior, probably fifteen, when she asked me to come and live with her, not at camp but wherever it was that she lived when she was not at Lenore. She promised to make me into a great Shakespearean actress. I scarcely heeded what she was saying—my response to her invitation was to giggle.

Fifteen was then, of course, a young age. Still, within a year I would enter college. How long could one continue to meet the confusions of life with a giggle?

There were few opportunities to raise our artistic consciousness which the directress left unexplored. One summer, she invited Robert Frost to speak to us at Lenore. The poet was staying in Pittsfield, only a dozen or so miles from Camp Lenore. His daughter ran a bookmobile in the surrounding countryside, and from it I purchased the first book I ever bought for myself, a volume of the poems of Rudyard Kipling. Though not yet the eminence that he would become, Frost was already a poet of repute. Yet it was actually not as a literary man but as a man of nature that Mrs. Spectorsky invited him to speak to us. A slithering green snake had been seen near one of the Intermediate bunks, and Lenore was on the brink of panic. The visit from the local woodsman was intended to assure us that our snakes would do us no harm. For his visit, Sunday Assembly was delayed until midmorning and held outdoors on the front lawn. I no longer recall how Frost dealt with our snake problem. I remember only what seemed to me to be his great height and the shine of his thick hair as it blew in the summer wind.

Any male visitor created a stir among us. Our non-female population was limited to four: the directress's husband; the directress's son, Auguste (his name must be given its French pronunciation); Dr. Saunders, husband of our camp nutritionist; and Steve, our Polish man-of-all-work. There are times now, looking back over my years at Lenore, when it seems to me that we were horrid to Auguste Spectorsky, though there are other times when I am struck by how unexpectedly thoughtful we were of him; we tried to spare him some of the embarrassment he must have felt as the only boy in a camp of a hundred and forty girls.

The whole of Auguste's name was Auguste Comte Spectorsky; he had been named for the French positivist philosopher. Auguste, too, like Mrs. Horn, had a bunk of his own, but his was situated at the other end of the camp from hers, not far from the camp's front gate. I have no idea what Auguste did throughout our long camp days. He had no friends and he shared in none of our activities. I have no memory of ever seeing him at an assembly or at our camp dramatic offerings. Where did he hide himself? To be the only boy in a camp of a hundred and forty girls: it is a test such as a child Turandot might have devised for her young suitors! How did Auguste survive it? He did survive it, to become a well-known book reviewer. Later, he worked at *Playboy* and—so I heard—became an habitué of Hugh Hefner's erotic Eden. One day when we were fully grown, Auguste and I ran into each other in a Manhattan bookstore. I, too, had become a book reviewer. At sight of me, he fled as from a ghost of the past.

Auguste was not the only child of the Spectorskys: he had an older sister, Miriam. But Miriam's presence didn't, like his, require explanation. Except that, at least as an adolescent, she had a troubling tendency to faint, she was in all respects her mother's spiritual heiress, and in due course she in fact became her mother's official adjutant. When, many years later, I would return to camp for a quick, anxious visit, there she would be. It was Rest Hour, a time for the picking up of loose threads, and, gentle but urgent, she was having an improving little talk with an errant Intermediate.

Sometimes, on summer evenings when the temperature had abruptly fallen, we would have a campfire night. On the Intermediate campus, near the tennis courts, Steve would make a giant pile of wooden crates and boxes that he had hoarded for just this purpose, and when it became sufficiently dark he would set the pile ablaze to our excited applause. In the roaring light of the fire, we huddled together in our thick camp sweaters, our rough Army blankets spread beneath us. These were the nights when Mr. Spectorsky came as far into his own as was ever allowed him. He stood in the light of the great fire and told us the tale of the Ring of the Nibelung. An ardent Wagnerian, he was bent on making little Wagnerians of us all. He brought us into the mythic company of Siegmund and Sieglinde, Siegfried, the Valkyrie, Brünnhilde and her fond Wotan. Year in and year out, I heard and forgot the saga of the Nibelung. With their glittering metal helmets and shields, their wildly rearing horses and sacred swords (those improbable chastity belts of theirs), Wagner's bold heroes and heroines are a muddle to me still.

It was frequent on parent weekends for a father to bring a gift of lollypops for the camp—dozens of them. If he was sufficiently imaginative, they would be of one flavor, so as not to cause a problem in their distribution. Mrs. Spectorsky set these gifts aside to be distributed at campfire. We cheered the absent donor. "Rah, rah, rah, Mr. Shapiro!" we roared in unison, led by our Senior cheerleader. Mr. Shapiro was Fritzi Shapiro's father, and at moments such as these I dearly wished that it were my father who was being celebrated. Sucking our lollypops, we older girls folded ourselves as closely as we could into our sweaters, and in the now blazing, now dying firelight tried to still our nameless yearnings. There was no one to tell us what it was that our young bodies, edging toward each other, longed for as we sat under the wide dark sky in the changing light of the fire, or where it was in the longings of our bodies that art might really have its source.

The words "Jew" and "Jewish" were never heard at Lenore. We were nevertheless a Jewish camp. Mr. and Mrs. Spectorsky were Jewish, and a hundred and thirty-nine of our hundred and forty girls were of the same faith and drawn from the newly successful business class of New York. Apart from our counsellors, most of whom were not Jewish, the single Gentile among us was Nancy Still, a blond wisp of a girl with a roguish grin that belied her simplicity. Nancy came from Staten Island, and I never found out— not that I tried—what accounted for her presence among us.

Nancy ranked high in popularity at Lenore. But she lacked subtlety, a quality that was much cherished by the older campers and much sought in our counsellors. The quality was hard to define, but its chief component was mystery. For a counsellor to be subtle, she had to possess some obscure characteristic of personality which at the same time defied and seduced us. Expectably enough, our nonathletic counsellors were more likely to meet this requirement than our counsellors in baseball or basketball, although there were exceptions, like Hermit, our head swimming counsellor, or Billy, who was camp bugler and also taught baseball and track. Hermit, for example, was set apart from most of our sports counsellors by her splendid good looks and her spare use of words. It was important if you were to be thought subtle not to let yourself be too easily drawn into careless conversation. Many of us had crushes on Hermit. I was myself in love with her for a whole summer.

While no note was taken of conventional religion at Lenore, the directress was far from a nonbeliever or lacking in religious sentiment. Scornful of sects and denominations, she had her own sacraments and was indubitably to be counted among the devout. Her immediate leanings were toward the religious teachings of the East, but in total she was a worshipper at the shrine of the immaterial. She aspired to the whole wide glorious universe of spirit.

If ever the directress's capacity for rising above the impositions of worldliness was tried, it was on parent weekends. Each summer, there were two weekends on which parents were permitted, even urged, to visit their children. For the few hours in which they were in possession, Lenore trembled under the intrusion of this alien culture. The mothers and fathers arrived at Lenore like an invasive horde in their shiny new Packards and Pierce-Arrows, the fathers wearing plaid golf knickers and broad-patterned Argyle socks, the mothers brilliant in their expensive summer outfits. Not even Mrs. Spectorsky's poise and cultivated speech could threaten the confidence of these noisy invaders—having paid for their children's summer tuition, the parents apparently felt that they had bought, if only for these few hours, the right to its lawns and lakes, its Assembly and Mess Halls.

At Monday morning Assembly after a parent weekend, the

directress would quietly address the daughters of the rich and noisy on how the voice and the heart were one: a hundred and forty girls were once more instructed in the difference between striving and aspiration, this ill-marked crossroads at which the directress took up her pedagogic post. Gravely, she explained to us that, while there was much that was laudable in being a good swimmer or tennis player, at Lenore the goal was a willing rather than a winning. Better to play the game poorly or run the race in which we suffered defeat than not to extend ourselves, not to try. Within each of us, she summed up, was an inner gleam that must guide us.

We might not easily unravel Mrs. Spectorsky's pedagogic syntax but we had no difficulty in comprehending the high intention she had for us. Unfortunately, the brave vault of mind to which she inspired us often had painful physical consequences. On ten-mile hikes I bore my aching legs and blistering heels in silence. No, not in silence. I burst into energetic song. Its vigor propelled us in our forward march!

Each season, small groups of Seniors would be taken on an overnight hike to the summit of nearby Mt. Greylock. Here were tests of another sort. We were driven to the base of Greylock by Steve in the camp truck; with two counsellors in charge, we climbed the short rest of the way. Supper was sandwiches and fruit, which we carried with us, along with our cumbersome bedrolls; by the time we had finished our picnic, it was dark, but we pressed together, resisting sleep. We were frightened by the darkness under this vast expanse of sky, and we filled the air with our forced gaiety. Our counsellors had difficulty in at last quieting us for sleep. A poncho and two Army blankets beneath us, two blankets and another poncho on top of us, we lay on the ground in pairs; from bed to makeshift bed, we went on calling to each other. Long after it might have been supposed that we were all of us asleep, I lay awake; I was shivering and I hunched down in my blankets as best I could. I felt alone and lost.

For all the directress's tireless teaching—"Girls, be kind to one another"—kindness was often in short supply among us, especially among the older girls. How cruelly we teased the girl in the next Senior bunk because, unlike the rest of us, she had not yet begun to menstruate! During one of my own menstrual periods, Mimi Pomeroy, who was the camp's fat girl and my enemy, said to me, threateningly, "I'll kick you and a pound will flow!" Without comprehending what the threat could mean, I was much troubled by its menace. Even now it disturbs me to recall it.

I knew little about my body. I complained one day to the camp nurse about a persistent pain in my side, and Dr. Saunders was sent to my bunk to examine me. "You've strained an ovary," he said. "Probably from diving."

I must have looked at him blankly. "Don't you know what an ovary is?" he demanded gruffly. I shook my head.

"How old are you?" he inquired.

"Fourteen," I admitted.

"My God!" The doctor summarized the situation, and stomped angrily from the bunk.

We were presumably not a competitive camp, but at the start of each summer we divided into two teams, the Greens and the Whites, and the two teams battled for supremacy throughout the season. One could score points by one's excellence in a sport. But there were other means of winning points for one's team. I earned points for my team, the Whites, by writing our camp songs, borrowing their tunes from music that was familiar to us. To the popular tune of "Avalon," I wrote one of my major point-winners:

> *The Whites are just like Chesterfields;*
> *They satisfy.*
> *And like Ward's bread, they are Tip Top;*
> *On us rely.*
> *Like razor's, Ever-Ready.*

My memory of the current advertising slogans that I incorporated into this lyric deserts me here, but I remember another song of mine, my lollypop song, set to the immortal tune of "Harrigan":

> *L-O-double-L-Y*
> *P-O-P spells lollypop.*
> *It's a special kind of candy;*
> *The man who made it was a dandy.*
> *L-O-double-L-Y-P-O-P, you see.*
> *It's a lick on a stick*
> *And it's guaranteed to make you sick.*
> *Lollypops for me!*

I had yet another means of contributing to the final score of the Whites. It was not for naught that I bore the name of the goddess of the hunt: I excelled at archery. When I became a counsellor, this was the sport I taught. Actually, I was teaching it at Lenore while I was still a camper. As Mrs. Spectorsky would have wished, I made archery into an art. Marksmanship? This was of but minor importance. I put my emphasis on form: the arm of the archer had precisely to line up with her unhunched shoulder; her head must be held high, the neck upstretched and proud; there must be uplift, aspiration in every line of our young bodies. Sometimes at the end of class, I lay on the ground and braced my bow between upraised feet. I shot arrows into the air. It was a brave and wasteful pastime.

One summer, a group of us at camp formed a clandestine society, the A.E.G.T.H. The letters stood for "Auntie Ella Go to Hell." With no small astonishment, I now recognize that when this sinister organization came into being we, its creators, were fifteen years old; in another year—as I have indicated—I would be entering college. We already had a secret society at Lenore, Rada Thron, which had been created by Mrs. Spectorsky. The presence of the A.E.G.T.H. was not announced until it was in action; that is, until we marched on the Mess Hall. To the music of Chopin's "Funeral March" I composed an appropriate dirge for our demonstrations:

> We—are—the girls—of—the—A.E.G.T.H.
> Ours—is—a meeting—of ghostly
> or—i—gin.

I insert the dashes to indicate the solemn pace at which we walked and sang.

Our camp disciplinarian, Auntie Ella, was a wiry little woman of middle age with sharp, darting eyes and unnaturally black hair, which she wore in thick loops over her ears. Her responsibilities at Lenore were many, her energies formidable. It was Auntie Ella's duty to see that our bunks were thoroughly swept out each morning and our beds freshly made. A ruthless perfectionist, she was not above pulling back the smoothest of top blankets to reveal the crumpled bedsheet that it was intended to hide. She was in charge of the collection of our laundry and regularly inspected the heads of the younger campers for nits or hair bugs. Of the older Intermediates and Seniors she assumed that we would report to her on our own if we suspected that our heads were unclean.

"If your head itzes," she would tell us, "go into the kitzen and get a pitzer of hot water, and I'll wass it." Dear Auntie Ella! We took her accent, as we took her inspection of our bunks, to be a form of personal attack.

I doubt that any of us in the A.E.G.T.H. had then heard of the Ku Klux Klan, but if we had its ugly message had been lost on us. For our grand march upon the Mess Hall, we wrapped ourselves, like Klan members, in our white bedsheets, covering our heads with pillowcases in which we had cut holes for our eyes. "We—are—the girls—of—the—A.E.G.T.H.," we chanted in dire unison as we entered the dining hall and took a table. Mid-meal, once more solemnly intoning our dirge, we rose and slowly lifted our table high over our heads until the dishes rattled like the bones of a skeleton.

I don't know what we supposed we were doing, and today I should like to believe that our demonstration was only an effort to josh our poor old disciplinarian. I fear, though, that this was not the case, and that we actually believed that we posed a threat to our camp monitor; that, indeed, we hoped to achieve a relaxation in our rules for neatness or for Rest Hour—and we weren't the babies of Camp Lenore, we were its Seniors, its big girls! We stood on the brink of young womanhood; in another few years, those of us who were not in college would be thinking of marriage and of having children of our own.

Auntie Ella was the only counsellor whom we addressed as a relation. Sometimes we addressed our counsellors formally—Miss Harrington or Miss Press—and sometimes by nicknames or by their last names alone, as in the case of Whittelsey, our riding counsellor, or our head counsellor, Beam. The directress was extraordinarily skilled in choosing her staff; they were as if designed to uphold the principles on which Lenore was founded. They were also almost universally good-looking: Red, with her tousled red curls; boy-girl Billy, with her strangely bruised lips; Jerry, the dance counsellor with whom I fell in love when I graduated from my crush on Hermit.

In general, Mrs. Spectorsky treated our crushes much as she treated the A.E.G.T.H.—she paid them no heed. She did intervene, however, in my crush on Jerry: she took me for one of her little walks and talks in which she probed the nature of the relationship. She was being careful not to upset me, but I understood that I was being warned against some untoward influence in my life. She left me with an unnamed fear that at moments would return to me well after Jerry had all but disappeared from memory.

We graded our counsellors by their subtlety: Jerry was subtler than Hermit, Billy was subtler still. Red was an uncommon mix of subtlety and practical good sense—when the high-school friend with whom I had planned to go to Radcliffe failed her admission examinations and urged me to go elsewhere with her, it was Red who advised me not to yield to this appeal.

And Beam, our head counsellor? How did Beam rate for subtlety? Only now, this many years later, does it occur to me to measure her on this yardstick of ours. Heaven knows, there was mystery enough about her. She kept herself well apart from the rest of the staff, far more than was demanded by her position as head counsellor. And she was as spare in speech as in body. Yet we would not have spoken of her as subtle, not in the sense in which the word was used at Lenore. Her pale good looks were without robustness. Her hair was a commonplace brown, thin and straight, and long before it was the fashion she wore it down her back, held by a wide tortoiseshell barrette. Her thin face always seemed to be tired, and although I recall her pleasant smile, I have no memory of her laughter.

And why should she have laughed, I now ask myself. Under the circumstances, it must surely have represented a miracle of self-control for her to do her job as she did and so thoroughly conceal her personal anguish. I reconstruct her story from old newspaper clippings and I realize that it was during these very months when she was at Lenore that her lover decided to end their relationship and reconcile with his wife. How much better it would have been for her if he had! According to the newspaper accounts, he did take his wife to Europe that summer on what was supposed to have been their second honeymoon. But after his return he once more sought out Beam and Beam once more joined the universe of his sick and sordid imagination.

It was in my first year as a Senior that Mrs. Spectorsky established our camp honor society, Rada Thron—I never saw the name in print and I am not sure that I spell it correctly. Because Mrs. Spectorsky always mentioned it in conjunction with our pursuit of the inner gleam, it was my belief that our camp motto, "Follow the Gleam," was what the words meant in one of the languages of India. But I now discover that Rada Thron is neither Hindi nor Sanskrit but that it vaguely suggests Tibetan, and thus may have come to Mrs. Spectorsky through the writings of the Theosophists, specifically those of Mme. Blavatsky; the conjecture is bolstered by the fact that in the early years of this century a poem by Tennyson, "Merlin and the Gleam," was excerpted in the *Theosophical Journal*. The poem exhorts us to follow our inner light to new heights of the spirit. Comte, Wagner, Theosophy—surely it was a rich and varied board at which we feasted at Lenore!

There were no counsellors in Rada Thron, only Seniors who had been at Lenore for at least two years. The wish to belong to our camp honor society brought many girls back to Lenore for a second season or more; indeed, there was a suspicion among some of us that this commercial purpose had its part in Mrs. Spectorsky's creation of the society. At Assembly early each August, the directress announced the names of the newly elected members—they were chosen by their predecessors in the society. Even the Bluebirds recognized the importance of the occasion; they applauded excitedly and stamped their feet. I am still puzzled by how long it took for me to be elected to Rada Thron. Apparently the delay embarrassed even Mrs. Spectorsky herself: the summer before I finally became a member, she took me aside to apologize for my continuing exclusion but without accounting for it.

I was sixteen when I was at last a member of Rada Thron but was not too old to enjoy its privileges. The camp honor society had its own clubhouse: Mrs. Spectorsky had had a log cabin built in the woods at the edge of the lake for its headquarters, and here the society held its secret meetings and had its overnight parties. The cabin had a large stone fireplace, but we preferred to cook outdoors; we contrived a fireplace before our door. In a large iron cauldron that we hung from a sturdy green stick, itself resting in the forks of two other stalwart saplings, we concocted something we called a Mulligan stew. It consisted of everything the kitchen could spare: beans, onions, carrots, bones or chunks of beef, tomatoes, potatoes, cabbage. As we ate, we heard the sound of taps being played at camp, but we stayed awake long into the night, putting fresh logs on our indoor fire against the mounting chill. We laughed and talked. Last thing before sleep, the girls asked me to sing, and I sang for them softly: "Nobody Knows De Trouble I've Seen," "Solveig's Song," Delilah's love song to Samson, that most womanly of love arias.

I piece the story together from the old newspaper accounts: It was the month after Beam had been head counsellor at Lenore, and shortly after her lover had returned from what was to have been a second honeymoon in Europe, that he began to poison his wife. The poisoning would seem to have continued throughout that fall and winter. The first report of the bizarre crime appears in the *Times* of April 27, 1924: A Westchester resident, Clarence O. Baring, has been arrested for an attempt to murder his wife. "A young woman" is involved in the Baring marital situation, but her name is not mentioned, nor are we given any clue to her identity. The story appears on a Sunday under a bold front-page headline: "ADMITS IN COURT HE GAVE ARSENIC TO HIS RICH WIFE." In smaller type there follows, "C.O. Baring of White Plains Pleads 'Guilty, Except as to Intent to Kill.'"

On Monday, April 28th, the Baring story appears again on the front page of the *Times*: "DIPHTHERIA GERMS FED TO MRS. BARING, PROSECUTOR SAYS." A smaller headline reads, "Declares Evidence Also Shows Pneumonia Microbes As Well As Arsenic. . . . Wife, Victim of Many Long Illnesses, Was Said to Have Been Obsessed by Jealousy."

Although there is another *Times* story on Tuesday, it is not until Wednesday, April 30th, that the "other woman" is identified. Her name is Mildred E. Beam, and she is a twenty-seven-year-old teacher of physical education in Elizabeth, New Jersey. She is the daughter, we learn, of a Maine sea captain who is no longer alive, and she is a graduate in physical training of Columbia's Teachers College. At the time of his arrest, on Friday, April 25th, Baring and Mildred Beam had just that afternoon returned from a five-day trip to Norfolk, Virginia.

Of Clarence Baring we are told that he is a man of good reputation in his business and residential communities, successful in his work; he is the Eastern director for a manufacturer of heating equipment, forty years of age, an avid amateur chemist and inventor.

He is sufficiently plausible in appearance and manner to have encountered no difficulty in obtaining germ cultures from the Willard Parker Hospital. In addition to feeding his wife arsenic, he has also given her the germs of pneumonia, diphtheria, typhoid, and scarlet fever. He introduced them into nighttime snacks of stuffed dates, malted milk, bread, and milk.

According to the *Times*, Baring's "other woman" was aware that her lover was married. He had promised to divorce his wife and marry her. He had, in fact, temporarily separated from his wife a few years earlier. But the Barings had reunited, and it was upon their reunion that Baring had decided to poison his wife. Mrs. Baring, after suffering undiagnosed illnesses, had come to suspect that her husband was trying to kill her. She began to secrete the foods he gave her and to send them to a toxicologist for analysis. Her suspicions were confirmed. She had not died of the arsenic and germs Baring had given her because the doses were too small. When he was arrested, Baring readily admitted that he had fed these poisons to his wife, but he denied any wish to kill her. In jail, he explained that he had intended only to make his wife so ill that he would have to take her to California to recuperate. This would have enabled him to break off his relations with his mistress. On further investigation, it was revealed that there had been other "other women" in Baring's life than Mildred Beam. He had kept an apartment in New York for his extramarital activities.

Mildred Beam would appear to have learned of Baring's arrest on Saturday, April 26th, the day after the two of them returned from Norfolk—she read about it in a newspaper on a train and collapsed. She took refuge with her mother and disappeared from public view. But she kept herself available to the Westchester County District Attorney.

Neither Baring's employer nor any of his friends ultimately rallied to his side; none offered to make bail for him. His story was unbelievable, and they refused to believe it. Baring never stood trial. On July 8, 1924, the *Times* proclaims, "BARING FOUND INSANE BY STATE ALIENISTS. . . . Experts Testify That Six in Family of Prisoner's Father Suffered from Mental Disease. Prisoner Had Illusions. Thought He Was Being Followed and Insisted His Wife Had a Child." On the testimony of the psychiatrists, Baring was remanded to the Matteawan Asylum for the Criminal Insane. Here, so far as we are told, the story ends.

Soon after Baring's arrest, Beam had run away from the press, but she never ran from the law. As I read her story today, it seems to me that she had much to be grateful for in the treatment accorded her by both the press and the law—she was not hounded by reporters and photographers or written about sensationally, and the District Attorney appears to have treated her with entire respect. Her front-page scandal was made as little scandalous as possible.

Nineteen twenty-four was the summer that Dorothy, my dormitory neighbor and close friend at Radcliffe, came to Lenore as a counsellor. Mrs. Spectorsky was in need of another pianist, and I recommended Dorothy, who was a serious student of music. I ask Dorothy now if she remembers the Beam story and she tells me that she has no recollection of it. This confirms my own recollection that Beam's name was never mentioned at camp even though it was during the camp season that Baring was sent to Matteawan and that his and Beam's awful story was being reported in the newspapers. In the twenties, it was not required of us that, in order to qualify as good citizens, we keep abreast of public events. We had no newspapers at Lenore. We were shielded from the world rather than urged to engage in it.

The counsellors at Lenore had a day off each week. I had now become a full-fledged counsellor. There was little we could do for recreation within walking distance of the camp, and we usually spent our free days hitchhiking. Dorothy and I hitchhiked to the college campuses in our New England area: Wellesley, Mount Holyoke, Smith, Amherst.

Although life was not then as hazardous as it is today, we sometimes encountered difficulty because of our venturesome means of travel. I remember one excursion, for instance, when it was already dark before we could get a lift. We found ourselves with two men who, it soon turned out, wanted more of us in friendliness than we were prepared to give. We had to cross the Mohawk Trail, where there was little traffic and virtually no illumination, and I had begun to be badly frightened when, by good fortune, a gas station loomed up ahead of us and our driver stopped for gas. There was another car at the station and simultaneously, without pause to explain our conduct, Dorothy and I jumped out and took refuge in it. The occupants were a middle-aged couple who quickly appreciated our plight. They drove many miles out of their way to deliver us at our camp gate. Several minutes had to pass before I realized that I was still clutching the Scout knife in my bloomer pocket.

As a full counsellor—and how many summers of hope and strenuous application it had taken to achieve this position!—I had two bunkloads of Intermediates in my charge; I also taught archery, helped with Intermediate basketball, and, like the rest of the athletic staff, was regularly on watch during swimming periods. In addition, I helped as I could in the preparation of our camp plays and pageants. Unfortunately, our growth isn't calibrated for us like a thermometer. I had no way of knowing whether or not I had at last reached maturity. Had I? Was I there?

Many girls came to camp with special needs. We would be made acquainted with these individual problems at the first staff meeting of the season: Edna Hartman must eat no tomatoes, Evelyn Kantor had had a mastoid operation and must not get water in her ears. Eleven-year-old Beatrice, a charge of mine, was clearly the most heavily burdened with physical and emotional disorders. Of Beatrice we were cautioned that she must be guarded against heat, cold, insects, ice water, acidity, and such a myriad of other perils that a wave of derisive laughter ran through the room as Mrs. Spectorsky went on with the list. Strangely, I was unable to laugh. One had perhaps to be oneself enough young, still in battle against excessive parental vigilance, to feel a quick sympathy for this child so overtended and ill-loved.

On rainy days at Lenore, when the camp lawns were suddenly transformed into shiny pools, the children would put on their bathing suits and run splashing and sliding in the downpour. It was on one such day of shrieking delight that I spied my Beatrice sitting in her bunk, a lone mute spectator at the fun. Beatrice must not be allowed to get her feet wet, Beatrice must not take a chill: I had not forgotten the instructions I had been given, but they suddenly had no bearing on the misery of this child, alone, excluded from everything that was allowed the other girls her age. Hurrying to her bunk, I told her that she must put on her bathing suit and—quick, quick, quick!—join the other girls in the rain. Heady with authority, I assured her that no harm would befall her. She had my promise that she wouldn't catch cold. When Beatrice returned to her bunk I was waiting with a towel. Her face was wreathed in her wet smile, water dripped from her hair. I rubbed her dry and hustled her into her clothes—I insisted that she wear a sweater. In the days that followed, I listened anxiously for tell-tale signs of illness, a cough or a sneeze. Beatrice and I were lucky: she was well. I doubt whether I have ever again been this courageous on behalf of freedom.

As a counsellor, I returned to Lenore for two more summers after that. Then Lionel and I were married, and I didn't again see Lenore or its directress until more than a decade had passed. In my mid-thirties, a settled married woman, I was driving in New England with Lionel when all at once it came to me that we were in the vicinity of my old camp. I burst out impulsively, "Let's go to Lenore!"

It was only much later, when we were driving away from camp and I was trying, not very successfully, to still my pain and anger at the scant notice that Mrs. Spectorsky had taken of me, that I realized that I had of course invited just such rejection by dropping in at Lenore this unexpectedly. Mrs. Spectorsky suffered with grace the intrusion of the parents at camp weekends; for the rest of the summer, the seclusion and routine of Lenore must not be interrupted. I was not part of this routine. I had once been part of Lenore but I no longer shared in it. Now it belonged to other girls, little girls like the Bluebirds and bigger girls as well, edging toward womanhood, making their way through the wilderness of their ignorance and their desires. I was no longer part of Mrs. Spectorsky's history as she was part of mine.

It was Rest Hour and the camp was deadly quiet. Mrs. Spectorsky was near the Mess Hall and when she caught sight of me she did no more than lift her hand in an ambiguous wave. While it could have been a wave of recognition, it was as likely a wave of dismissal. This was the full extent of the recognition I earned from her, and even this little was more than the response I earned from her surrogate, her daughter. A short distance away, Miriam stood talking to a little camper. She was bent over the child, gentle and attentive. In the sympathetic lines of her body, she was a replica of her mother's concern.

I had left Lionel in our parked car and I had proceeded alone to the Lodge. I moved through a silent universe. Obedient to whoever was today's Auntie Ella, the campers at Rest Hour were quiet in their bunks, resting on their beds, perhaps writing home to their families. In a flash of sweet memory, there had come back to me the recollection of the summer when Mrs. Spectorsky had employed the Rest Hour to read aloud to the girls in my bunk from H. G. Wells's new bestseller, *The Outline of History*. We had been the most ordinary-minded of adolescents yet we had realized that we were being improved and, uncomprehending as we might be, this had flattered us.

Apart from the soft sounds of summer, I could hear only the distant whirring of a lawnmower. Was it still Steve, I wondered, who had the care of the camp lawns, and had he now been provided with a power mower? How proud this would make him!

I had rapped on the door of Mrs. Spectorsky's office in the Lodge and it had been opened to me by Mr. Spectorsky. For a moment he had stood vacantly staring.

"Hello, Mr. Spectorsky," I murmured. I was finding it difficult to speak clearly. "Don't you remember me?" I asked.

The directress's husband didn't ask me to identify myself. He drew me into the room and to the window where he lifted my chin and turned my face to the light. He was still tall and straightlimbed, though he now moved a bit heavily. Chiefly one saw his age in his blurred eyes. They had lost their old glitter. At last, he said, "It's my little Diana." He folded me in his arms.

So here we have it, and here, I suppose, it should be left, with me in the embrace of "Spec," who had meant so little to me that I couldn't even remember the stories he had so often told us at campfire—how poorly I must have listened! My thoughts must have been elsewhere. But where? Where do our thoughts go when we are growing up and suppose that we have no further use for them?

Horse Camp

Ursula K. Le Guin

All the other Seniors were over at the street side of the parking lot, but Sal stayed with her sister Norah while they waited for the bus drivers. "Maybe you'll be in the creek cabin," Sal said, quiet and serious. "I had it second year. It's the best one. Number Five."

"How do they—when do you, like, like, find out what cabin?" asked Norah.

"They better remember we're in the same cabin," Ev said, sounding shrill. Norah did not look at her. She and Ev had planned for months and known for weeks that they were to be cabinmates, but what good was that if they never found their cabin, and also Sal was not looking at Ev, only at Norah. Sal was cool, a tower of ivory.

"They show you around as soon as you get there," she said, her quiet voice speaking directly to Norah's dream last night of never finding the room where she had to take a test she was late for and looking among endless thatched barracks in a forest of thin black trees growing very close together, like hair under a hand lens. Norah had told no one the dream, and now remembered and forgot it. "Then you have dinner, and First Campfire," Sal said. "Kimmy's going to be a counsellor again. She's really neat. Listen, you tell old Meredy . . ."

Norah drew breath. In all the histories of Horse Camp which she had asked for and heard over and over for three years—the thunderstorm story, the horse-thief story, the wonderful Stevens Mountain stories—in all of them Meredy the handler had been: Meredy said, Meredy did, Meredy knew . . .

"Tell him I said hi," Sal said, with a shadowy smile, looking across the parking lot at the far, insubstantial towers of downtown. Behind them the doors of the Junior Girls bus gasped open. One after another the engines of the four buses roared and spewed. Across the asphalt, in the hot morning light, small figures were lining up and climbing into the Junior Boys bus. High, rough, faint voices bawled. "O.K., hey, have fun," Sal said. She hugged Norah and then, keeping a hand on her arm, looked down at her intently for a moment from the tower of ivory. She turned away. Norah watched her walk, light-foot and buxom, across the black gap to the others of her kind, who enclosed her, greeting her, "Sal! Hey, Sal!"

Ev was twitching and nickering, "Come on, Nor, come on. We'll have to sit way at the back. Come on!" Side by side, they pressed into the line below the gaping doorway of the bus.

273

. . .

In Number Five cabin, four iron cots, thin-mattressed, gray-blanketed, stood strewn with bottles of insect repellent and styling mousse, T-shirts lettered "UCSD" and "I ♥ Teddy Bears," a flashlight, an apple, a comb with hair caught in it, a paperback book open facedown: *The Black Colt of Pirate Island*. Over the shingle roof huge second-growth redwoods cast deep shade, and a few feet below the porch the creek ran out into sunlight over brown stones streaming bright-green weed. Behind the cabin Jim Meredith, the horse-handler, a short man of fifty who had ridden as a jockey in his teens, walked along the well-beaten path, quick and a bit bowlegged. Meredith's lips were pressed firmly together. His eyes, narrow and darting, glanced from cabin to cabin, from side to side. Far through the trees high voices cried.

The counsellors know what is to be known. Red Ginger, blond Kimmy, and beautiful Black Sue: they know the vices of Pal, and how to keep Trigger from putting her head down and drinking for ten minutes from every creek. They strike the great shoulders smartly: "Aw, get over, you big lunk!" They know how to swim underwater, how to sing in harmony, how to get seconds, and when a shoe is loose. They know where they are. They know where the rest of Horse Camp is. "Home Creek runs into Little River here," Kimmy says, drawing lines in the soft dust with a redwood twig that breaks. "Senior Girls here, Senior Boys across there, Junior Birdmen about here."

"Who needs 'em?" says Sue, yawning. "Come on, who's going to help me walk the mares?"

. . .

They were all around the campfire on Quartz Meadow after the long first day of the First Overnight. The counsellors were still singing, but very soft, so soft you almost couldn't hear them, lying in the sleeping bag listening to One Spot stamp and Trigger snort and the shifting at the pickets, standing in the fine, cool alpine grass listening to the soft voices and the sleepers shifting and, later, one coyote down the mountain singing all alone.

"Nothing wrong with you. Get up!" said Meredy, and slapped her hip. Turning her long, delicate head to him with a deprecating gaze, Philly got to her feet. She stood a moment, shuddering the reddish silk of her flank as if to dislodge flies, tested her left foreleg with caution, and then walked on, step by step. Step by step, watching, Norah went with her. Inside her body there was still a deep trembling. As she passed him, the handler just nodded. "You're all right," he meant. She was all right.

Freedom, the freedom to run, freedom is to run. Freedom is galloping. What else can it be? Only other ways to run, imitations of galloping across great highlands with the wind. Oh, Philly, sweet Philly, my love! If Ev and Trigger couldn't keep up she'd slow down and come round in a while, after a while, over there, across the long, long field of grass, once she had learned this by heart and knew it forever, the purity, the pure joy.

"Right leg, Nor," said Meredy. And passed on to Cass and Tammy.
  You have to start with the right fore. Everything else is all

right. Freedom depends on this, that you start with the right fore, that long leg well balanced on its elegant pastern, that you set down that tiptoe middle fingernail, so hard and round, and spurn the dirt. High-stepping, trot past old Meredy, who always hides his smile.

Shoulder to shoulder, she and Ev, in the long heat of afternoon, in a trance of light, across the home creek in the dry wild oats and cow parsley of the Long Pasture. I was afraid before I came here, thinks Norah, incredulous, remembering childhood. She leans her head against Ev's firm and silken side. The sting of small flies awakens, the swish of long tails sends to sleep. Down by the creek, in a patch of coarse grass, Philly grazes and dozes. Sue comes striding by, winks wordless, beautiful as a burning coal, lazy and purposeful, bound for the shade of the willows. Is it worth getting up to go down to get your feet in the cool water? Next year Sal will be too old for a camper, but can come back as a counsellor, come back here. Norah will come back a second-year camper, Sal a counsellor. They will be here. This is what freedom is, what goes on—the sun in summer, the wild grass, coming back each year.

Coming back from the long pack trip to Stevens Mountain, weary and dirty, thirsty and in bliss, coming down from the high places, in line, Sue jogging just in front of her and Ev half asleep behind her—some sound or motion caught and turned Norah's head to look across the alpine field. On the far side, under dark firs, a line of horses, mounted and with packs: "Look!"

Ev snorted. Sue flicked her ears and stopped. Norah halted in

line behind her, stretching her neck to see. She saw her sister going first in the distant line, the small head proudly borne. She was
walking light-foot and easy, fresh, just starting up to the high
passes of the mountain. On her back a young man sat erect, his
fine, fair head turned a little aside, to the forest. One hand was on
his thigh, the other on the reins, guiding her. Norah called out
and then broke from the line, going to Sal, calling out to her.
"No, no, no, no!" she called. Behind her, Ev and then Sue called
to her, "Nor! Nor!"

Sal did not hear or heed. Going straight ahead, the color of
ivory, distant in the clear, dry light, she stepped into the shadow
of the trees. The others and their riders followed, jogging one after the other till the last was gone.

Norah had stopped in the middle of the meadow, and stood in
grass in sunlight. Flies hummed.

She tossed her head, turned, and trotted back to the line. She
went along it from one to the next, teasing, chivying, Kimmy
yelling at her to get back in line, till Sue broke out of line to chase
her and she ran, and then Ev began to run, whinnying shrilly, and
then Cass and Philly and all the rest, the whole bunch, cantering
first and then running flat out, running wild, racing, heading for
Horse Camp and the Long Pasture, for Meredy and the long
evening standing in the fenced field, in the sweet dry grass, in the
fetlock-shallow water of the home creek.

Brownies

ZZ Packer

By our second day at Camp Crescendo, the girls in my Brownie troop had decided to kick the asses of each and every girl in Brownie Troop 909. Troop 909 was doomed from the first day of camp; they were white girls, their complexions a blend of ice cream: strawberry, vanilla. They turtled out from their bus in pairs, their rolled-up sleeping bags chromatized with Disney characters: Sleeping Beauty, Snow White, Mickey Mouse; or the generic ones cheap parents bought: washed-out rainbows, unicorns, curly-eyelashed frogs. Some clutched Igloo coolers and still others held on to stuffed toys like pacifiers, looking all around them like tourists determined to be dazzled.

Our troop was wending its way past their bus, past the ranger station, past the colorful trail guide drawn like a treasure map, locked behind glass.

"Man, did you smell them?" Arnetta said, giving the girls a slow once-over, "They smell like Chihuahuas. *Wet* Chihuahuas." Their troop was still at the entrance, and though we had passed them by yards, Arnetta raised her nose in the air and grimaced.

Arnetta said this from the very rear of the line, far away from Mrs. Margolin, who always strung our troop behind her like a brood of obedient ducklings. Mrs. Margolin even looked like a mother duck—she had hair cropped close to a small ball of a head, almost no neck, and huge, miraculous breasts. She wore enormous belts that looked like the kind that weightlifters wear, except hers would be cheap metallic gold or rabbit fur or covered with gigantic fake sunflowers, and often these belts would become nature lessons in and of themselves. "See," Mrs. Margolin once said to us, pointing to her belt, "this one's made entirely from the feathers of baby pigeons."

The belt layered with feathers was uncanny enough, but I was more disturbed by the realization that I had never actually *seen* a baby pigeon. I searched weeks for one, in vain—scampering after pigeons whenever I was downtown with my father.

But nature lessons were not Mrs. Margolin's top priority. She saw the position of troop leader as an evangelical post. Back at the A.M.E. church where our Brownie meetings were held, Mrs. Margolin was especially fond of imparting religious aphorisms by means of acrostics—"Satan" was the "Serpent Always Tempting and Noisome"; she'd refer to the "Bible" as "Basic Instructions Before Leaving Earth." Whenever she quizzed us on these, expecting to hear the acrostics parroted back to her, only Arnetta's correct replies soared over our vague mumblings. "Jesus?" Mrs. Margolin might ask expectantly, and Arnetta alone would dutifully answer, "Jehovah's Example, Saving Us Sinners."

Arnetta always made a point of listening to Mrs. Margolin's religious talk and giving her what she wanted to hear. Because of this, Arnetta could have blared through a megaphone that the white girls of Troop 909 were "wet Chihuahuas" without so much as a blink from Mrs. Margolin. Once, Arnetta killed the troop goldfish by feeding it a french fry covered in ketchup, and when Mrs. Margolin demanded that she explain what had happened, claimed the goldfish had been eyeing her meal for *hours*, then the fish—giving in to temptation—had leapt up and snatched a whole golden fry from her fingertips.

"*Serious* Chihuahua," Octavia added, and though neither Arnetta nor Octavia could *spell* "Chihuahua," had ever *seen* a Chihuahua, trisyllabic words had gained a sort of exoticism within our fourth-grade set at Woodrow Wilson Elementary. Arnetta and Octavia would flip through the dictionary, determined to work the vulgar-sounding ones like "Djibouti" and "asinine" into conversation.

"*Caucasian* Chihuahuas," Arnetta said.

That did it. The girls in my troop turned elastic: Drema and Elise doubled up on one another like inextricably entwined kites; Octavia slapped her belly; Janice jumped straight up in the air, then did it again, as if to slam-dunk her own head. They could not stop laughing. No one had laughed so hard since a boy named Martez had stuck a pencil in the electric socket and spent the whole day with a strange grin on his face.

"Girls, girls," said our parent helper, Mrs. Hedy. Mrs. Hedy was Octavia's mother, and she wagged her index finger perfunctorily, like a windshield wiper. "Stop it, now. Be good." She said this loud enough to be heard, but lazily, bereft of any feeling or indication that she meant to be obeyed, as though she could say these words again at the exact same pitch if a button somewhere on her were pressed.

But the rest of the girls didn't stop; they only laughed louder. It was the word "Caucasian" that got them all going. One day at school, about a month before the Brownie camping trip, Arnetta turned to a boy wearing impossibly high-ankled floodwater jeans and said, "What are you? *Caucasian?*" The word took off from there, and soon everything was Caucasian. If you ate too fast you ate like a Caucasian, if you ate too slow you ate like a Caucasian. The biggest feat anyone at Woodrow Wilson could do was to jump off the swing in midair, at the highest point in its arc, and if you fell (as I had, more than once) instead of landing on your feet, knees bent Olympic gymnast–style, Arnetta and Octavia were prepared to comment. They'd look at each other with the silence of passengers who'd narrowly escaped an accident, then nod their heads, whispering with solemn horror, "*Caucasian.*"

Even the only white kid in our school, Dennis, got in on the Caucasian act. That time when Martez stuck a pencil in the socket, Dennis had pointed and yelled, "That was *so* Caucasian!"

When you lived in the south suburbs of Atlanta, it was easy to forget about whites. Whites were like those baby pigeons: real and existing, but rarely seen or thought about. Everyone had been to

Rich's to go clothes shopping, everyone had seen white girls and their mothers coo-cooing over dresses; everyone had gone to the downtown library and seen white businessmen swish by importantly, wrists flexed in front of them to check the time as though they would change from Clark Kent into Superman at any second. But those images were as fleeting as cards shuffled in a deck, whereas the ten white girls behind us—*invaders*, Arnetta would later call them—were instantly real and memorable, with their long, shampoo-commercial hair, straight as spaghetti from the box. This alone was reason for envy and hatred. The only black girl most of us had ever seen with hair that long was Octavia, whose hair hung past her butt like a Hawaiian hula dancer's. The sight of Octavia's mane prompted other girls to listen to her reverentially, as though whatever she had to say would somehow activate their own follicles. For example, when, on the first day of camp, Octavia made as if to speak, and everyone fell silent. "Nobody," Octavia said, "calls us niggers."

At the end of that first day, when half of our troop made their way back to the cabin after tag-team restroom visits, Arnetta said she'd heard one of the Troop 909 girls call Daphne a nigger. The other half of the girls and I were helping Mrs. Margolin clean up the pots and pans from the campfire ravioli dinner. When we made our way to the restrooms to wash up and brush our teeth, we met up with Arnetta midway.

"Man, I completely heard the girl," Arnetta reported. "Right, Daphne?"

Daphne hardly ever spoke, but when she did, her voice was petite and tinkly, the voice one might expect from a shiny new earring. She'd written a poem once, for Langston Hughes Day, a poem brimming with all the teacher-winning ingredients—trees and oceans, sunsets and moons—but what cinched the poem for the grown-ups, snatching the win from Octavia's musical ode to Grandmaster Flash and the Furious Five, were Daphne's last lines:

> *You are my father, the veteran*
> *When you cry in the dark*
> *It rains and rains and rains in my heart*

She'd always worn clean, though faded, jumpers and dresses when Chic jeans were the fashion, but when she went up to the dais to receive her prize journal, pages trimmed in gold, she wore a new dress with a velveteen bodice and a taffeta skirt as wide as an umbrella. All the kids clapped, though none of them understood the poem. I'd read encyclopedias the way others read comics, and I didn't get it. But those last lines pricked me, they were so eerie, and as my father and I ate cereal, I'd whisper over my Froot Loops, like a mantra, *"You are my father, the veteran. You are my father, the veteran, the veteran, the veteran,"* until my father, who acted in plays as Caliban and Othello and was not a veteran, marched me up to my teacher one morning and said, "Can you tell me what's wrong with this kid?"

I thought Daphne and I might become friends, but I think she grew spooked by me whispering those lines to her, begging her to tell me what they meant, and I soon understood that two quiet people like us were better off quiet alone.

"Daphne? Didn't you hear them call you a nigger?" Arnetta asked, giving Daphne a nudge.

The sun was setting behind the trees, and their leafy tops formed a canopy of black lace for the flame of the sun to pass through. Daphne shrugged her shoulders at first, then slowly nodded her head when Arnetta gave her a hard look.

Twenty minutes later, when my restroom group returned to the cabin, Arnetta was still talking about Troop 909. My restroom group had passed by some of the 909 girls. For the most part, they deferred to us, waving us into the restrooms, letting us go even though they'd gotten there first.

We'd seen them, but from afar, never within their orbit enough to see whether their faces were the way all white girls appeared on TV—ponytailed and full of energy, bubbling over with love and money. All I could see was that some of them rapidly fanned their faces with their hands, though the heat of the day had long passed. A few seemed to be lolling their heads in slow circles, half purposefully, as if exercising the muscles of their necks, half ecstatically, like Stevie Wonder.

"We can't let them get away with that," Arnetta said, dropping her voice to a laryngitic whisper. "We can't let them get away with calling us niggers. I say we teach them a lesson." She sat down cross-legged on a sleeping bag, an embittered Buddha, eyes glimmering acrylic-black. "We can't go telling Mrs. Margolin, either. Mrs. Margolin'll say something about doing unto others and the path of righteousness and all. Forget that shit." She let her eyes flutter irreverently till they half closed, as though ignoring an insult not worth returning. We could all hear Mrs. Margolin outside, gathering the last of the metal campware.

Nobody said anything for a while. Usually people were quiet after Arnetta spoke. Her tone had an upholstered confidence that was somehow both regal and vulgar at once. It demanded a few moments of silence in its wake, like the ringing of a church bell or the playing of taps. Sometimes Octavia would ditto or dissent to whatever Arnetta had said, and this was the signal that others could speak. But this time Octavia just swirled a long cord of hair into pretzel shapes.

"Well?" Arnetta said. She looked as if she had discerned the hidden severity of the situation and was waiting for the rest of us to catch up. Everyone looked from Arnetta to Daphne. It was, after all, Daphne who had supposedly been called the name, but Daphne sat on the bare cabin floor, flipping through the pages of the Girl Scout handbook, eyebrows arched in mock wonder, as if the handbook were a catalogue full of bright and startling foreign costumes. Janice broke the silence. She clapped her hands to broach her idea of a plan.

"They gone be sleeping," she whispered conspiratorially, "then we gone sneak into they cabin, then we'll put daddy longlegs in they sleeping bags. Then they'll wake up. Then we gone beat 'em up till they're as flat as frying pans!" She jammed her fist into the palm of her hand, then made a sizzling sound.

Janice's country accent was laughable, her looks homely, her jumpy acrobatics embarrassing to behold. Arnetta and Octavia volleyed amused, arrogant smiles whenever Janice opened her mouth, but Janice never caught the hint, spoke whenever she wanted, fluttered around Arnetta and Octavia futilely offering her opinions to their departing backs. Whenever Arnetta and Octavia shooed her away, Janice loitered until the two would finally sigh and ask, "What *is* it, Miss Caucausoid? What do you *want?*"

"Shut up, Janice," Octavia said, letting a fingered loop of hair fall to her waist as though just the sound of Janice's voice had ruined the fun of her hair twisting.

Janice obeyed, her mouth hung open in a loose grin, unflappable, unhurt.

"All right," Arnetta said, standing up. "We're going to have a secret meeting and talk about what we're going to do."

Everyone gravely nodded her head. The word "secret" had a built-in importance, the modifier form of the word carried more clout than the noun. A secret meant nothing; it was like gossip: just a bit of unpleasant knowledge about someone who happened to be someone other than yourself. A secret *meeting*, or a secret *club* was entirely different.

That was when Arnetta turned to me as though she knew that doing so was both a compliment and a charity.

"Snot, you're not going to be a bitch and tell Mrs. Margolin, are you?"

I had been called "Snot" ever since first grade, when I'd sneezed in class and two long ropes of mucus had splattered a nearby girl.

"Hey," I said. "Maybe you didn't hear them right—I mean—"

"Are you gonna tell on us or not?" was all Arnetta wanted to know, and by the time the question was asked, the rest of our Brownie troop looked at me as though they'd already decided their course of action, me being the only impediment.

Camp Crescendo used to double as a high-school-band and field hockey camp until an arcing field hockey ball landed on the clasp of a girl's metal barrette, knifing a skull nerve and paralyzing the right side of her body. The camp closed down for a few years and the girl's teammates built a memorial, filling the spot on which the girl fell with hockey balls, on which they had painted—all in nail polish—get-well tidings, flowers, and hearts. The balls were still stacked there, like a shrine of ostrich eggs embedded in the ground.

On the second day of camp, Troop 909 was dancing around the mound of hockey balls, their limbs jangling awkwardly, their cries like the constant summer squeal of an amusement park. There was a stream that bordered the field hockey lawn, and the girls from my troop settled next to it, scarfing down the last of lunch: sandwiches made from salami and slices of tomato that had gotten waterlogged from the melting ice in the cooler. From the stream bank, Arnetta eyed the Troop 909 girls, scrutinizing their movements to glean inspiration for battle.

"Man," Arnetta said, "we could bumrush them right now if that damn lady would *leave*."

The 909 troop leader was a white woman with the severe page-boy hairdo of an ancient Egyptian. She lay on a picnic blanket, sphinxlike, eating a banana, sometimes holding it out in front of her like a microphone. Beside her sat a girl slowly flapping one hand like a bird with a broken wing. Occasionally, the leader would call out the names of girls who'd attempted leapfrogs and flips, or of girls who yelled too loudly or strayed far from the circle.

"I'm just glad Big Fat Mama's not following us here," Octavia said. "At least we don't have to worry about her." Mrs. Margolin, Octavia assured us, was having her Afternoon Devotional, shrouded in mosquito netting, in a clearing she'd found. Mrs. Hedy was cleaning mud from her espadrilles in the cabin.

"I handled them." Arnetta sucked on her teeth and proudly grinned. "I told her we was going to gather leaves."

"Gather leaves," Octavia said, nodding respectfully. "That's a good one. Especially since they're so mad-crazy about this camping thing." She looked from ground to sky, sky to ground. Her hair hung down her back in two braids like a squaw's. "I mean, I really don't know why it's even called *camping*—all we ever do with Nature is find some twigs and say something like, 'Wow, this fell from a tree.'" She then studied her sandwich. With two disdainful fingers, she picked out a slice of dripping tomato, the sections congealed with red slime. She pitched it into the stream embrowned with dead leaves and the murky effigies of other dead things, but in the opaque water, a group of small silver-brown fish appeared. They surrounded the tomato and nibbled.

"Look!" Janice cried. "Fishes! Fishes!" As she scrambled to the edge of the stream to watch, a covey of insects threw up tantrums from the wheatgrass and nettle, a throng of tiny electric machines, all going at once. Octavia sneaked up behind Janice as if push her in. Daphne and I exchanged terrified looks. It seemed as though only we knew that Octavia was close enough—and bold enough—

to actually push Janice into the stream. Janice turned around quickly, but Octavia was already staring serenely into the still water as though she was gathering some sort of courage from it. "What's so funny?" Janice said, eyeing them all suspiciously.

Elise began humming the tune to "Karma Chameleon," all the girls joining in, their hums light and facile. Janice also began to hum, against everyone else, the high-octane opening chords of "Beat It."

"I love me some Michael Jackson," Janice said when she'd finished humming, smacking her lips as though Michael Jackson were a favorite meal. "I *will* marry Michael Jackson."

Before anyone had a chance to impress upon Janice the impossibility of this, Arnetta suddenly rose, made a sun visor of her hand, and watched Troop 909 leave the field hockey lawn.

"Dammit!" she said. "We've got to get them *alone*."

"They won't ever be alone," I said. All the rest of the girls looked at me, for I usually kept quiet. If I spoke even a word, I could count on someone calling me Snot. Everyone seemed to think that we could beat up these girls; no one entertained the thought that they might fight *back*. "The only time they'll be unsupervised is in the bathroom."

"Oh shut up, Snot," Octavia said.

But Arnetta slowly nodded her head. "The bathroom," she said. "The bathroom," she said, again and again. "The bathroom! The bathroom!"

According to Octavia's watch, it took us five minutes to hike to the restrooms, which were midway between our cabin and Troop

909's. Inside, the mirrors above the sinks returned only the vaguest of reflections, as though someone had taken a scouring pad to their surfaces to obscure the shine. Pine needles, leaves, and dirty, flattened wads of chewing gum covered the floor like a mosaic. Webs of hair matted the drain in the middle of the floor. Above the sinks and below the mirrors, stacks of folded white paper towels lay on a long metal counter. Shaggy white balls of paper towels sat on the sinktops in a line like corsages on display. A thread of floss snaked from a wad of tissues dotted with the faint red-pink of blood. One of those white girls, I thought, had just lost a tooth.

Though the restroom looked almost the same as it had the night before, it somehow seemed stranger now. We hadn't noticed the wooden rafters coming together in great V's. We were, it seemed, inside a whale, viewing the ribs of the roof of its mouth.

"Wow. It's a mess," Elise said.

"You can say that again."

Arnetta leaned against the doorjamb of a restroom stall. "This is where they'll be again," she said. Just seeing the place, just having a plan seemed to satisfy her. "We'll go in and talk to them. You know, 'How you doing? How long'll you be here?' That sort of thing. Then Octavia and I are gonna tell them what happens when they call any one of us a nigger."

"I'm going to say something, too," Janice said.

Arnetta considered this. "Sure," she said. "Of course. Whatever you want."

Janice pointed her finger like a gun at Octavia and rehearsed the line she'd thought up. "'We're gonna teach you a *lesson*!'

That's what I'm going to say." She narrowed her eyes like a TV mobster. " 'We're gonna teach you little girls a lesson!' "

With the back of her hand, Octavia brushed Janice's finger away. "You couldn't teach me to shit in a toilet."

"But," I said, "what if they say, 'We didn't say that? We didn't call anyone an N-I-G-G-E-R.' "

"Snot," Arnetta said, and then sighed. "Don't think. Just fight. If you even know how."

Everyone laughed except Daphne. Arnetta gently laid her hand on Daphne's shoulder. "Daphne. You don't have to fight. We're doing this for you."

Daphne walked to the counter, took a clean paper towel, and carefully unfolded it like a map. With it, she began to pick up the trash all around. Everyone watched.

"C'mon," Arnetta said to everyone. "Let's beat it." We all ambled toward the doorway, where the sunshine made one large white rectangle of light. We were immediately blinded, and we shielded our eyes with our hands and our forearms.

"Daphne?" Arnetta asked. "Are you coming?"

We all looked back at the bending girl, the thin of her back hunched like the back of a custodian sweeping a stage, caught in limelight. Stray strands of her hair were lit near-transparent, thin fiber-optic threads. She did not nod yes to the question, nor did she shake her head no. She abided, bent. Then she began again, picking up leaves, wads of paper, the cotton fluff innards from a torn stuffed toy. She did it so methodically, so exquisitely, so humbly, she must have been trained. I thought of those dresses she wore, faded and old, yet so pressed and clean. I then saw the poverty in them; I then could imagine her mother, cleaning the houses of others, returning home, weary.

"I guess she's not coming."

We left her and headed back to our cabin, over pine needles and leaves, taking the path full of shade.

"What about our secret meeting?" Elise asked.

Arnetta enunciated her words in a way that defied contradiction: "We just had it."

It was nearing our bedtime, but the sun had not yet set.

"Hey, your mama's coming," Arnetta said to Octavia when she saw Mrs. Hedy walk toward the cabin, sniffling. When Octavia's mother wasn't giving bored, parochial orders, she sniffled continuously, mourning an imminent divorce from her husband. She might begin a sentence, "I don't know what Robert will do when Octavia and I are gone. Who'll buy him cigarettes?" and Octavia would hotly whisper, "*Mama*," in a way that meant: Please don't talk about our problems in front of everyone. Please shut up.

But when Mrs. Hedy began talking about her husband, thinking about her husband, seeing clouds shaped like the head of her husband, she couldn't be quiet, and no one could dislodge her from the comfort of her own woe. Only one thing could perk her up—Brownie songs. If the girls were quiet, and Mrs. Hedy was in her dopey, sorrowful mood, she would say, "Y'all know I like those songs, girls. Why don't you sing one?" Everyone would groan, except me and Daphne. I, for one, liked some of the songs.

"C'mon, everybody," Octavia said drearily. "She likes the Brownie song best."

We sang, loud enough to reach Mrs. Hedy:

"I've got something in my pocket;
It belongs across my face.
And I keep it very close at hand in a most convenient place.
I'm sure you couldn't guess it
If you guessed a long, long while.
So I'll take it out and put it on—
It's a great big Brownie smile!"

The Brownie song was supposed to be sung cheerfully, as though we were elves in a workshop, singing as we merrily cobbled shoes, but everyone except me hated the song so much that they sang it like a maudlin record, played on the most sluggish of rpms.

"That was good," Mrs. Hedy said, closing the cabin door behind her. "Wasn't that nice, Linda?"

"Praise God," Mrs. Margolin answered without raising her head from the chore of counting out Popsicle sticks for the next day's craft session.

"Sing another one," Mrs. Hedy said. She said it with a sort of joyful aggression, like a drunk I'd once seen who'd refused to leave a Korean grocery.

"God, Mama, get over it," Octavia whispered in a voice meant only for Arnetta, but Mrs. Hedy heard it and started to leave the cabin.

"Don't go," Arnetta said. She ran after Mrs. Hedy and held her by the arm. "We haven't finished singing." She nudged us with a single look. "Let's sing the 'Friends Song.' For Mrs. Hedy."

Although I liked some of the songs, I hated this one:

> *Make new friends*
> *But keep the o-old,*
> *One is silver*
> *And the other gold.*

If most of the girls in the troop could be any type of metal, they'd be bunched-up wads of tinfoil, maybe, or rusty iron nails you had to get tetanus shots for.

"No, no, no," Mrs. Margolin said before anyone could start in on the "Friends Song." "An uplifting song. Something to lift her up and take her mind off all these earthly burdens."

Arnetta and Octavia rolled their eyes. Everyone knew what song Mrs. Margolin was talking about, and no one, no one, wanted to sing it.

"Please, no," a voice called out. "Not 'The Doughnut Song.'"

"Please not 'The Doughnut Song,'" Octavia pleaded.

"I'll brush my teeth two times if I don't have to sing 'The Doughnut—'"

"Sing!" Mrs. Margolin demanded.

We sang:

> *"Life without Jesus is like a do-ough-nut!*
> *Like a do-ooough-nut!*
> *Like a do-ooough-nut!*
> *Life without Jesus is like a do-ough-nut!*
> *There's a hole in the middle of my soul!"*

There were other verses, involving other pastries, but we stopped after the first one and cast glances toward Mrs. Margolin to see if we could gain a reprieve. Mrs. Margolin's eyes fluttered blissfully. She was half asleep.

"Awww," Mrs. Hedy said, as though giant Mrs. Margolin were a cute baby, "Mrs. Margolin's had a long day."

"Yes indeed," Mrs. Margolin answered. "If you don't mind, I might just go to the lodge where the beds are. I haven't been the same since the operation."

I had not heard of this operation, or when it had occurred, since Mrs. Margolin had never missed the once-a-week Brownie meetings, but I could see from Daphne's face that she was concerned, and I could see that the other girls had decided that Mrs. Margolin's operation must have happened long ago in some remote time unconnected to our own. Nevertheless, they put on sad faces. We had all been taught that adulthood was full of sorrow and pain, taxes and bills, dreaded work and dealings with whites, sickness and death. I tried to do what the others did. I tried to look silent.

"Go right ahead, Linda," Mrs. Hedy said. "I'll watch the girls." Mrs. Hedy seemed to forget about divorce for a moment; she looked at us with dewy eyes, as if we were mysterious, furry creatures. Meanwhile, Mrs. Margolin walked through the maze of sleeping bags until she found her own. She gathered a neat stack of clothes and pajamas slowly, as though doing so was almost painful. She took her toothbrush, her toothpaste, her pillow. "All right!" Mrs. Margolin said, addressing us all from the threshold of the cabin. "Be in bed by nine." She said it with a twinkle in her voice, letting us know she was allowing us to be naughty and stay up till nine-fifteen.

"C'mon everybody," Arnetta said after Mrs. Margolin left. "Time for us to wash up."

Everyone watched Mrs. Hedy closely, wondering whether she would insist on coming with us since it was night, making a fight with Troop 909 nearly impossible. Troop 909 would soon be in the bathroom, washing their faces, brushing their teeth— completely unsuspecting of our ambush.

"We won't be long," Arnetta said. "We're old enough to go to the restrooms by ourselves."

Ms. Hedy pursed her lips at this dilemma. "Well, I guess you Brownies are almost Girl Scouts, right?"

"Right!"

"Just one more badge," Drema said.

"And about," Octavia droned, "a million more cookies to sell." Octavia looked at all of us, *Now's our chance*, her face seemed to say, but our chance to do *what*, I didn't exactly know.

Finally, Mrs. Hedy walked to the doorway where Octavia stood dutifully waiting to say goodbye but looking bored doing it. Mrs. Hedy held Octavia's chin. "You'll be good?"

"Yes, Mama."

"And remember to pray for me and your father? If I'm asleep when you get back?"

"Yes, Mama."

When the other girls had finished getting their toothbrushes and washcloths and flashlights for the group restroom trip, I was drawing pictures of tiny birds with too many feathers. Daphne was sitting on her sleeping bag, reading.

"You're not going to come?" Octavia asked.

Daphne shook her head.

"I'm gonna stay, too," I said. "I'll go to the restroom when Daphne and Mrs. Hedy go."

Arnetta leaned down toward me and whispered so that Mrs. Hedy, who'd taken over Mrs. Margolin's task of counting Popsicle sticks, couldn't hear. "No, Snot. If we get in trouble, you're going to get in trouble with the rest of us."

We made our way through the darkness by flashlight. The tree branches that had shaded us just hours earlier, along the same path, now looked like arms sprouting menacing hands. The stars sprinkled the sky like spilled salt. They seemed fastened to the darkness, high up and holy, their places fixed and definite as we stirred beneath them.

Some, like me, were quiet because we were afraid of the dark; others were talking like crazy for the same reason.

"Wow!" Drema said, looking up. "Why are all the stars out here? I never see stars back on Oneida Street."

"It's a camping trip, that's why," Octavia said. "You're supposed to see stars on camping trips."

Janice said, "This place smells like my mother's air freshener."

"These woods are *pine*," Elise said. "Your mother probably uses *pine* air freshener."

Janice mouthed an exaggerated "Oh," nodding her head as though she just then understood one of the world's great secrets.

No one talked about fighting. Everyone was afraid enough just walking through the infinite deep of the woods. Even though I didn't want to fight, was afraid of fighting, I felt I was part of the rest of the troop; like I was defending something. We trudged against the slight incline of the path, Arnetta leading the way.

"You know," I said, "their leader will be there. Or they won't even be there. It's dark already. Last night the sun was still in the sky. I'm sure they're already finished."

Arnetta acted as if she hadn't heard me. I followed her gaze with my flashlight, and that's when I saw the squares of light in the darkness. The bathroom was just ahead.

But the girls were there. We could hear them before we could see them.

"Octavia and I will go in first so they'll think there's just two of us, then wait till I say, 'We're gonna teach you a lesson,'" Arnetta said. "Then, bust in. That'll surprise them."

"That's what I was supposed to say," Janice said.

Arnetta went inside, Octavia next to her. Janice followed, and the rest of us waited outside.

They were in there for what seemed like whole minutes, but something was wrong. Arnetta hadn't given the signal yet. I was with the girls outside when I heard one of the Troop 909 girls say, "No. That did NOT happen!"

That was to be expected, that they'd deny the whole thing. What I hadn't expected was *the voice* in which the denial was said. The girl sounded as though her tongue were caught in her mouth. "That's a BAD word!" the girl continued. "We don't say BAD words!"

"Let's go in," Elise said.

"No," Drema said, "I don't want to. What if we get beat up?"

"Snot?" Elise turned to me, her flashlight blinding. It was the first time anyone had asked my opinion, though I knew they were just asking because they were afraid.

"I say we go inside, just to see what's going on."

"But Arnetta didn't give us the signal," Drema said. "She's supposed to say, 'We're gonna teach you a lesson,' and I didn't hear her say it."

"C'mon," I said. "Let's just go in."

We went inside. There we found the white girls—about five girls huddled up next to one big girl. I instantly knew she was the owner of the voice we'd heard. Arnetta and Octavia inched toward us as soon as we entered.

"Where's Janice?" Elise asked, then we heard a flush. "Oh."

"I think," Octavia said, whispering to Elise, "they're retarded."

"We ARE NOT retarded!" the big girl said, though it was obvious that she was. That they all were. The girls around her began to whimper.

"They're just pretending," Arnetta said, trying to convince herself. "I know they are."

Octavia turned to Arnetta. "Arnetta. Let's just leave."

Janice came out of a stall, happy and relieved, then she suddenly remembered her line, pointed to the big girl, and said, "We're gonna teach you a lesson."

"Shut up, Janice," Octavia said, but her heart was not in it. Arnetta's face was set in a lost, deep scowl. Octavia turned to the big girl and said loudly, slowly, as if they were all deaf, "We're going to leave. It was nice meeting you, O.K.? You don't have to tell any-one that we were here. O.K.?"

"Why not?" said the big girl, like a taunt. When she spoke, her lips did not meet, her mouth did not close. Her tongue grazed the roof of her mouth, like a little pink fish. "You'll get in trouble. I know. *I* know."

Arnetta got back her old cunning. "If you said anything, then you'd be a tattletale."

The girl looked sad for a moment, then perked up quickly. A flash of genius crossed her face. "I *like* tattletale."

"It's all right, girls. It's gonna be all right!" the 909 troop leader said. All of Troop 909 burst into tears. It was as though someone had instructed them all to cry at once. The troop leader had girls under her arm, and all the rest of the girls crowded about her. It reminded me of a hog I'd seen on a field trip, where all the little hogs gathered about the mother at feeding time, latching on to her teats. The 909 troop leader had come into the bathroom, shortly after the big girl had threatened to tell. Then the ranger came, then, once the ranger had radioed the station, Mrs. Margolin arrived with Daphne in tow.

The ranger had left the restroom area, but everyone else was huddled just outside, swatting mosquitoes.

"Oh. They *will* apologize," Mrs. Margolin said to the 909 troop leader, but she said this so angrily, I knew she was speaking more to us than to the other troop leader. "When their parents find out, every one a them will be on punishment."

"It's all right, it's all right," the 909 troop leader reassured Mrs.

Margolin. Her voice lilted in the same way it had when addressing the girls. She smiled the whole time she talked. She was like one of those TV-cooking-show women who talk and dice onions and smile all at the same time.

"See. It could have happened. I'm not calling your girls fibbers or anything." She shook her head ferociously from side to side, her Egyptian-style pageboy flapping against her cheeks like heavy drapes. "It *could* have happened. See. Our girls are *not* retarded. They are *delayed* learners." She said this in a syrupy instructional voice, as though our troop might be delayed learners as well. "We're from the Decatur Children's Academy. Many of them just have special needs."

"Now we won't be able to walk to the bathroom by ourselves!" the big girl said.

"Yes you will," the troop leader said, "but maybe we'll wait till we get back to Decatur—"

"I don't want to wait!" the girl said. "I want my Independence badge!"

The girls in my troop were entirely speechless. Arnetta looked stoic, as though she were soon to be tortured but was determined not to appear weak. Mrs. Margolin pursed her lips solemnly and said, "Bless them, Lord. Bless them."

In contrast, the Troop 909 leader was full of words and energy. "Some of our girls are echolalic—" She smiled and happily presented one of the girls hanging on to her, but the girl widened her eyes in horror, and violently withdrew herself from the center of attention, sensing she was being sacrificed for the village sins. "Echolalic," the troop leader continued. "That means they will

ZZ Packer

say whatever they hear, like an echo—that's where the word comes from. It comes from 'echo.'" She ducked her head apologetically, "I mean, not all of them have the most *progressive* of parents, so if they heard a bad word, they might have repeated it. But I guarantee it would not have been *intentional*."

Arnetta spoke. "I saw her say the word. I heard her." She pointed to a small girl, smaller than any of us, wearing an oversized T-shirt that read: "Eat Bertha's Mussels."

The troop leader shook her head and smiled, "That's impossible. She doesn't speak. She can, but she doesn't."

Arnetta furrowed her brow. "No. It wasn't her. That's right. It was *her*."

The girl Arnetta pointed to grinned as though she'd been paid a compliment. She was the only one from either troop actually wearing a full uniform: the mocha-colored A-line shift, the orange ascot, the sash covered with badges, though all the same one—the Try-It patch. She took a few steps toward Arnetta and made a grand sweeping gesture toward the sash. "See," she said, full of self-importance, "I'm a Brownie." I had a hard time imagining this girl calling anyone a "nigger"; the girl looked perpetually delighted, as though she would have cuddled up with a grizzly if someone had let her.

On the fourth morning, we boarded the bus to go home.

The previous day had been spent building miniature churches from Popsicle sticks. We hardly left the cabin. Mrs. Margolin and Mrs. Hedy guarded us so closely, almost no one talked for the entire day.

302

Even on the day of departure from Camp Crescendo, all was serious and silent. The bus ride began quietly enough. Arnetta had to sit beside Mrs. Margolin; Octavia had to sit beside her mother. I sat beside Daphne, who gave me her prize journal without a word of explanation.

"You don't want it?"

She shook her head no. It was empty.

Then Mrs. Hedy began to weep. "Octavia," Mrs. Hedy said to her daughter without looking at her, "I'm going to sit with Mrs. Margolin. All right?"

Arnetta exchanged seats with Mrs. Hedy. With the two women up front, Elise felt it safe to speak. "Hey," she said, then she set her face into a placid, vacant stare, trying to imitate that of a Troop 909 girl. Emboldened, Arnetta made a gesture of mock pride toward an imaginary sash, the way the girl in full uniform had done. Then they all made a game of it, trying to do the most exaggerated imitations of the Troop 909 girls, all without speaking, all without laughing loud enough to catch the women's attention.

Daphne looked down at her shoes, white with sneaker polish. I opened the journal she'd given me. I looked out the window, trying to decide what to write, searching for lines, but nothing could compare with what Daphne had written, "*My father, the veteran,*" my favorite line of all time. It replayed itself in my head, and I gave up trying to write.

By then, it seemed that the rest of the troop had given up making fun of the girls in Troop 909. They were now quietly gossiping about who had passed notes to whom in school. For a moment the gossiping fell off, and all I heard was the hum of the bus as we sped down the road and the muffled sounds of Mrs. Hedy and Mrs. Margolin talking about serious things.

"You know," Octavia whispered, "why did *we* have to be stuck at a camp with retarded girls? You know?"

"*You* know why," Arnetta answered. She narrowed her eyes like a cat. "My mama and I were in the mall in Buckhead, and this white lady just kept looking at us. I mean, like we were foreign or something. Like we were from China."

"What did the woman say?" Elise asked.

"Nothing," Arnetta said. "She didn't say nothing."

A few girls quietly nodded their heads.

"There was this time," I said, "when my father and I were in the mall and—"

"Oh shut up, Snot," Octavia said.

I stared at Octavia, then rolled my eyes from her to the window. As I watched the trees blur, I wanted nothing more than to be through with it all: the bus ride, the troop, school—all of it. But we were going home. I'd see the same girls in school the next day. We were on a bus, and there was nowhere else to go.

"Go on, Laurel," Daphne said to me. It seemed like the first time she'd spoken the whole trip, and she'd said my name. I turned to her and smiled weakly so as not to cry, hoping she'd remember when I'd tried to be her friend, thinking maybe that her gift of the journal was an invitation of friendship. But she didn't smile back. All she said was, "What happened?"

I studied the girls, waiting for Octavia to tell me to shut up again before I even had a chance to utter another word, but everyone was amazed that Daphne had spoken. The bus was silent. I gathered my voice. "Well," I said. "My father and I were in this mall, but *I* was the one doing the staring." I stopped and glanced from face to face. I continued. "There were these white people dressed like Puritans or something, but they weren't Puritans. They were Mennonites. They're these people who, if you ask them to do a favor, like paint your porch or something, they have to do it. It's in their rules."

"That sucks," someone said.

"C'mon," Arnetta said. "You're lying."

"I am not."

"How do you know that's not just some story someone made up?" Elise asked, her head cocked full of daring. "I mean, who's gonna do whatever you ask?"

"It's not made up. I know because when I was looking at them, my father said, 'See those people? If you ask them to do something, they'll do it. Anything you want.'"

No one would call anyone's father a liar—then they'd have to fight the person. But Drema parsed her words carefully. "How does your *father* know that's not just some story? Huh?"

"Because," I said, "he went up to the man and asked him would he paint our porch, and the man said yes. It's their religion."

"Man, I'm glad I'm a Baptist," Elise said, shaking her head in sympathy for the Mennonites.

"So did the guy do it?" Drema asked, scooting closer to hear if the story got juicy.

"Yeah," I said. "His whole family was with him. My dad drove them to our house. They all painted our porch. The woman and girl were in bonnets and long, long skirts with buttons up to their necks. The guy wore this weird hat and these huge suspenders."

"Why," Arnetta asked archly, as though she didn't believe a word, "would someone pick a *porch*? If they'll do anything, why not make them paint the whole *house*? Why not ask for a hundred bucks?"

I thought about it, and then remembered the words my father had said about them painting our porch, though I had never seemed to think about his words after he'd said them.

"He said," I began, only then understanding the words as they uncoiled from my mouth, "it was the only time he'd have a white man on his knees doing something for a black man for free."

I now understood what he meant, and why he did it, though I didn't like it. When you've been made to feel bad for so long, you jump at the chance to do it to others. I remembered the Mennonites bending the way Daphne had bent when she was cleaning the restroom. I remembered the dark blue of their bonnets, the black of their shoes. They painted the porch as though scrubbing a floor. I was already trembling before Daphne asked quietly, "Did he thank them?"

I looked out the window. I could not tell which were the thoughts and which were the trees. "No," I said, and suddenly knew there was something mean in the world that I could not stop.

Arnetta laughed. "If I asked them to take off their long skirts and bonnets and put on some jeans, would they do it?"

And Daphne's voice, quiet, steady: "Maybe they would. Just to be nice."

Contributors

James Atlas is the author of *Delmore Schwartz: The Life of an American Poet*, which was nominated for a National Book Award; *The Great Pretender*, a novel; *Battle of the Books: The Curriculum Debate in America*; *Bellow: A Biography*; and, most recently, *My Life in the Middle Ages: A Survivor's Tale*. He has been a staff writer for *Time*, an editor at *The New York Times Book Review* and *The New York Times Magazine*, and a staff writer at *The Atlantic*, *Vanity Fair*, and *The New Yorker*. He is the founding editor of the Penguin Lives series, and president of Atlas Books. He lives in New York City with his wife and two children.

Margaret Atwood was born in Ottawa in 1939, and grew up in northern Quebec and Ontario, and later in Toronto. She has lived in numerous cities in Canada, the U.S., and Europe. She is the author of more than thirty books—novels, short stories, poetry, literary criticism, social history, and books for children. Atwood's work is acclaimed internationally and has been published around the world. Her novels include *The Handmaid's Tale* and *Cat's Eye*—both shortlisted for the Booker Prize; *The Robber Bride*; *Alias Grace*, winner of the prestigious Giller Prize in Canada and the Premio Mondello in Italy, and a finalist for the Booker Prize, the Orange Prize, and the International IMPAC Dublin Literary Award; and *The Blind Assassin*, winner of the Booker Prize and a finalist for the International IMPAC Dublin Literary Award. Her newest novel is *Oryx and Crake* (2003). She is the recipient of numerous honors, such as *The Sunday Times* Award for Literary Excellence in the U.K., the National Arts Club Medal of Honor for Literature in the U.S., Le Chevalier dans l'Ordre des Arts et des Lettres in France, and she was the first winner of the London Literary Prize. She has received honorary degrees from universities across Canada, and one from Oxford University in England. Margaret Atwood lives in Toronto with novelist Graeme Gibson.

Kevin Canty is the award-winning author of the novels *Into the Great Wide Open* and *Nine Below Zero*, and the short story collections *Honeymoon and Other Stories* and *A Stranger in This World*. His work has been published in *The New Yorker*, *Esquire*, *GQ*, *Details*, *Story*, *The New York Times Magazine*, and *Glimmer Train*. His latest novel is *Winslow in Love*. He lives in Missoula, Montana.

Terry Galloway is a deaf, queer writer, director, and performer who writes, directs, and performs. She was born in Stuttgart, Germany, and grew up in Berlin. She received a degree in American Studies from the University of Texas in Austin and was a Heckscher Scholar in Theater Arts at Columbia University. She lives in the part of Florida that is not Miami Beach.

Lev Grossman is the book critic at *Time* magazine and the author of two novels, *Warp* and *Codex*. He lives in Brooklyn, New York.

Cynthia Kaplan, author of *Why I'm Like This: True Stories*, is a writer and an actress. She lives in New York City with her family.

Josh Lambert was born in 1979 in Toronto and spent twelve summers at Canadian Young Judea camps in Ontario, Quebec, and Nova Scotia. His book reviews have appeared in the *National Post*, *Globe and Mail*, *San*

Francisco Chronicle, and *Forward*. He spent March 2003 at the Mac-Dowell Colony in New Hampshire, working on a novel.

Andrea Lee was born in Philadelphia and received her bachelor's and master's degrees from Harvard University. Her fiction and nonfiction writing appear regularly in *The New Yorker*, as well as in *The New York Times Magazine*, *The New York Times Book Review*, *Vogue*, *Time*, and *The Oxford American*. She is the author of the novels *Sarah Phillips* and *Russian Journal*, which was nominated for a National Book Award and won the Jean Stein Award from the National Academy of Arts and Letters. Her book of short stories *Interesting Women* was published in April 2002. She lives with her husband and two children in Torino, Italy.

Ursula K. Le Guin lives in Portland, Oregon. Among her honors are a National Book Award, five Hugo and five Nebula Awards, the Kafka Award, a Pushcart Prize, and the Harold D. Vursell Memorial Award from the American Academy of Arts and Letters.

Wendy McClure, the author of *I'm Not the New Me*, holds an M.F.A. in poetry from the Iowa Writers' Workshop. She is the creator of the on-line journal *Pound*, as well as the humor site *Candyboots*. A columnist for *Bust* and a regular contributor to the website *Television Without Pity*, she lives in Chicago.

Thisbe Nissen is a graduate of Oberlin College and the Iowa Writers' Workshop, and she is a former James Michener Fellow. A native New Yorker, she now lives, writes, gardens, and collages in Iowa City, Iowa. She is the author of two novels, *The Good People of New York* and *Osprey Island*, and a collection of short stories, *Out of the Girls' Room and into the Night*.

Sharon Olds was born in San Francisco and educated at Stanford and Columbia universities. Her books include *The Unswept Room*; *Blood*,

Tin, Straw; The Dead and the Living; The Father; The Gold Cell; and *The Wellspring.* Ms. Olds teaches at New York University and helps run its writing workshop program at Goldwater Hospital, a public facility for the severely physically challenged. Ms. Olds served as the New York State Poet Laureate from 1998 to 2000.

Mark Oppenheimer's essays have appeared in the *American Scholar*, the *Yale Review*, and *Southwest Review*. He is the editor of the *New Haven Advocate* and the author of *Thirteen and a Day: The Bar and Bat Mitzvah Across America.*

ZZ Packer's stories have appeared in *The New Yorker*, *Harper's*, and *Story*, have been published in *The Best American Short Stories*, and have been read on NPR's Selected Shorts. Packer is the recipient of a Whiting Writers Award and a Rona Jaffe Foundation Writers' Award. A graduate of Yale, the Iowa Writers' Workshop, and the Writing Seminar at Johns Hopkins University, she has been a Wallace Stegner–Truman Capote fellow at Stanford University where she is currently a Jones Lecturer. Her collection *Drinking Coffee Elsewhere* was a finalist for the PEN/Faulkner Award.

Steven Rinehart is the recipient of an NEA grant and a Michener Fellowship. He is the author of a novel, *Built in a Day*, and a collection of short stories, *Kick in the Head*. He lives in New York City.

David Sedaris is a playwright and a regular commentator for National Public Radio. He is also the author of the bestselling *Barrel Fever, Naked, Holidays on Ice, Me Talk Pretty One Day*, and *Dress Your Family in Corduroy and Denim*. He travels extensively through Europe and the United States on lecture tours and lives in France.

A member of the New York intellectuals, a group of writers and critical thinkers of the 1930s, '40s and '50s, **Diana Trilling** wrote reviews and essays for *The Nation*, *The New Yorker*, *Harper's*, and *The Saturday Review*, as well as five books. She was married to Lionel Trilling, one of the country's best known and respected thinkers of the twentieth century. Until the time of her death, Diana Trilling wrote daily from 9 A.M. to 1 P.M. She died in 1996.

Ellen Umansky's fiction and nonfiction have appeared in the *New York Times*, the *New York Sun*, *Playboy*, *Jane*, the *Forward*, and the anthology *Lost Tribe*, among other publications. A graduate of Columbia's M.F.A. program, she lives in Brooklyn, New York, where she is at work on her first novel.

Gahan Wilson, author of numerous books for adults and children, is a regular contributor to *The New Yorker* magazine. He is the recipient of a Lifetime Achievement Award from the World Fantasy Association. His next children's book, *Didn't*, written with Bradford Morrow, will be published in 2006.

Dan Zanes grew up in New Hampshire and squandered his twenties playing in a rock and roll band called the Del Fuegos. When Anna Zanes was born nine years ago, Dan began recording the kind of family music that he heard in his head but couldn't find in the stores. He has released six CDs with guests including Sheryl Crow, Philip Glass, Lou Reed, Suzanne Vega, and Debbie Harry. Dan Zanes and Friends, as the band is known, has toured the country extensively and has been featured in *The New York Times Magazine*, *People*, *Rolling Stone*, and *Entertainment Weekly*, as well as on NPR. Dan's music videos have been played on Noggin and *Sesame Street*. His newest CD entitled *Parades and Panoramas: 25 Songs Collected by Carl Sandburg for the American Songbag* has been featured on NPR's *All Things Considered* and on the *Diane Rehm Show*. He is also the author of the picture book *Hello Hello*.

Credits

Credits